# Workshop on Linguistic Distances 2006



**Held in conjunction with COLING/ACL 2006**

## Sydney, Australia
## 23 July 2006

ISBN: 978-1-61738-507-0

**Printed from e-media with permission by:**

Curran Associates, Inc.
57 Morehouse Lane
Red Hook, NY 12571
www.proceedings.com

**Some format issues inherent in the e-media version may also appear in this print version.**



Printed by Curran Associates, Inc. (2010)



Association for Computational Linguistics
209 N. Eighth Street
Stroudsburg, Pennsylvania 18360

Phone: 1-570-476-8006
Fax: 1-570-476-0860

acl@aclweb.org

# Table of Contents

# Preface

Welcome to the proceedings of 'Linguistic Distances' a workshop held in conjunction with ACL/COLING 2006 in Sydney. An introductory article explains our motivation for holding the workshop, which attracted 30 submissions, of which thirteen are included in these proceedings. We are gratified by this level of interest. In fact we restricted the remit of the workshop to exclude the use of distance (or its inverse, similarity) in evaluation because it was felt that evaluation was already regularly the subject of several focused workshops. So the topic of 'Linguistic Distances' seems to resonate within the computational linguistics community.

Perhaps we should add that we also hoped to attract computational interest in (non-applied) linguistic topics, and that this, too, emerged in the submissions, although it is not strongly reflected in the choice of articles. We'll poll participants about interest in a possible follow-up, but we have no plans in that direction at this writing.

Our thanks are largely given in the acknowledgments section of the introductory article, but let's add thanks to Suzanne Stevenson, the workshop chair of the conference, and to her review committee.

John Nerbonne and Erhard Hinrichs

# Organizers

**Chairs:**

John Nerbonne, Groningen
Erhard Hinrichs, Tübingen

**Program Committee:**

Harald Baayen, Nijmegen
Walter Daelemans, Antwerp
Ido Dagan, Technion, Haifa
Wilbert Heeringa, Groningen
Ed Hovy, ISI, Los Angeles
Grzegorz Kondrak, Alberta
Sandra Kübler, Tübingen
Rada Mihalcea, North Texas
Ted Pedersen, Minnesota
Dan Roth, Illinois
Hinrich Schütze, Stuttgart
Junichi Tsujii, Tokyo
Menno van Zaanen, Macquarie, Sydney

**Additional Reviewers:**

Gosse Bouma, Groningen
Gertjan van Noord, Groningen
and anonymous reviewers

**Invited Speaker:**

Ido Dagan, Bar Ilan University

**Sponsor:**

Netherlands Organisation for Scientific Research (NWO), Grant 200-02100, for cooperation with the *Seminar für Sprachwissenschaft*, Tübingen.

# Workshop Program

**Sunday, 23 July 2006**

| | |
|---|---|
| 8:45–9:00 | Opening Remarks:<br>*Linguistic Distances*<br>John Nerbonne and Erhard Hinrichs |
| | **Session 1: Semantics I** |
| 9:00–10:00 | Invited Talk:<br>*Semantic Similarity: What for?*<br>Ido Dagan |
| 10:00–10:30 | *Similarity Judgments: Philosophical, Psychological and Mathematical Investigations*<br>Claude St-Jacques and Caroline Barrière |
| 10:30–11:00 | Break |
| | **Session 2: Semantics II** |
| 11:00–11:30 | *Automatically Creating Datasets for Measures of Semantic Relatedness*<br>Torsten Zesch and Iryna Gurevych |
| 11:30–12:00 | *Comparison of Similarity Models for the Relation Discovery Task*<br>Ben Hachey |
| 12:00–12:30 | *Sentence Comparison Using Robust Minimal Recursion Semantics and an Ontology*<br>Rebecca Dridan and Francis Bond |
| 12:30–14:00 | Lunch |

**Sunday, 23 July 2006 (continued)**

**Session 3: Pronunciation and Language Variation**

14:00–14:30 *Evaluation of Several Phonetic Similarity Algorithms on the Task of Cognate Identification*
Grzegorz Kondrak and Tarek Sherif

14:30–15:00 *Evaluation of String Distance Algorithms for Dialectology*
Wilbert Heeringa, Peter Kleiweg, Charlotte Gooskens and John Nerbonne

15:00–15:30 *Study of Some Distance Measures for Language and Encoding Identification*
Anil Kumar Singh

15:30–16:00 Break

**Session 4: Syntax**

16:00–16:30 *Towards Case-Based Parsing: Are Chunks Reliable Indicators for Syntax Trees?*
Sandra Kübler

16:30–17:00 *A Measure of Aggregate Syntactic Distance*
John Nerbonne and Wybo Wiersma

17:00–17:30 *A Structural Similarity Measure*
Petr Homola and Vladislav Kuboň

17:30–18:00 *Variants of Tree Similarity in a Question Answering Task*
Martin Emms

**Reserve Paper**

*Total Rank Distance and Scaled Total Rank Distance: Two Alternative Metrics in Computational Linguistics*
Anca Dinu and Liviu P. Dinu

# Linguistic Distances

**John Nerbonne**
Alfa-informatica
University of Groningen
j.nerbonne@rug.nl

**Erhard Hinrichs**
Seminar für Sprachwissenschaft
Universität Tübingen
eh@sfs.uni-tuebingen.de

## Abstract

In many theoretical and applied areas of computational linguistics researchers operate with a notion of linguistic distance or, conversely, linguistic similarity, which is the focus of the present workshop. While many CL areas make frequent use of such notions, it has received little focused attention, an honorable exception being Lebart & Rajman (2000). This workshop brings a number of these strands together, highlighting a number of common issues.

## 1 Introduction

In many theoretical and applied areas of computational linguistics researchers operate with a notion of linguistic distance or, conversely, linguistic similarity, which is the focus of the present workshop. While many CL areas make frequent use of such notions, it has received little focused attention, an honorable exception being Lebart & Rajman (2000).

In information retrieval (IR), also the focus of Lebart & Rajman's work, similarity is at heart of most techniques seeking an optimal match between query and document. Techniques in vector space models operationalize this via (weighted) cosine measures, but older tf/idf models were also arguably aiming at a notion of similarity.

Word sense disambiguation models often work with a notion of similarity among the contexts within which word (senses) appear, and MT identifies candidate lexical translation equivalents via a comparable measure of similarity. Many learning algorithms currently popular in CL, including not only supervised techniques such as memory-based learning (k-nn) and support-vector machines, but also unsupervised techniques such as Kohonen maps and clustering, rely essentially on measures of similarity for their processing.

Notions of similarity are often invoked in linguistic areas such as dialectology, historical linguistics, stylometry, second-language learning (as a measure of learners' proficiency), psycholinguistics (accounting for lexical "neighborhood" effects, where neighborhoods are defined by similarity) and even in theoretical linguistics (novel accounts of the phonological constraints on semitic roots).

This volume reports on a workshop aimed at bringing together researchers employing various measures of linguistic distance or similarity, including novel proposals, especially to demonstrate the importance of the abstract properties of such measures (consistency, validity, stability over corpus size, computability, fidelity to the mathematical distance axioms), but also to exchange information on how to analyze distance information further.

We assume that there is always a "hidden variable" in the similarity relation, so that we should always speak of similarity with respect to some property, and we suspect that there is such a plethora of measures in part because researchers are often inexplicit on this point. It is useful to tease the different notions apart. Finally, it is most intriguing to try to make a start on understanding how some of the different notions might construed as alternative realizations of a single abstract notion.

## 2 Pronunciation

John Laver, the author of the most widely used textbook in phonetics, claimed that "one of the



*Proceedings of the Workshop on Linguistic Distances*, pages 1–6,
Sydney, July 2006. 

most basic concepts in phonetics, and one of the least discussed, is that of **phonetic similarity** [boldface in original, JN & EH]" (Laver, 1994, p. 391), justifying the attention the workshop pays to it. Laver goes on to sketch the work that has been done on phonetic similarity, or, more exactly, phonetic distance, in particular, the empirical derivation of confusion matrices, which indicate the likelihood with which people or speech recognition systems confusion one sound for another. Miller & Nicely (1955) founded this approach with studies of how humans confused some sounds more readily than others. Although "confusability" is a reasonable reflection of phonetic similarity, it is perhaps worth noting that confusion matrices are often asymmetric, suggesting that something more complex is at play. Clark & Yallop (1995, p. 319ff) discuss this line of work further, suggesting more sophisticated analyses which aggregate confusion matrices based on segments.

In addition to the phonetic interest (above), phonologists have likewise shown interest in the question of similarity, especially in recent work. Albright and Hayes (2003) have proposed a model of phonological learning which relies on "minimal generalization". The idea is that children learn e.g. rules of allomorphy on the basis not merely of rules and individual lexical exceptions (the earlier standard wisdom), but rather on the basis of slight but reliable generalizations. An example is the formation of the past tense of verbs ending in [••], 'ing' (fling, sing, sting, spring, string) that build past tenses as 'ung' [••]. We omit details but note that the "minimal generalization" is minimally DISTANT in pronunciation.

Frisch, Pierrehumbert & Broe (2004) have also kindled an interest in segmental similarity among phonologists with their claim that syllables in Semitic languages are constrained to have unlike consonants in syllable onset and coda. Their work has not gone unchallenged (Bailey and Hahn, 2005; Hahn and Bailey, 2005), but it has certainly created further theoretical interest in phonological similarity.

There has been a great deal of attention in psycholinguistics to the the problem of word recognition, and several models appeal explicitly to the "degree of phonetic similarity among the words" (Luce and Pisoni, 1998, p. 1), but most of these models employ relatively simple notions of sequence similarity and/or, e.g., the idea that distance may be operationalized by the number or replacements needed to derive one word from another—ignoring the problem of similarity among words of different lengths (Vitevitch and Luce, 1999). Perhaps more sophisticated computational models of pronunciation distance could play a role in these models in the future.

Kessler (1995) showed how to employ edit distance to operationalize pronunciation difference in order to investigate dialectology more precisely, an idea which, particular, Heeringa (2004) pursued at great length. Kondrak (2002) created a variant of the dynamic programming algorithm used to compute edit distance which he used to identify cognates in historical linguistics. McMahon & McMahon (2005) include investigations of pronunciation similarity in their recent book on phylogenetic techniques in historical linguistics. Several of the contributions to this volume build on these earlier efforts or are relevant to them.

Kondrak and Sherif (this volume) continue the investigation into techniques for identifying cognates, now comparing several techniques which rely solely on parameters set by the researcher to machine learning techniques which automatically optimize those parameters. They show the the machine learning techniques to be superior, in particular, techniques basic on hidden Markov models and dynamic Bayesian nets.

Heeringa et al. (this volume) investigate several extensions of the fundamental edit distance algorithm for use in dialectology, including sensitivity to order and context as well syllabicity constraints, which they argue to be preferable, and length normalization and graded weighting schemes, which they argue against.

Dinu & Dinu (this volume) investigate metrics on string distances which attach more importance to the initial parts of the string. They embed this insight into a scheme in which $n$-grams are ranked (sorted) by frequency, and the difference in the rankings is used to assay language differences. Their paper proves that difference in rankings is a proper mathematical metric.

Singh (this volume) investigates the technical question of identifying languages and character encoding systems from limited amounts of text. He collects about $1,000$ or so of the most frequent $n$-grams of various sizes and then classifies next texts based on the similarity between the frequency distributions of the known texts with those of texts to be classified. His empirical results show "mutual cross entropy" to identify similarity most reliably, but there are several close competitors.

## 3 Syntax

Although there is less interest in similarity at the syntactic level among linguistic theorists, there is still one important areas of theoretical research in which it could play an important role and several interdisciplinary studies in which similarity and/or distant is absolutely crucial. Syntactic TYPOLOGY is an area of linguistic theory which seeks to identify syntactic features which tend to be associated with one another in all languages (Comrie, 1989; Croft, 2001). The fundamental vision is that some sorts of languages may be more similar to one another—typologically—than would first appear.

Further, there are two interdisciplinary linguistic studies in which similarity and/or distance plays a great role, including similarity at the syntactic level (without, however, exclusively focusing on syntax). LANGUAGE CONTACT studies seek to identify the elements of one language which have been adopted in a second in a situation in which two or more languages are used in the same community (Thomason and Kaufmann, 1988; van Coetsem, 1988). Naturally, these may be non-syntactic, but syntactic CONTAMINATION is a central concept which is recognized in contaminated varieties which have become more similar to the languages which are the source of contamination.

Essentially the same phenomena is studied in SECOND-LANGUAGE LEARNING, in which syntactic patterns from a dominant, usually first, language are imposed on a second. Here the focus is on the psychology of the individual language user as opposed to the collective habits of the language community.

Nerbonne and Wiersma (this volume) collect frequency distributions of part-of-speech (POS) trigrams and explore simple measures of distance between these. They approach issues of statistical significance using permutation tests, which requires attention to tricky issues of normalization between the frequency distributions.

Homola & Kuboň (this volume) join Nerbonne and Wiersma in advocating a surface-oriented measure of syntactic difference, but base their measure on dependency trees rather than POS tags, a more abstract level of analysis. From there they propose an analogue to edit distance to gauge the degree of difference. The difference between two tree is the sum of the costs of the tree-editing operations needed to obtain one tree from another (Noetzel and Selkow, 1999).

Emms (this volume) concentrates on applications of the notion 'tree similarity' in particular in order to identify text which is syntactically similar to questions and which may therefore be expected to constitute an answer to the question. He is able to show that the tree-distance measure outperforms sequence distance measures, at least if lexical information is also emphasized.

Kübler (this volume) uses the similarity measure in memory-based learning to parse. This is a surprising approach, since memory-based techniques are normally used in classification tasks where the target is one of a small number of potential classifications. In parsing, the targets may be arbitrarily complex, so a key step is select an initial structure in a memory-based way, and then to adapt it further. In this paper Kübler first applies chunking to the sentence to be parsed and selects an initial parse based on chunk similarity.

## 4 Semantics

While similarity as such has not been a prominent term in theoretical and computational research on natural language semantics, the study of LEXICAL SEMANTICS, which attempts to identify regularities of and systematic relations among word meanings, is more often than not predicated on an implicit notion of 'semantic similarity'. Research on the lexical semantics of verbs tries to identify verb classes whose members exhibit similar syntactic and semantic behavior. In logic-based theories of word meaning (e.g., Vendler (1967) and Dowty (1979)), verb classes are identified by similarity patterns of inference, while Levin's (1993) study of English verb classes demonstrates that similarities of word meanings for verbs can be gleaned from their syntactic behavior, in particular from their ability or inability to participate in diatheses, i.e. patterns of argument alternations.

With the increasing availability of large electronic corpora, recent computational research on word meaning has focused on capturing the notion of 'context similarity' of words. Such studies follow the empiricist approach to word meaning summarized best in the famous dictum of the British linguist J.R. Firth: "You shall know a word by the company it keeps." (Firth, 1957, p. 11) Context similarity has been used as a means of extracting collocations from corpora, e.g. by Church & Hanks (1990) and by Dunning (1993), of identifying word senses, e.g. by Yarowski (1995) and by Schütze (1998), of clustering verb classes, e.g. by Schulte im Walde (2003), and of inducing selectional restrictions of verbs, e.g. by Resnik (1993), by Abe & Li (1996), by Rooth et al. (1999) and by Wagner (2004).

A third approach to lexical semantics, developed by linguists and by cognitive psychologists, primarily relies on the intuition of lexicographers for capturing word meanings, but is also informed by corpus evidence for determining word usage and word senses. This type of approach has led to two highly valued semantic resources: the Princeton WordNet (Fellbaum, 1998) and the Berkeley Framenet (Baker et al., 1998). While originally developed for English, both approaches have been successfully generalized to other languages.

The three approaches to word meaning discussed above try to capture different aspects of the notion of semantic similarity, all of which are highly relevant for current and future research in computational linguistics. In fact, the five papers that discuss issues of semantic similarity in the present volume build on insights from these three frameworks or address open research questions posed by these frameworks. Zesch and Gurevych (this volume) discuss how measures of semantic similarity—and more generally: semantic relatedness—can be obtained by similarity judgments of informants who are presented with word pairs and who, for each pair, are asked to rate the degree of semantic relatedness on a predefined scale. Such similarity judgments can provide important empirical evidence for taxonomic models of word meanings such as wordnets, which thus far rely mostly on expert knowledge of lexicographers. To this end, Zesch and Gurevych propose a corpus-based system that supports fast development of relevant data sets for large subject domains.

St-Jacques and Barrière (this volume) review and contrast different philosophical and psychological models for capturing the notion of semantic similarity and different mathematical models for measuring semantic distance. They draw attention to the fact that, depending on which underlying models are in use, different notions of semantic similarity emerge and conjecture that different similarity metrics may be needed for different NLP tasks. Dagan (this volume) also explores the idea that different notions of semantic similarity are needed when dealing with semantic disambiguation and language modeling tasks on the one hand and with applications such as information extraction, summarization, and information retrieval on the other hand.

Dridan and Bond (this volume) and Hachey (this volume) both consider semantic similarity from an application-oriented perspective. Dridan and Bond employ the framework of robust minimal recursion semantics in order to obtain a more adequate measure of sentence similarity than can be obtained by word-overlap metrics for bag-of-words representations of sentences. They show that such a more fine-grained measure, which is based on compact representations of predicate-logic, yields better performance for paraphrase detection as well as for sentence selection in question-answering tasks than simple word-overlap metrics. Hachey considers an automatic content extraction (ACE) task, a particular subtask of information extraction. He demonstrates that representations based on term co-occurrence outperform representations based on term-by-document matrices for the task of identifying relationships between named objects in texts.

## Acknowledgments

We are indebted to our program committee and to the incidental reviewers named in the organizational section of the book, and to others who remain anonymous. We thank Peter Kleiweg for managing the production of the book and Therese Leinonen for discussions about phonetic similarity. We are indebted to the Netherlands Organization for Scientific Research (NWO), grant 200-02100, for cooperation between the Center for Language and Cognition, Groningen, and the *Seminar für Sprachwissenschaft*, Tübingen, for support of the work which is reported on here. We are also indebted to the Volkswagen Stiftung for their support of a joint project "Measuring Linguistic Unity and Diversity in Europe" that is carried out in cooperation with the Bulgarian Academy of Science, Sofia. The work reported here is directly related to the research objectives of this project.

## References


Naoki Abe and Hang Li. 1996. Learning word association norms using tree cut pair models. In *Proceedings of 13th International Conference on Machine Learning*.

Adam Albright and Bruce Hayes. 2003. Rules vs. analogy in English past tenses: A computational/experimental study. *Cognition*, 90:119–161.

Todd M. Bailey and Ulrike Hahn. 2005. Phoneme Similarity and Confusability. *Journal of Memory and Language*, 52(3):339–362.

Collin F. Baker, Charles J. Fillmore, and John B. Lowe. 1998. The Berkeley FrameNet project. In Christian Boitet and Pete Whitelock, editors, *Proceedings of the Thirty-Sixth Annual Meeting of the Association for Computational Linguistics and Seventeenth International Conference on Computational Linguistics*, pages 86–90, San Francisco, California. Morgan Kaufmann Publishers.

Kenneth Ward Church and Patrick Hanks. 1990. Word association norms, mutual information, and lexicography. *Computational Linguistics*, 16(1):22–29.

John Clark and Colin Yallop. 1995. *An Introduction to Phonetics and Phonology*. Blackwell, Oxford.

Bernard Comrie. 1989. *Language Universals and Linguistic Typology:Syntax and Morphology*. Oxford, Basil Blackwell.

William Croft. 2001. *Radical Construction Grammar: Syntactic Theory in Typological Perspective*. Oxford University Press, Oxford.

David Dowty. 1979. *Word Meaning and Montague Grammar*. Reidel, Dordrecht.

Ted Dunning. 1993. Accurate methods for the statistics of surprise and coincidence. *Computational Linguistics*, 19(1):61–74.

Christiane Fellbaum. 1998. *WordNet: An Electronic Lexical Database*. MIT Press.

J. R. Firth. 1957. A synopsis of linguistic theory. *Oxford: Philological Society*. Reprinted in F. Palmer (ed.)(1968). Studies in Linguistic Analysis 1930-1955. Selected Papers of J.R. Firth., Harlow: Longman.

Stefan A. Frisch, Janet B. Pierrehumbert, and Michael B. Broe. 2004. Similarity Avoidance and the OCP. *Natural Language & Linguistic Theory*, 22(1):179–228.

Ulrike Hahn and Todd M. Bailey. 2005. What Makes Words Sound Similar? *Cognition*, 97(3):227–267.

Wilbert Heeringa. 2004. *Measuring Dialect Pronunciation Differences using Levenshtein Distance*. Ph.D. thesis, Rijksuniversiteit Groningen.

Brett Kessler. 1995. Computational dialectology in Irish Gaelic. In *Proc. of the European ACL*, pages 60–67, Dublin.

Grzegorz Kondrak. 2002. *Algorithms for Language Reconstruction*. Ph.D. thesis, University of Toronto.

John Laver. 1994. *Principles of Phonetics*. Cambridge Univeristy Press, Cambridge.

Ludovic Lebart and Martin Rajman. 2000. Computing similarity. In Robert Dale, Hermann Moisl, and Harold Somers, editors, *Handbook of Natural Language Processing*, pages 477–505. Dekker, Basel.

Beth Levin. 1993. *English Verb Classes and Alternations: a Preliminary Investigation*. University of Chicago Press, Chicago and London.

Paul A. Luce and David B. Pisoni. 1998. Recognizing spoken words: The neighborhood activation model. *Ear and Hearing*, 19(1):1–36.

April McMahon and Robert McMahon. 2005. *Language Classification by the Numbers*. Oxford University Press, Oxford.

George A. Miller and Patricia E. Nicely. 1955. An Analysis of Perceptual Confusions Among Some English Consonants. *The Journal of the Acoustical Society of America*, 27:338–352.

Andrew S. Noetzel and Stanley M. Selkow. 1999. An analysis of the general tree-editing problem. In David Sankoff and Joseph Kruskal, editors, *Time Warps, String Edits and Macromolecules: The Theory and Practice of Sequence Comparison*, pages 237–252. CSLI, Stanford. [1]1983.

Philip Stuart Resnik. 1993. *Selection and Information: A Class-Based Approach to Lexical Relationships*. Ph.D. thesis, University of Pennsylvania.

Mats Rooth, Stefan Riezler, Detlef Prescher, Glenn Carroll, and Franz Beil. 1999. Inducing an semantically annotated lexicon via em-based clustering. In *Proceedings of the 37th Annual Meeting of the Association for Computational Linguistics*, Maryland.

Sabine Schulte im Walde. 2003. *Experiments on the Automatic Induction of German Semantic Verb Classes*. Ph.D. thesis, Institut für Maschinelle Sprachverarbeitung, Universität Stuttgart. Published as AIMS Report 9(2).

Hinrich Schütze. 1998. Automatic word sense discrimination. *Computational Linguistics*, 24(1):97–123.

Sarah Thomason and Terrence Kaufmann. 1988. *Language Contact, Creolization, and Genetic Linguistics*. University of California Press, Berkeley.

Frans van Coetsem. 1988. *Loan Phonology and the Two Transfer Types in Language Contact*. Publications in Language Sciences. Foris Publications, Dordrecht.

Zeno Vendler. 1967. *Linguistics in Philosophy*. Cornell University Press, Ithaca, NY.

Michael S. Vitevitch and Paul A. Luce. 1999. Probabilistic Phonotactics and Neighborhood Activation in Spoken Word Recognition. *Journal of Memory and Language*, 40(3):374–408.

Andreas Wagner. 2004. *Learning Thematic Role Relations for Lexical Semantic Nets*. Ph.D. thesis, Universität Tübingen.

David Yarowsky. 1995. Unsupervised word sense disambiguation rivaling supervised methods. In *Proceedings of 33rd Annual Meeting of the Association for Computational Linguistics*, pages 189–196, Cambridge, MA.

# Semantic Similarity: What for?

**Ido Dagan**
Bar Ilan University
dagan@macs.biu.ac.il

## Abstract

Linguistic similarity has been a prominent notion and tool in computational linguistics and related areas, as elaborated nicely in the announcement of this workshop. Yet, what exactly counts as "similarity", or when two linguistic concepts should be regarded as similar, often remains rather vague and ill posed, which is in fact quite typical for unsupervised notions. This talk will focus on similarity at the semantic level, and will explore the perspective that different notions of similarity may be defined relative to concrete modeling goals. In particular, I will refer to the two major goals in semantic modeling: predicting likelihood of occurrence, which is the typical goal in disambiguation and language modeling, and recognizing target meanings, which is the typical semantic goal in text understanding applications such as question answering, information extraction, summarization and information retrieval. We will discuss each goal and present corresponding semantic similarity approaches.



*Proceedings of the Workshop on Linguistic Distances*, page 7,
Sydney, July 2006. 

# Similarity judgments: philosophical, psychological and mathematical investigations

**Claude St-Jacques**
Institute for Information Technology
National Research Council of Canada
Gatineau, QC, Canada
Claude.St-Jacques@nrc.gc.ca

**Caroline Barrière**
Institute for Information Technology
National Research Council of Canada
Gatineau, QC, Canada
Caroline.Barriere@nrc.gc.ca

**Abstract**

This study investigates similarity judgments from two angles. First, we look at models suggested in the psychology and philosophy literature which capture the essence of concept similarity evaluation for humans. Second, we analyze the properties of many metrics which simulate such evaluation capabilities. The first angle reveals that non-experts can judge similarity and that their judgments need not be based on predefined traits. We use such conclusions to inform us on how gold standards for word sense disambiguation tasks could be established. From the second angle, we conclude that more attention should be paid to metric properties before assigning them to perform a particular task.

## 1 Introduction

The task of word sense disambiguation has been at the heart of Natural Language Processing (NLP) for many years. Recent Senseval competitions (Mihalcea and Edmonds, 2004; Preiss and Yarowsky, 2001) have stimulated the development of algorithms to tackle different lexical disambiguation tasks. Such tasks require at their core a judgment of similarity as a word's multiple definitions and its contexts of occurrences are compared. Similarity judgment algorithms come in many different forms. One angle of this article is to analyze the assumptions behind such similarity metrics by looking at different shared or non-shared properties. Among the interesting properties we note symmetry and transitivity, which are fundamental to the understanding of similarity. This angle is investigated in Section 4 and 5, looking respectively at two broad classes of mathematical models of similarity and then more closely at different similarity metrics.

As Senseval and other similar competitions need a gold standard for evaluating the competing systems, the second angle of our research looks into literature in philosophy and psychology to gain insight on the human capability in performing a similarity judgment. From the first discipline explored in Section 2, we discover that philosophers have divergent views on concept identification, ranging from scientific definitions to human perception of concepts. From the second discipline, explored in Section 3, we discover different psychological models for concept identification and implicitly concept comparison, this time ranging from continuous concepts being positioned in multi-dimensional spaces to concrete concepts being grasped as entities.

The two angles (metrics and humans) converge in the conclusion of Section 6 with general observations and future work.

## 2 Philosophical evidence

Children have a natural eagerness to recognize regularities in the world and to mimic the behavior of competent members of their linguistic community. It is in these words that Wittgenstein (1980) simply expresses how infants acquire the community's language. What underlies the activities surrounding a common use of language is similar to our usage of words to express something: "Consider for example the proceedings that we call *games*. I mean board-games, card-games, ball-games, Olympic games, and so on. What is common to them all?" (Wittgenstein, 1968: 66). Wittgenstein answers that these expressions are characterized by similarities he calls *family resemblances*.



*Proceedings of the Workshop on Linguistic Distances*, pages 8–15,
Sydney, July 2006. 

Given that a dictionary's purpose is to define concepts, we could hope to see such family resemblances among its definitions. Contrarily to this intuition, Table 1 shows definitions and examples for a few senses of *game* in Wordnet[1], from which resemblance cannot be found in terms of common words in the definitions or examples. Nevertheless, humans are able to give different judgments of similarity between different senses of the word *game*. For example, similarity between sense 1 and sense 3 is intuitively larger than between sense 1 and sense 4.

Table 1: Some senses of *game* in Wordnet

| | Definition + *Example* |
|---|---|
| 1 | A single play of a sport or other contest. *The game lasted two hours.* |
| 2 | A contest with rules to determine a winner. *You need four people to play this game.* |
| 3 | The game equipment needed in order to play a particular game. *The child received several games for his birthday.* |
| 4 | Your occupation or line of work *He's in the plumbing game.* |
| 5 | A secret scheme to do something (especially something underhand or illegal). [...] *I saw through his little game from the start.* |

Before being tempted to call up gigabytes of corpus evidence data and computational strength to help us identify the family of resemblance emerging here, let us further look at the nature of that notion from a philosophical point of view. Possible senses of individual things could be traced back to Aristotle's work and identified "without qualification" as the primary substance of a thing (Cassam, 1986). What accounts for the substance of an object, for Aristotle, was the thing itself, namely its essence. Taking a slightly different view on the notion of family of objects, Putnam (1977) instead pursues a quest for *natural kinds* and according to him, the distinguishing characteristics that "hold together" natural kinds are the "core facts [...] conveying the use of words of that kind" (Putnam, 1977: 118). Putnam disagrees with any analytical approaches sustaining that the meaning of a word $X$ is given by a conjunction of properties $P = \{P_1, P_2, \ldots P_n\}$ in such a way that $P$ is the essence of $X$. The problem is that a "natural kind may have *abnormal members*" (Putnam, 1977: 103). For instance, normal lemons have a yellow peel but let's suppose in accordance with Putnam, that a new environmental condition makes lemon peel become blue. An analytical view will be unable to state which one amongst the yellow or the blue ones is now the normal member of the natural class of lemons. Putnam rather relies on a "scientific theory construction" to define what an object of natural kind is, and therefore, does not see that dictionaries "are *cluttered up* [...] with pieces of empirical information" (Putnam, 1977: 118) as a defect to convey core facts about a natural class.

In contrast to Putnam, Fodor (1998) is a virulent opponent to a mind-independent similarity semantics subject to scientific discoveries. With his ostentatious *doorknob* example, Fodor shows that there is not any natural kind, hidden essence or peculiar structure that makes a doorknob *a doorknob*. "No doubt, some engineer might construct a counter-example–a mindless doorknob detector; and we might even come to rely on such a thing when groping for a doorknob in the dark" (Fodor, 1998: 147). However, the construct will have to be done on what strikes us as *doorknobhood* or satisfying the *doorknob stereotype*, i.e. "the gadget would have to be calibrated to us since there is nothing else in nature that responds selectively to doorknobs" (Fodor, 1998: 147). According to Fodor, our capacity to acquire the concept of *doorknob* involves a similarity metric, and it is the human innate capacity to determine the concepts similar to *doorknob* that allow the characterization of *doorknobhood*. Therefore, Fodor states that the meaning of concepts is mind-dependent and that individuation is not intractable since members of a language community, although experiencing diverse forms of a concept will tend to acquire similar stereotypes of such a concept.

This brief exploration into philosophical approaches for concept representation and delimitation can inform us on the establishment of a gold standard by humans for the word sense disambiguation (WSD) task. In fact, the adherence to one model rather than another has an impact on who should be performing the evaluation[2]. Senseval-2 was in line with Putnam's view of 'division of linguistic labour' by relying on lexicographers' judgments to build a gold standard (Kilgarrif, 1998). On the other hand, Senseval-3 collected data via Open-Mind Initiative[3], which was much more in line with Fodor's view that any common people can use their own *similarity*

[1] See http://wordnet.princeton.edu/

[2] The evaluation consists in performing sense tagging of word occurrences in context.

[3] See http://www.openmind.org/, a web site where anyone can perform the sense tagging "games".

*metric* to disambiguate polysemous terms. Interestingly, a recent empirical study (Murray and Green 2004) showed how judgments by ordinary people were consistent among themselves but different from the one of lexicographers. It is important to decide who the best judges are; a decision which can certainly be based on the foreseen application, but also, as we suggest here, on some theoretical grounds.

## 3 Psychological Evidence

We pursue our quest for insights in the establishment of gold standards by humans for the WSD task, now trying to answer the "how" question rather then the "who" question. Indeed, Fodor's view might influence us in deciding that non-experts can perform similarity judgments, but this does not tell us how these judgments should be performed. Different psychological models will give possible answers. In fact, similarity judgments have been largely studied by experimental psychologists and distinctive theories give some evidence about the existence of a human internal cognitive mechanism for such judgments. In this section, we present three approaches: *subjective scaling* and *objective scaling* (Voinov, 2002), and *semantic differential* (Osgood et al. 1957).

### 3.1 Subjective Scaling

In *subjective scaling* (Voinov, 2002), the subjective human judgment is considered as a convenient raw material to make comparison between empirical studies of similarity. Subjects are asked to point out the "similarities among $n$ objects of interest – whether concepts, persons, traits, symptoms, cultures or species" (Shepard, 1974: 373). Then the similarity judgments are represented in an $n \times n$ matrix of objects by a multidimensional scaling (MDS) of the distance between each object. Equation 1 shows the evaluation of similarity, where $d(x_{ik}, x_{jk})$ stands for the distance between objects $x_i$ and $x_j$ on stimulus (dimension) $k$ and $w_k$ is the psychological salience of that stimulus $k$:

$$D(x_i, x_j) = \sum_{k=1}^{m} w_k (d(x_{ik}, x_{jk})). \quad (1)$$

Shepard's MDS theory assumes that a monotonic transformation should be done from a nonmetric psychological salience of a stimulus to a metric space model. By definition, the resulting metric function over a set $X$ should fullfill the following conditions:

$\forall x, y, z \in X$ :

1. $d(x, y) \geq d(x, x) = 0$ (minimality),
2. $d(x, y) = d(y, x)$ (symmetry),
3. $d(x, y) \geq d(x, z) + d(z, y)$ (triangle ineq.).

Accordingly to Shepard (1974), the distance in equation (1) can be computed with different metrics. Some of these metrics are given in Lebart and Rajman (2000). The *Euclidean metric* is the best known:

$$d_E(x_i, x_j) = \left( \sum_{k=1}^{m} w_k (x_{ik} - x_{jk})^2 \right)^{1/2}. \quad (2)$$

The *city block metric* is another one:

$$d_C(x_i, x_j) = \sum_{k=1}^{m} w_k \left| x_{ik} - x_{jk} \right|. \quad (3)$$

Another yet is the *Minkowski metric*:

$$d_N(x_i, x_j) = \sum_{k=1}^{m} w_k \left( (x_{ik} - x_{jk})^n \right)^{\frac{1}{n}}. \quad (4)$$

There is a main concern with the MDS model. Tversky (1977) criticized the adequacy of the metric distance functions as he showed that the three conditions of minimality, symmetry and triangle inequality are sometimes empirically violated. For instance, Tversky and Gati showed empirically that assessment of the similarity between pairs of countries was asymetric when they asked for "the degree to which Red China is similar to North Korea" (1978: 87) and in the reverse order, i.e. similarity between North Korea and Red China.

### 3.2 Objective Scaling

The second approach is called *objective scaling* by Voinov "though this term is not widely accepted" (Voinov, 2002). According to him, the objectivity of the method comes from the fact that similarity measures are calculated from the ratio of objective features that describe objects under analysis. So, subjects are asked to make qualitative judgments on common or distinctive features of objects and the comparison is then made by any distance axioms. Tversky's (1977) *contrast model* (CM) is the best known formalization of this approach. In his model, the measure of similarity is computed by:

$$S(A, B) = \alpha f(A \cap B) - \beta f(A - B) - \chi f(B - A) \quad (5)$$

where $f(A \cap B)$ represents a function of the common features of both entities $A$ and $B$, $f(A-B)$ is the function of the features belonging to $A$ but not $B$, $f(B-A)$ is the function of the features belonging to $B$ but not $A$ and $\alpha, \beta, \chi$ are their respective weighting parameters. Equation (5) is the *matching* axiom of the CM. A second fundamental property of that model is given by the axiom of *monotonicity*:

$$S(A,B) \geq S(A,C) \tag{6}$$

If $A \cap C \subset A \cap B$, $A-B \subset A-C$, and $B-A \subset C-A$, then (6) is satisfied. With these two axioms (5-6), Tversky (1977) defined the basis of what he called the *matching function* using the theoretical notion of feature sets rather then the geometric concept of similarity distance. Interesting empirical studies followed this research on CM and aimed at finding the correlation between human judgments of similarity and difference. Although some results show a correlation between these judgments, there is limitation to their complementarity: "the relative weights of the common and distinctive features vary with the nature of the task and support the focusing hypothesis that people attend more to the common features in judgments of similarity than in judgments of the difference" (Tverski and Gati, 1978: 84). Later on, Medin et al. (1990) also reported cases when judgments of similarity and difference are not inverses: first, when entities differ in their number of features, and second when similarity/difference judgments involve distinction of both attributes and relations. "Although sameness judgments are typically described as more global or non-analytic than difference judgments, an alternative possibility is that they focus on relations rather than attributes" (Medin et al., 1990: 68).

### 3.3 Semantic Differential

One standard psycholinguistic method to measure the similarity of meaning combines the use of *subjective scaling* transposed in a semantic space. One well-known method is *Semantic Differential* (SD) developed by Osgood et al. (1957).

The SD methodology measures the meanings that individual subjects grant to words and concepts according to a series of factor analyses. These factor analyses are bipolar adjectives put at each end of a *Likert scale* (Likert, 1932) devised to rate the individual reaction to the contrasted stimulus. For instance, the SD of a concept can be rated with two stimuli of goodness and temperature:

$$\textit{Good}\ \underset{3}{\_}:\underset{2}{\_}:\underset{1}{\overset{\times}{\_}}:\underset{0}{\_}:\underset{1}{\_}:\underset{2}{\_}:\underset{3}{\_}\ \textit{Bad}$$

$$\textit{Cold}\ \underset{3}{\_}:\underset{2}{\_}:\underset{1}{\_}:\underset{0}{\_}:\underset{1}{\overset{\times}{\_}}:\underset{2}{\_}:\underset{3}{\_}\ \textit{Hot}$$

If the subject feels that the observed concept is neutral with regards to the polar terms, his check-mark should be at the position 0. In our example, the mark on the *good-bad* scale being at the 1 on the left side of the neutral point 0, the judgment means *slighthy good*. Positions 2 and 3 on that same side would be respectively *quite good* and *extremely good*. A similar analysis applies for the *cold-hot* scale shown.

The theoretical background of that methodology, which tries to standardize across subjects the meaning of the same linguistic stimulus, relies on psychological research on synestesia. Simply explained, synestesia is similar to a double reaction to a stimulus. For example, when presented with images of concepts, subjects do not only have a spontaneous reaction to the images, but they are also able to characterize the associated concept in terms of almost any bipolar adjective pairs (hot-cold, pleasant-unpleasant, simple-complex, vague-precise, dull-sharp, static-dynamic, sweet-bitter, emotional-rational, etc.). According to Osgood et al. "the imagery found in synesthesia is intimately tied up with language metaphor, and both represent *semantic* relations" (1957: 23).

In SD, bipolar adjectives used in succession can mediate a generalization to the meaning of a sign, as uncertainty on each scale is reduced with the successive process of elicitation. By postulating representation in a semantic space, each orthogonal axis of selection produces a semantic differentiation when the subjects rate the semantic alternatives on a bipolar scale. Although that space could be multidimensional, empirical studies (Osgood et al., 1957) on factor analysis showed stability and relative importance of three particular dimensions labeled as Evaluation, Potency, and Activity (EPA). We refer the reader to Osgood et al. (1957) for further explanation on these EPA dimensions.

### 3.4 WSD and human judgments

Table 2 emphasizes commonalities and differences between the three psychological models explored.

Table 2 – Psychological Models

| | Continuous | Predefined traits | Similarity/ Difference |
|---|---|---|---|
| MDS | Yes | Yes | No |
| CM | No | Yes | Yes |
| SD | No | No | Possible |

In Table 2, we show that both MDS (Shepard, 1974) and CM (Tversky, 1977) rely on a set of predefined traits. This is a major problem, as it leads to the necessity of defining in advance such a set of traits on which to judge similarity between objects. On the other hand, SD (Osgood et al. 1957), although using a few bipolar scales for positioning concepts, argues that these scales are not concept-dependent, but rather they can be used for grasping the meaning of all concepts. A second major difference highlighted in Table 2 is that MDS is the only approach looking at continuous perceptual dimensions of stimulus, contrarily to CM in which the scaling procedes with discrete conceptual traits, and even more in opposition to SD which considers entities as primitives. Finally, Table 2 shows the interesting observation brought forth by Tversky and later empirical studies of Medin et al. (1980) of the non-equivalence between the notion of similarity and difference.

Coming back to the question of "how" human evaluation could be performed to provide a gold standard for the WSD task, considering the pros and cons of the different models lead us to suggest a particular strategy of sense attribution. Combining the similarity/difference of Tversky with the successive elucidation of Osgood et al., two bipolar Likert scales could be used to delimit a similarity concept: a resembling axis and a contrasting axis. In this approach, the similarity concept still stays general, avoiding the problems of finding specific traits for each instance on which to have a judgment.

Already in the empirical studies of Murray and Green (2004), a Likert scale is used, but on an "applying" axis. Subjects are asked for each definition of a word to decide whether it "applies perfectly" or rather "barely applies" to a context containing the word. The choice of such an axis has limitations in its applicability for mapping senses on examples. More general resembling and contrasting axis would allow for similarity judgments on any statements whether they are two sense definitions, two examples or a sense definition with an example.

# 4 Mathematical Models of Similarity

Logic and mathematics are extremely prolific in similarity measurement models. According to Dubois et al (1997), they are used for cognitive tasks like classification, case-based reasoning and interpolation. In the present study, we restrict our investigation to the classification task as representative on the unsupervised WSD task. The other approaches are inferential strategies, using already solved problems to extrapolate or interpolate solutions to new problems. Those would be appropriate for WSD in a supervised context (provided training data), but due to space constraints, we postpone discussion of those models to a later study. Our present analysis divides classification models into two criteria: the *cardinality of sets* and the *proximity-based* similarity measures.

## 4.1 Cardinality of sets

In line with De Baets et al. (2001), similarity measures can be investigated under a rational *cardinality*-based criterion of *sets*. In an extensive study of 28 similarity measures for ordinary sets, this research showed that measures can be classified on the basis of only a few properties. They proposed at first to build the class of cardinality-based similarity measures from one generic formula:

$$S(X,Y) = \frac{w\alpha_{X,Y} + x\beta_{X,Y} + y\chi_{X,Y} + z\delta_{X,Y}}{w'\alpha_{X,Y} + x'\beta_{X,Y} + y'\chi_{X,Y} + z'\delta_{X,Y}}, \tag{8}$$

where $\alpha_{X,Y} = \min\{\#(X-Y), \#(Y-X)\}$, $\beta_{X,Y} = \max\{\#(X-Y), \#(Y-X)\}$, $\chi_{X,Y} = \#(X \cap Y)$ and $\delta_{X,Y} = \#(X \cup Y)^c$, and all $w$, $x$, $y$, $z$, $w'$, $x'$, $y'$, $z' \in \{0,1\}$. It follows that $\#(X \cap Y)$ is the number of couples $(1,1)$ and $X - Y$ denotes the sets difference $(X-Y) = (X \cap Y^c)$.

The classification of these 28 similarity measures (which can all be linked to the general formula) becomes possible by borrowing from the framework of fuzzy sets the concepts of $T$ for t-norm (*fuzzy intersection*) operators and *T-equivalence* for the property of *T*-indistinguishability (De Baets et al., 2001). So, a typical measure $M$ of *T-equivalence* under the universe $U$ must satisfy the following conditions for any $(x, y, z) \in U$: (i) $M(x,x) = 1$ (reflexivity); (ii) $M(x,y) = M(y,x)$ (Symmetry);

(iii) $T(M(x,y), M(y,z)) \le M(x,z)$ (*T*-transitivity).

All 28 measures show reflexivity and symmetry but they vary on the type of transitivity they achieve. In fact, studying boundary and monotonicity behavior of the different measures, De Baets et al. (2001) group them under four types corresponding to four different formulas of fuzzy intersections (t-norms): the standard intersection $Z(a,b) = \min(a,b)$, the Lukasiewicz t-norm $L(a,b) = \max(0, a+b-1)$, the algebraic product $P(a,b) = ab$ and the drastic intersection $D(a,b) = (a$ when $b = 1$, $b$ when $a = 1$ and 0 otherwise). We refer the reader to De Baets et al. (2001) to get the full scope of their results. Accordingly, Jaccard's coefficient *J* (equation 9) and Russel-Rao's coefficient *R* (equation 10) are both, for example, *L*-transivive (Lukasiewicz' type):

$$S_J(X,Y) = \frac{\#(X \cap Y)}{\#(X \cup Y)} \quad (9)$$

$$S_R(X,Y) = \frac{\#(X \cap Y)}{n} \quad . \quad (10)$$

On the other hand, the overlapping coefficient *O* (equation 11) is not even *D*-transitive, knowing that *D* is the lower transitive condition $(D \le L \le P \le Z)$ in the framework:

$$S_O(X,Y) = \frac{\#(X \cap Y)}{\min(\#X, \#Y)} \quad . \quad (11)$$

### 4.2 Proximity-based

Following our second criterion of classification, mathematics also uses diverse *proximity-based* similarity measures. We subdivide these mathematical measures into three groups: the distance model, the probabilistic model, and the angular coefficients. The first one, the distance model, overlaps in part with the subjective scaling of similarity as presented in the psychological approaches (section 3.1). The mathematical model is the same with a metric of distance $d(x, y)$ computed between the objects in a space. Algorithms like formulae (2), (3) and (4) of section 3.1 are amongst the *proximity-based* similarity measures.

Second, the probabilistic model is based on the statistical analysis of objects and their attributes in a data space. Lebart & Rajman (2000) gave many examples of that kind of proximity measures, such as the Kullback-Leiber distance $D_K$ between two documents *A* and *B*, given the probability distribution $P = \{p_1, p_2, ..., p_n\}$:

$$D_K(A,B) = \sum_{p_{ak} \times p_{bk} \neq 0} (p_{ak} - p_{bk})(\log p_{ak} - \log p_{bk}) \quad (12)$$

The third mathematical model is also a metric space model but it uses angular measures between vectors of features to determine the similarity between objects. A well-known measure from that group is the cosine-correlation:

$$S_C(x,y) = \frac{\sum_{k=1}^{n} x_k y_k}{\sqrt{\left[\sum_{k=1}^{n} x_k^2\right]\left[\sum_{k=1}^{n} y_k^2\right]}} \quad . \quad (13)$$

Although conditions applying on proximity-based measures are shortly described in Cross and Sudkamp (2002) and Miyamoto (1990) for fuzzy sets, we are not aware of an extensive research such as the one by De Baets et al. (2001), presented in section 4.1, for classifying cardinality of sets types. We make such an attempt in the following section.

## 5 Analysis of similarity metrics

In this section, we perform a classification and analysis exercise for similarity measure[4], possibly used for WSD, but more generally used in any task where similarity between words is required. Table 3 shows the measures classified in the four categories of the mathematical model presented in section 4: measures of cardinality (Card), of distance (Dist), of probability (Prob) and of angle (Ang).

We sustain that these groupings can be further justified based on two criteria: the psychological model of meaning (Table 2) and the typical properties of the classes (Table 4). The first criterion refers to the representation of concepts distinguishing between the dense-state and the discrete-state[5] of concept (meaning) attributes. That psychological distinction is helpful to categorize some metrics, like Gotoh, which seems hybrid (Card and Dist). In such a metric, the penalty for the gap between two concepts applies on the defect of the dense-state, such as for a blurred im-

[4] We use the list of the following web page: http:// www.dcs.shef.ac.uk/~sam/stringmetrics.html#sellers

[5] This differentiation is based on Tenenbaum's (1996) idea that MDS better suits continuous perceptual domains and set-theoretic accommodate discrete features like in the CM.

age rather then the absence of the discrete-state, i.e. of a feature; it is therefore classified in the Dist category.

Table 3: Classification of Similarity Metrics

| Metric | Card | Dist | Prob | Ang |
|---|---|---|---|---|
| Hamming distance | | X | | |
| Levenshtein distance | | X | | |
| Needleman-Wunch | | X | | |
| Smith-Waterman | | X | | |
| Gotoh distance | | X | | |
| Block distance | | X | | |
| Monge Elkan dist. | | X | | |
| Jaro distance | | | X | |
| Jaro Winkler | | | X | |
| SoundEx distance | | | X | |
| Matching coefficient | X | | | |
| Dice's coefficient | X | | | |
| Jaccard similarity | X | | | |
| Overlap coefficient | X | | | |
| Euclidean distance | | X | | |
| Cosine similarity | | | | X |
| Variational distance | | | X | |
| Hellinger distance | | | X | |
| Information radius | | | X | |
| Harmonic mean | | | X | |
| Skew divergence | | | X | |
| Confusion probability | | | X | |
| Tau | | | X | |
| Fellegi & Sunters | | | X | |
| TFIDF | | | | X |
| FastA | | | X | |
| BlastP | | | X | |
| Maximal matches | | | X | |
| q-gram | | | X | |
| Ukkonen algorithms | | | X | |

The second criterion is a study on shared properties for each category of the mathematical model. Table 4 summarizes the properties using the following schema: (m) minimality, (r) reflexivity, (s) symmetry, (ti) triangle inequality, (tr) transitivity.

Table 4 – Typical Properties of Metrics

| | (m) | (r) | (s) | (ti) | (tr) |
|---|---|---|---|---|---|
| **Card** | | Yes | Yes | | Yes |
| **Dist** | Yes | | Yes | Yes | Possible |
| **Prob** | | No | Possible | | Yes |
| **Ang** | Yes | | Yes | | Yes |

From Table 4, we see for instance that reflexivity is a basic property for cardinality measures because we wish to regularly count discrete objects in a set. On the opposite side, the minimality property is a characteristic of a distance measure, since it is noticeable by the displacement or the change, for example, in distinctive images. According to Fodor (1998), we say that statistical or probabilistic approaches exhibit several necessary and sufficient conditions for the inclusion of elements in the extension of a concept, but the dominant element, such as the pattern of comparison (in Maximal matches for instance) is anti-reflexive and asymmetric with the resulting elements. However, there is symmetry in the resultant, but there is still anti-reflexivity.

We also single out the angular metrics from distance measures even though they use a similar analysis of the qualitative variation of entities. According to Ekman & Sjöberg (1965), a method using similarity converted into cosine representation has the advantage to reveal two components of percepts, i.e. the two-dimensional vector is a modeling in magnitude and direction. Thus, angular metrics can be a means used to contrast two semantic features of entities.

### 5.1 A closer look at properties

Finding out that different sets of properties can serve as dividing lines between groups of metrics is interesting in itself, but does not answer the question as to which set is more appropriate than others. We do not wish to answer this question here as we believe it is application-dependent, but we do wish to emphasize that a questioning should take place before choosing a particular measure. In fact, for each property, there is an appropriate question that can be asked, as is summarized in Table 5.

Table 5 – Questioning for Measure Selection

| Property | Question |
|---|---|
| Minimality | Is the minimal distance between objects the distance of an object with itself? |
| Symmetry | Is it true that the distance between x and y is always the same as the distance between y and x? |
| Triangle Inequality | Is it appropriate that a direct distance between x and z is always smaller than a composed distance from x to y and y to z? |
| Reflexivity | Is it true that the relation that it holds between an object and itself is always the same? |
| Transitivity | Is it necessarily the case that when x is similar to y and y is similar to z, that x be similar to z? |

For the task of WSD investigated in this paper, we hope to open the debate as to which properties are to be taken into consideration.

## 6 Conclusion and future work

This paper presented some ideas from two angles of study (human and metrics) into the intricate problem of similarity judgments. A larger study is under way on both angles. First, we suggested, based on some psychological and philosophical model analysis, a two-axis Osgood-like benchmarking approach for "ordinary human" word-sense judgments. We intend to perform an empirical experiment to validate this idea by looking at inter-judge agreement.

On the algorithm side, although the approaches based on the cardinality of sets are not central to WSD, we presented them first as we find it inspiring to see an effort of classification on those measures. We then attempted a somewhat more broad classification by emphasizing properties of different groups of similarity measures: cardinality of sets, distance, probabilistic measures and angular metrics. Although each group has a particular subset of properties, we noted that all of them share a property of transitivity. This is interestingly different from the psychological contrast model of Tversky where differences and similarities are measured differently on different criteria. We think investigations into similarity measures which reproduce such a non-transitive differentiation approach should be performed. We are on that path in our larger study. We also suggest that any proposal of a measure for a task should be preceded by a study of which properties seem adequate for such a task. We conclude by opening up the debate for the WSD task.

## References


Bernard De Baets, Hans De Meyer and Helga Naessens. 2001. A class of rational cardinality-based similarity measures. *Journal of Computational and Applied Mathematics*, 132:51-69.

Quassim Cassam. 1986. Science and Essence. *Philosophy*, 61:95-107.

Valerie V. Cross and Thomas A. Sudkamp. 2002. *Similarity and Compatibility in Fuzzy Set Theory*. Heidelberg, Germany: Physica-Verlag..

Didier Dubois, Henri Prade, Francesc Esteva, Pere Garcia and Lluis Godo. 1997. A Logical Approach to Interpolation Based on Similarity Relations. *International Journal of Approximate Reasoning*, 17:1-36.

Cösta Ekman and Lennart Sjöberg. 1965. Scaling. *Annual Review of Psychology*, 16, 451-474.

Jerry A. Fodor. 1998. *Concepts. Where Cognitive Science Went Wrong*. Oxford: Clarendon Press.

Adam Kilgarriff. 1998. Gold standard datasets for evaluating word sense disambiguation programs. *Computer Speech and Language*, 12:453-472.

Ludovic Lebart and Martin Rajman. 2000. Computing Similarity in R. Dale, H. Moisl & H. Somers eds. *Handbook of Natural Language Processing*. New York: Marcel Dekker, Inc., 477-505.

Rensis Likert. 1932. A technique for the measurement of attitudes. Archives of Psychology 140, 5-53.

Douglas L. Medin, Robert L. Goldstone and Dedre Gentner. 1990. Similarity Involving Attributes and Relations: Judgments of Similarity and Difference are not Inverses. *Psychological Science*, 1(1):64-69

Rada Mihalcea and Phil Edmonds. 2004. *Proceedings of SENSEVAL-3, Association for Computational Linguistics Workshop*, Barcelona, Spain.

Sadaaki Miyamoto. 1990. *Fuzzy Sets in Information Retrieval and Cluster Analysis*. Dordrecht: Kluwer Academic Publisher.

G. Craig Murray and Rebecca Green. 2004. Lexical knowledge and human disagreement on a WSD task, *Computer Speech and Language* 18, 209-222.

Charles E. Osgood, George J. Suci and Percy H. Tannenbaum. 1957. *The measurement of meaning*. Urbana: University of Illinois Press

Judita Preiss and David Yarowsky (eds). 2001. *Proceedings of SENSEVAL-2, Association for Computational Linguistics Workshop*, Toulouse, France.

Hilary Putnam. 1977. Is Semantics Possible? in Stephen P. Schwartz ed. *Naming, Necessity, and Natural Kinds*. Ithaca and London: Cornell University Press, 102-118.

Roger N. Shepard. 1974. Representation of structure in similarity data: Problems and prospects. *Psychometrika*, 39(4):373-421.

Joshua B. Tenenbaum. 1996. Learning the structure of similarity. In D. S. Touretzky, M. C. Mozer and M. E. Hasselmo (Eds), *Advances in neural information processing systems*, (Vol. 8, pp. 3-9), Cambridge, MA: MIT Press.

Amos Tversky. 1977. Features of Similarity. *Psychological Review*, 84, 79-98.

Amos Tversky and Itamar Gati. 1978. Studies of Similarity in E. Rosch & B. B. Lloyd eds. *Cognition and Categorization*. New York: John Wiley & Sons, Inc., 79-98.

Alexander V. Voinov. 2002. The Role of Similarity Judgment in Intuitive Problem Solving and its Modeling in a Sheaf-Theoretic Framework. *Proceedings of the 1st Int. Conf. on FSKD'02*, 1:753-757.

Ludwig Wittgenstein. 1968. *Philosophical Investigations*. Oxford: Basil Blackwell.

Ludwig Wittgenstein. 1980. *Remarks on the Philosophy of Psychology*. Chicago: University of Chicago Press; Oxford: Basil Blackwell.

# Automatically creating datasets for measures of semantic relatedness

**Torsten Zesch** and **Iryna Gurevych**
Department of Telecooperation
Darmstadt University of Technology
D-64289 Darmstadt, Germany
{zesch,gurevych} (at) tk.informatik.tu-darmstadt.de

**Abstract**

Semantic relatedness is a special form of linguistic distance between words. Evaluating semantic relatedness measures is usually performed by comparison with human judgments. Previous test datasets had been created analytically and were limited in size. We propose a corpus-based system for automatically creating test datasets.[1] Experiments with human subjects show that the resulting datasets cover all degrees of relatedness. As a result of the corpus-based approach, test datasets cover all types of lexical-semantic relations and contain domain-specific words naturally occurring in texts.

## 1 Introduction

Linguistic distance plays an important role in many applications like information retrieval, word sense disambiguation, text summarization or spelling correction. It is defined on different kinds of textual units, e.g. documents, parts of a document (e.g. words and their surrounding context), words or concepts (Lebart and Rajman, 2000).[2] Linguistic distance between words is inverse to their semantic similarity or relatedness.

Semantic similarity is typically defined via the lexical relations of synonymy ($automobile$ – $car$) and hypernymy ($vehicle$ – $car$), while semantic relatedness (SR) is defined to cover any kind of lexical or functional association that may exist between two words (Gurevych, 2005).[3] Dissimilar words can be semantically related, e.g. via functional relationships ($night$ – $dark$) or when they are antonyms ($high$ – $low$). Many NLP applications require knowledge about semantic relatedness rather than just similarity (Budanitsky and Hirst, 2006).

A number of competing approaches for computing semantic relatedness of words have been developed (see Section 2). A commonly accepted method for evaluating these approaches is to compare their results with a gold standard based on human judgments on word pairs. For that purpose, relatedness scores for each word pair have to be determined experimentally. Creating test datasets for such experiments has so far been a labor-intensive manual process.

We propose a corpus-based system to automatically create test datasets for semantic relatedness experiments. Previous datasets were created analytically, preventing their use to gain insights into the nature of SR and also not necessarily reflecting the reality found in a corpus. They were also limited in size. We provide a larger annotated test set that is used to better analyze the connections and differences between the approaches for computing semantic relatedness.

The remainder of this paper is organized as follows: we first focus on the notion of semantic relatedness and how it can be evaluated. Section 3 reviews related work. Section 4 describes our system for automatically extracting word pairs from a corpus. Furthermore, the experimental setup leading to human judgments of semantic relatedness

[1] In the near future, we are planning to make the software available to interested researchers.

[2] In this paper, *word* denotes the graphemic form of a token and *concept* refers to a particular sense of a word.

[3] Nevertheless the two terms are often (mis)used interchangeably. We will use semantic relatedness in the remainder of this paper, as it is the more general term that subsumes semantic similarity.



*Proceedings of the Workshop on Linguistic Distances*, pages 16–24,
Sydney, July 2006. ©2006 Association for Computational Linguistics

is presented. Section 5 discusses the results, and finally we draw some conclusions in Section 6.

## 2 Evaluating SR measures

Various approaches for computing semantic relatedness of words or concepts have been proposed, e.g. dictionary-based (Lesk, 1986), ontology-based (Wu and Palmer, 1994; Leacock and Chodorow, 1998), information-based (Resnik, 1995; Jiang and Conrath, 1997) or distributional (Weeds and Weir, 2005). The knowledge sources used for computing relatedness can be as different as dictionaries, ontologies or large corpora.

According to Budanitsky and Hirst (2006), there are three prevalent approaches for evaluating SR measures: mathematical analysis, application-specific evaluation and comparison with human judgments.

Mathematical analysis can assess a measure with respect to some formal properties, e.g. whether a measure is a metric (Lin, 1998).[4] However, mathematical analysis cannot tell us whether a measure closely resembles human judgments or whether it performs best when used in a certain application.

The latter question is tackled by application-specific evaluation, where a measure is tested within the framework of a certain application, e.g. word sense disambiguation (Patwardhan et al., 2003) or malapropism detection (Budanitsky and Hirst, 2006). Lebart and Rajman (2000) argue for application-specific evaluation of similarity measures, because measures are always used for some task. But they also note that evaluating a measure as part of a usually complex application only indirectly assesses its quality. A certain measure may work well in one application, but not in another. Application-based evaluation can only state the fact, but give little explanation about the reasons.

The remaining approach - comparison with human judgments - is best suited for application independent evaluation of relatedness measures. Human annotators are asked to judge the relatedness of presented word pairs. Results from these experiments are used as a gold standard for evaluation. A further advantage of comparison with human judgments is the possibility to gain deeper insights into the nature of semantic relatedness.

However, creating datasets for evaluation has so far been limited in a number of respects. Only a small number of word pairs was manually selected, with semantic similarity instead of relatedness in mind. Word pairs consisted only of noun-noun combinations and only general terms were included. Polysemous and homonymous words were not disambiguated to concepts, i.e. humans annotated semantic relatedness of words rather than concepts.

## 3 Related work

In the seminal work by Rubenstein and Goodenough (1965), similarity judgments were obtained from 51 test subjects on 65 noun pairs written on paper cards. Test subjects were instructed to order the cards according to the "similarity of meaning" and then assign a continuous similarity value (0.0 - 4.0) to each card. Miller and Charles (1991) replicated the experiment with 38 test subjects judging on a subset of 30 pairs taken from the original 65 pairs. This experiment was again replicated by Resnik (1995) with 10 subjects. Table 1 summarizes previous experiments.

A comprehensive evaluation of SR measures requires a higher number of word pairs. However, the original experimental setup is not scalable as ordering several hundred paper cards is a cumbersome task. Furthermore, semantic relatedness is an intuitive concept and being forced to assign fine-grained continuous values is felt to overstrain the test subjects. Gurevych (2005) replicated the experiment of Rubenstein and Goodenough with the original 65 word pairs translated into German. She used an adapted experimental setup where test subjects had to assign discrete values {0,1,2,3,4} and word pairs were presented in isolation. This setup is also scalable to a higher number of word pairs (350) as was shown in Gurevych (2006). Finkelstein et al. (2002) annotated a larger set of word pairs (353), too. They used a 0-10 range of relatedness scores, but did not give further details about their experimental setup. In psycholinguistics, relatedness of words can also be determined through association tests (Schulte im Walde and Melinger, 2005). Results of such experiments are hard to quantify and cannot easily serve as the basis for evaluating SR measures.

Rubenstein and Goodenough selected word pairs analytically to cover the whole spectrum of

[4]That means, whether it fulfills some mathematical criteria: $d(x, y) \geq 0$; $d(x, y) = 0 \Leftrightarrow x = y$; $d(x, y) = d(y, x)$; $d(x, z) \leq d(x, y) + d(y, z)$.

| Paper | Language | Pairs | POS | Rel-type | Scores | # Subjects | Correlation Inter | Correlation Intra |
|---|---|---|---|---|---|---|---|---|
| R/G (1965) | English | 65 | N | sim | continuous 0–4 | 51 | - | .850 |
| M/C (1991) | English | 30 | N | sim | continuous 0–4 | 38 | - | - |
| Res (1995) | English | 30 | N | sim | continuous 0–4 | 10 | .903 | - |
| Fin (2002) | English | 353 | N, V, A | relat | continuous 0–10 | 16 | - | - |
| Gur (2005) | German | 65 | N | sim | discrete {0,1,2,3,4} | 24 | .810 | - |
| Gur (2006) | German | 350 | N, V, A | relat | discrete {0,1,2,3,4} | 8 | .690 | - |
| Z/G (2006) | German | 328 | N, V, A | relat | discrete {0,1,2,3,4} | 21 | .478 | .647 |

Table 1: Comparison of previous experiments. R/G=Rubenstein and Goodenough, M/C=Miller and Charles, Res=Resnik, Fin=Finkelstein, Gur=Gurevych, Z/G=Zesch and Gurevych

similarity from "not similar" to "synonymous". This elaborate process is not feasible for a larger dataset or if domain-specific test sets should be compiled quickly. Therefore, we automatically create word pairs using a corpus-based approach. We assume that due to lexical-semantic cohesion, texts contain a sufficient number of words related by means of different lexical and semantic relations. Resulting from our corpus-based approach, test sets will also contain domain-specific terms. Previous studies only included general terms as opposed to domain-specific vocabularies and therefore failed to produce datasets that can be used to evaluate the ability of a measure to cope with domain-specific or technical terms. This is an important property if semantic relatedness is used in information retrieval where users tend to use specific search terms (*Porsche*) rather than general ones (*car*).

Furthermore, manually selected word pairs are often biased towards highly related pairs (Gurevych, 2006), because human annotators tend to select only highly related pairs connected by relations they are aware of. Automatic corpus-based selection of word pairs is more objective, leading to a balanced dataset with pairs connected by all kinds of lexical-semantic relations. Morris and Hirst (2004) pointed out that many relations between words in a text are non-classical (i.e. other than typical taxonomic relations like synonymy or hypernymy) and therefore not covered by semantic similarity.

Previous studies only considered semantic relatedness (or similarity) of *words* rather than concepts. However, polysemous or homonymous words should be annotated on the level of *concepts*. If we assume that *bank* has two meanings ("financial institution" vs. "river bank")[5] and it is paired with *money*, the result is two sense qualified pairs ($bank_{financial} - money$) and ($bank_{river}$ – $money$). It is obvious that the judgments on the two concept pairs should differ considerably. Concept annotated datasets can be used to test the ability of a measure to differentiate between senses when determining the relatedness of polysemous words. To our knowledge, this study is the first to include concept pairs and to automatically generate the test dataset.

In our experiment, we annotated a high number of pairs similar in size to the test sets by Finkelstein (2002) and Gurevych (2006). We used the revised experimental setup (Gurevych, 2005), based on discrete relatedness scores and presentation of word pairs in isolation, that is scalable to the higher number of pairs. We annotated semantic relatedness instead of similarity and included also non noun-noun pairs. Additionally, our corpus-based approach includes domain-specific technical terms and enables evaluation of the robustness of a measure.

## 4 Experiment

### 4.1 System architecture

Figure 1 gives an overview of our automatic corpus-based system for creating test datasets for evaluating SR measures.

In the first step, a source corpus is preprocessed using tokenization, POS-tagging and lemmatization resulting in a list of POS-tagged lemmas. Randomly generating word pairs from this list would result in too many unrelated pairs, yielding an unbalanced dataset. Thus, we assign weights to each word (e.g. using tf.idf-weighting). The most important document-specific words get the highest weights and due to lexical cohesion of the documents many related words can be found among the top rated. Therefore, we randomly generate a user-defined number of word pairs from the $r$ words with the highest weights for each document.

[5] WordNet lists 10 meanings.

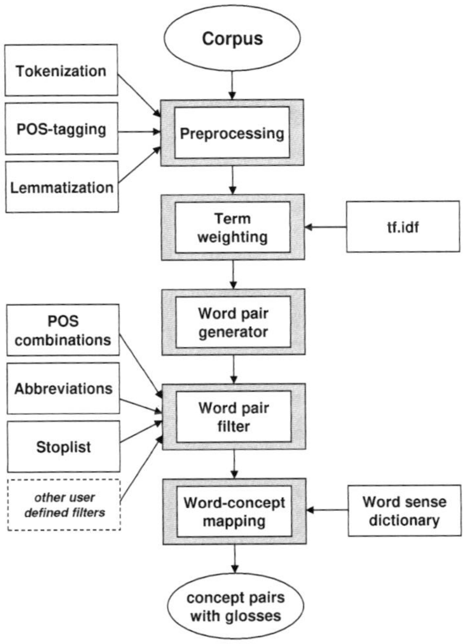


Figure 1: System architecture for extraction of concept pairs.

In the next step, user defined filters are applied to the initial list of word pairs. For example, a filter can remove all pairs containing only uppercase letters (mostly acronyms). Another filter can enforce a certain fraction of POS combinations to be present in the result set.

As we want to obtain judgment scores for semantic relatedness of concepts instead of words, we have to include all word sense combinations of a pair in the list. An external dictionary of word senses is necessary for this step. It is also used to add a gloss for each word sense that enables test subjects to distinguish between senses.

If differences in meaning between senses are very fine-grained, distinguishing between them is hard even for humans (Mihalcea and Moldovan, 2001).[6] Pairs containing such words are not suitable for evaluation. To limit their impact on the experiment, a threshold for the maximal number of senses can be defined. Words with a number of senses above the threshold are removed from the list.

The result of the extraction process is a list of sense disambiguated, POS-tagged pairs of concepts.

[6]E.g. the German verb "halten" that can be translated as hold, maintain, present, sustain, etc. has 26 senses in GermaNet.

## 4.2 Experimental setup

### 4.2.1 Extraction of concept pairs

We extracted word pairs from three different domain-specific corpora (see Table 2). This is motivated by the aim to enable research in information retrieval incorporating SR measures. In particular, the "Semantic Information Retrieval" project (SIR Project, 2006) systematically investigates the use of lexical-semantic relations between words or concepts for improving the performance of information retrieval systems.

The *BERUFEnet* (BN) corpus[7] consists of descriptions of 5,800 professions in Germany and therefore contains many terms specific to professional training. Evaluating semantic relatedness on a test set based on this corpus may reveal the ability of a measure to adapt to a very special domain. The *GIRT* (German Indexing and Retrieval Testdatabase) corpus (Kluck, 2004) is a collection of abstracts of social science papers. It is a standard corpus for evaluating German information retrieval systems. The third corpus is compiled from 106 arbitrarily selected *scientific PowerPoint presentations* (SPP). They cover a wide range of topics from bio genetics to computer science and contain many technical terms. Due to the special structure of presentations, this corpus will be particularly demanding with respect to the required preprocessing components of an information retrieval system.

The three preprocessing steps (tokenization, POS-tagging, lemmatization) are performed using TreeTagger (Schmid, 1995). The resulting list of POS-tagged lemmas is weighted using the SMART 'ltc'[8] tf.idf-weighting scheme (Salton, 1989).

We implemented a set of filters for word pairs. One group of filters removed unwanted word pairs. Word pairs are filtered if they contain at least one word that a) has less than three letters b) contains only uppercase letters (mostly acronyms) or c) can be found in a stoplist. Another filter enforced a specified fraction of combinations of nouns (N), verbs (V) and adjectives (A) to be present in the result set. We used the following parameters: $NN = 0.5$, $NV = 0.15$, $NA = 0.15$, $VV = 0.1$, $VA = 0.05$, $AA = 0.05$. That means 50% of the resulting word pairs for each corpus

[7]http://berufenet.arbeitsagentur.de

[8]l=logarithmic term frequency, t=logarithmic inverse document frequency, c=cosine normalization.

| CORPUS | # DOCS | # TOKENS | DOMAIN |
|---|---|---|---|
| BN | 9,022 | 7,728,501 | descriptions of professions |
| GIRT | 151,319 | 19,645,417 | abstracts of social science papers |
| SPP | 106 | 144,074 | scientific .ppt presentations |

Table 2: Corpus statistics.

were noun-noun pairs, 15% noun-verb pairs and so on.

Word pairs containing polysemous words are expanded to concept pairs using GermaNet (Kunze, 2004), the German equivalent to WordNet, as a sense inventory for each word. It is the most complete resource of this type for German.

GermaNet contains only a few conceptual glosses. As they are required to enable test subjects to distinguish between senses, we use artificial glosses composed from synonyms and hypernyms as a surrogate, e.g. for *brother*: "brother, male sibling" vs. "brother, comrade, friend" (Gurevych, 2005). We removed words which had more than three senses.

Marginal manual post-processing was necessary, since the lemmatization process introduced some errors. Foreign words were translated into German, unless they are common technical terminology. We initially selected 100 word pairs from each corpus. 11 word pairs were removed because they comprised non-words. Expanding the word list to a concept list increased the size of the list. Thus, the final dataset contained 328 automatically created concept pairs.

### 4.2.2 Graphical User Interface

We developed a web-based interface to obtain human judgments of semantic relatedness for each automatically generated concept pair. Test subjects were invited via email to participate in the experiment. Thus, they were not supervised during the experiment.

Gurevych (2006) observed that some annotators were not familiar with the exact definition of semantic relatedness. Their results differed particularly in cases of antonymy or distributionally related pairs. We created a manual with a detailed introduction to SR stressing the crucial points. The manual was presented to the subjects before the experiment and could be re-accessed at any time.

Figure 2: Screenshot of the GUI. Polysemous words are defined by means of synonyms and related words.

During the experiment, one concept pair at a time was presented to the test subjects in random ordering. Subjects had to assign a discrete relatedness value {0,1,2,3,4} to each pair. Figure 2 shows the system's GUI.

In case of a polysemous word, synonyms or related words were presented to enable test subjects to understand the sense of a presented concept. Because this additional information can lead to undesirable priming effects, test subjects were instructed to deliberately decide only about the relatedness of a concept pair and use the gloss solely to understand the sense of the presented concept.

Since our corpus-based approach includes domain-specific vocabulary, we could not assume that the subjects were familiar with all words. Thus, they were instructed to look up unknown words in the German Wikipedia.[9]

Several test subjects were asked to repeat the experiment with a minimum break of one day. Results from the repetition can be used to measure intra-subject correlation. They can also be used to obtain some hints on varying difficulty of judgment for special concept pairs or parts-of-speech.

## 5 Results and discussion

21 test subjects (13 males, 8 females) participated in the experiment, two of them repeated it. The average age of the subjects was 26 years. Most subjects had an IT background. The experiment took 39 minutes on average, leaving about 7 seconds for rating each concept pair.

The summarized inter-subject correlation between 21 subjects was r=.478 (cf. Table 3), which

[9] http://www.wikipedia.de

| | Concepts | | Words | |
|---|---|---|---|---|
| | Inter | Intra | Inter | Intra |
| all | .478 | .647 | .490 | .675 |
| BN | .469 | .695 | .501 | .718 |
| GIRT | .451 | .598 | .463 | .625 |
| SPP | .535 | .649 | .523 | .679 |
| AA | .556 | .890 | .597 | .887 |
| NA | .547 | .773 | .511 | .758 |
| NV | .510 | .658 | .540 | .647 |
| NN | .463 | .620 | .476 | .661 |
| VA | .317 | .318 | .391 | .212 |
| VV | .278 | .494 | .301 | .476 |

Table 3: Summarized correlation coefficients for all pairs, grouped by corpus and grouped by POS combinations.

is statistically significant at $p < .05$. This correlation coefficient is an upper bound of performance for automatic SR measures applied on the same dataset.

Resnik (1995) reported a correlation of r=.9026.[10] The results are not directly comparable, because he only used noun-noun pairs, words instead of concepts, a much smaller dataset, and measured semantic similarity instead of semantic relatedness. Finkelstein et al. (2002) did not report inter-subject correlation for their larger dataset. Gurevych (2006) reported a correlation of r=.69. Test subjects were trained students of computational linguistics, and word pairs were selected analytically.

Evaluating the influence of using concept pairs instead of word pairs is complicated because word level judgments are not directly available. Therefore, we computed a lower and an upper bound for correlation coefficients. For the lower bound, we always selected the concept pair with highest standard deviation from each set of corresponding concept pairs. The upper bound is computed by selecting the concept pair with the lowest standard deviation. The differences between correlation coefficient for concepts and words are not significant. Table 3 shows only the lower bounds.

Correlation coefficients for experiments measuring semantic relatedness are expected to be lower than results for semantic similarity, since the former also includes additional relations (like co-occurrence of words) and is thus a more complicated task. Judgments for such relations strongly depend on experience and cultural background of the test subjects. While most people may agree

[10]Note that Resnik used the averaged correlation coefficient. We computed the summarized correlation coefficient using a Fisher Z-value transformation.

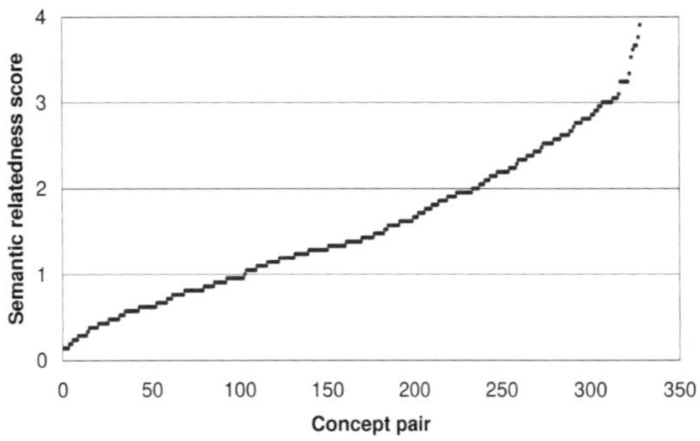


Figure 3: Distribution of averaged human judgments.

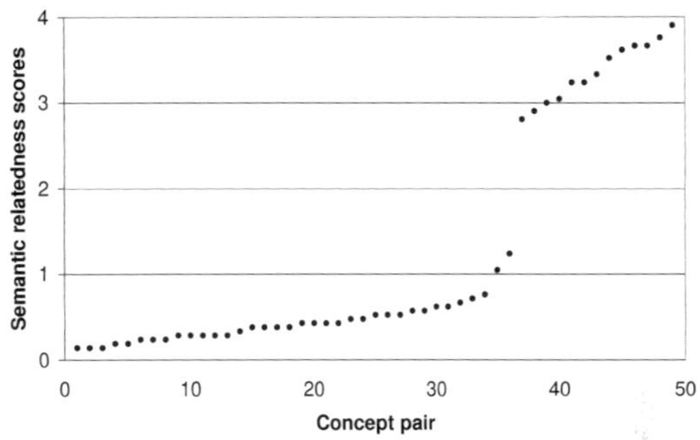


Figure 4: Distribution of averaged human judgments with standard deviation < 0.8.

that (*car – vehicle*) are highly related, a strong connection between (*parts – speech*) may only be established by a certain group. Due to the corpus-based approach, many domain-specific concept pairs are introduced into the test set. Therefore, inter-subject correlation is lower than the results obtained by Gurevych (2006).

In our experiment, intra-subject correlation was r=.670 for the first and r=.623 for the second individual who repeated the experiment, yielding a summarized intra-subject correlation of r=.647. Rubenstein and Goodenough (1965) reported an intra-subject correlation of r=.85 for 15 subjects judging the similarity of a subset (36) of the original 65 word pairs. The values may again not be compared directly. Furthermore, we cannot generalize from these results, because the number of participants which repeated our experiment was too low.

The distribution of averaged human judgments on the whole test set (see Figure 3) is almost balanced with a slight underrepresentation of highly related concepts. To create more highly related concept pairs, more sophisticated weighting schemes or selection on the basis of lexical chain-

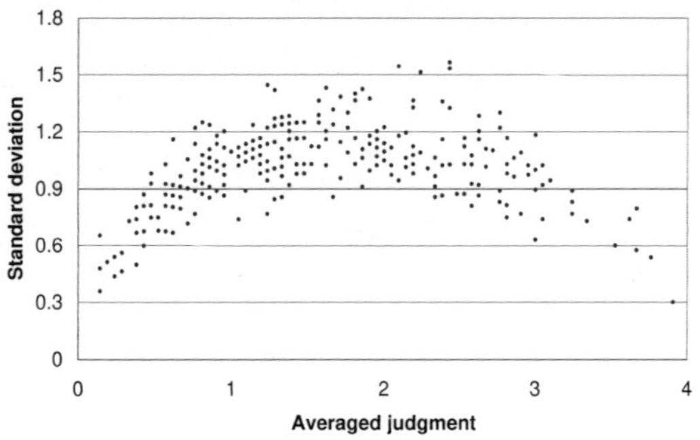


Figure 5: Averaged judgments and standard deviation for all concept pairs. Low deviations are only observed for low or high judgments.

ing could be used. However, even with the present setup, automatic extraction of concept pairs performs remarkably well and can be used to quickly create balanced test datasets.

Budanitsky and Hirst (2006) pointed out that distribution plots of judgments for the word pairs used by Rubenstein and Goodenough display an empty horizontal band that could be used to separate related and unrelated pairs. This empty band is not observed here. However, Figure 4 shows the distribution of averaged judgments with the highest agreement between annotators (standard deviation < 0.8). The plot clearly shows an empty horizontal band with no judgments. The connection between averaged judgments and standard deviation is plotted in Figure 5.

When analyzing the concept pairs with lowest deviation there is a clear tendency for particularly highly related pairs, e.g. hypernymy: *Universität – Bildungseinrichtung* (*university – educational institution*); functional relation: *Tätigkeit – ausführen* (*task – perform*); or pairs that are obviously not connected, e.g. *logisch – Juni* (*logical – June*). Table 4 lists some example concept pairs along with averaged judgments and standard deviation.

Concept pairs with high deviations between judgments often contain polysemous words. For example, $Quelle$ ($source$) was disambiguated to $Wasserquelle$ ($spring$) and paired with $Text$ ($text$). The data shows a clear distinction between one group that rated the pair low (0) and another group that rated the pair high (3 or 4). The latter group obviously missed the point that *textual source* was not an option here. High deviations were also common among special technical terms like ($Mips – Core$), proper names ($Georg – August$ – two common first names in German) or functionally related pairs ($agieren – mobil$). Human experience and cultural background clearly influence the judgment of such pairs.

The effect observed here and the effect noted by Budanitsky and Hirst is probably caused by the same underlying principle. Human agreement on semantic relatedness is only reliable if two words or concepts are highly related or almost unrelated. Intuitively, this means that classifying word pairs as related or unrelated is much easier than numerically rating semantic relatedness. For an information retrieval task, such a classification might be sufficient.

Differences in correlation coefficients for the three corpora are not significant indicating that the phenomenon is not domain-specific. Differences in correlation coefficients for different parts-of-speech are significant (see Table 3). Verb-verb and verb-adjective pairs have the lowest correlation. A high fraction of these pairs is in the problematic medium relatedness area. Adjective-adjective pairs have the highest correlation. Most of these pairs are either highly related or not related at all.

## 6 Conclusion

We proposed a system for automatically creating datasets for evaluating semantic relatedness measures. We have shown that our corpus-based approach enables fast development of large domain-specific datasets that cover all types of lexical and semantic relations. We conducted an experiment to obtain human judgments of semantic relatedness on concept pairs. Results show that averaged human judgments cover all degrees of relatedness with a slight underrepresentation of highly related concept pairs. More highly related concept pairs could be generated by using more sophisticated weighting schemes or selecting concept pairs on the basis of lexical chaining.

Inter-subject correlation in this experiment is lower than the results from previous studies due to several reasons. We measured semantic relatedness instead of semantic similarity. The former is a more complicated task for annotators because its definition includes all kinds of lexical-semantic relations not just synonymy. In addition, concept pairs were automatically selected eliminating the bias towards strong classical relations with high agreement that is introduced into the dataset by a manual selection process. Furthermore, our dataset contains many domain-specific

| Pair | | | | |
| --- | --- | --- | --- | --- |
| German | English | Corpus | Avg | St-dev |
| Universität – Bildungseinrichtung | university – educational institution | GIRT | 3.90 | 0.30 |
| Tätigkeit – ausführen | task – to perform | BN | 3.67 | 0.58 |
| strafen – Paragraph | to punish – paragraph | GIRT | 3.00 | 1.18 |
| Quelle – Text | spring – text | GIRT | 2.43 | 1.57 |
| Mips – Core | mips – core | SPP | 2.10 | 1.55 |
| elektronisch – neu | electronic – new | GIRT | 1.71 | 1.15 |
| verarbeiten – dichten | to manipulate – to caulk | BN | 1.29 | 1.42 |
| Leopold – Institut | Leopold – institute | SPP | 0.81 | 1.25 |
| Outfit – Strom | outfit – electricity | GIRT | 0.24 | 0.44 |
| logisch – Juni | logical – June | SPP | 0.14 | 0.48 |

Table 4: Example concept pairs with averaged judgments and standard deviation. Only one sense is listed for polysemous words. Conceptual glosses are omitted due to space limitations.

concept pairs which have been rated very differently by test subjects depending on their experience. Future experiments should ensure that domain-specific pairs are judged by domain experts to reduce disagreement between annotators caused by varying degrees of familiarity with the domain.

An analysis of the data shows that test subjects more often agreed on highly related or unrelated concept pairs, while they often disagreed on pairs with a medium relatedness value. This result raises the question whether human judgments of semantic relatedness with medium scores are reliable and should be used for evaluating semantic relatedness measures. We plan to investigate the impact of this outcome on the evaluation of semantic relatedness measures. Additionally, for some applications like information retrieval it may be sufficient to detect highly related pairs rather than accurately rating word pairs with medium values.

There is also a significant difference between the correlation coefficient for different POS combinations. Further investigations are needed to elucidate whether these differences are caused by the new procedure for corpus-based selection of word pairs proposed in this paper or are due to inherent properties of semantic relations existing between word classes.

## Acknowledgments

We would like to thank Sabine Schulte im Walde for her remarks on experimental setups. We are grateful to the *Bundesagentur für Arbeit* for providing the BERUFEnet corpus. This work was carried out as part of the "Semantic Information Retrieval" (SIR) project funded by the German Research Foundation.

## References

Alexander Budanitsky and Graeme Hirst. 2006. Evaluating WordNet-based Measures of Semantic Distance. *Computational Linguistics*, 32(1).

Lev Finkelstein, Evgeniy Gabrilovich, Yossi Matias, Ehud Rivlin, Zach Solan, and Gadi Wolfman. 2002. Placing Search in Context: The Concept Revisited. *ACM Transactions on Information Systems*, 20(1):116–131.

Iryna Gurevych. 2005. Using the Structure of a Conceptual Network in Computing Semantic Relatedness. In *Proceedings of the 2nd International Joint Conference on Natural Language Processing*, pages 767–778, Jeju Island, Republic of Korea.

Iryna Gurevych. 2006. Computing Semantic Relatedness Across Parts of Speech. Technical report, Darmstadt University of Technology, Germany, Department of Computer Science, Telecooperation.

Jay J. Jiang and David W. Conrath. 1997. Semantic Similarity Based on Corpus Statistics and Lexical Taxonomy. In *Proceedings of the 10th International Conference on Research in Computational Linguistics*.

Michael Kluck. 2004. The GIRT Data in the Evaluation of CLIR Systems - from 1997 Until 2003. *Lecture Notes in Computer Science*, 3237:376–390, January.

Claudia Kunze, 2004. *Lexikalisch-semantische Wortnetze*, chapter Computerlinguistik und Sprachtechnologie, pages 423–431. Spektrum Akademischer Verlag.

Claudia Leacock and Martin Chodorow, 1998. *WordNet: An Electronic Lexical Database*, chapter Combining Local Context and WordNet Similarity for Word Sense Identification, pages 265–283. Cambridge: MIT Press.

Ludovic Lebart and Martin Rajman. 2000. Computing Similarity. In Robert Dale, editor, *Handbook of NLP*. Dekker: Basel.

Michael Lesk. 1986. Automatic Sense Disambiguation Using Machine Readable Dictionaries: How to tell a pine cone from an ice cream cone. In *Proceedings of the 5th Annual International Conference on Systems Documentation*, pages 24–26, Toronto, Ontario, Canada.

Dekang Lin. 1998. An Information-Theoretic Definition of Similarity. In *Proceedings of International Conference on Machine Learning*, Madison, Wisconsin.

Rada Mihalcea and Dan Moldovan. 2001. Automatic Generation of a Coarse Grained WordNet. In *Proceedings of NAACL Workshop on WordNet and Other Lexical Resources*, Pittsburgh, PA, June.

George A. Miller and Walter G. Charles. 1991. Contextual Correlates of Semantic Similarity. *Language and Cognitive Processes*, 6(1):1–28.

Jane Morris and Graeme Hirst. 2004. Non-Classical Lexical Semantic Relations. In *Workshop on Computational Lexical Semantics, Human Language Technology Conference of the North American Chapter of the ACL*, Boston.

Siddharth Patwardhan, Satanjeev Banerjee, and Ted Pedersen. 2003. Using Measures of Semantic Relatedness for Word Sense Disambiguation. In *Proceedings of the Fourth International Conference on Intelligent Text Processing and Computational Linguistics*, Mexico City.

Philip Resnik. 1995. Using Information Content to Evaluate Semantic Similarity. In *Proceedings of the 14th International Joint Conference on Artificial Intelligence*, pages 448–453, Montreal, Canada.

Herbert Rubenstein and John B. Goodenough. 1965. Contextual Correlates of Synonymy. *Communications of the ACM*, 8(10):627–633.

Gerard Salton. 1989. *Automatic Text Processing: the Transformation, Analysis, and Retrieval of Information by Computer*. Addison-Wesley Longman Publishing, Boston, MA, USA.

Helmut Schmid. 1995. Probabilistic Part-of-Speech Tagging Using Decision Trees. In *International Conference on New Methods in Language Processing*, Manchester, UK.

Sabine Schulte im Walde and Alissa Melinger. 2005. Identifying Semantic Relations and Functional Properties of Human Verb Associations. In *Proceedings of the Joint Conference on Human Language Technology and Empirical Methods in NLP*, pages 612–619, Vancouver, Canada.

SIR Project. 2006. Project 'Semantic Information Retrieval'. URL `http://www.cre-elearning.tu-darmstadt.de/elearning/sir/`.

Julie Weeds and David Weir. 2005. Co-occurrence Retrieval: A Flexible Framework For Lexical Distributional Similarity. *Computational Linguistics*, 31(4):439–475, December.

Zhibiao Wu and Martha Palmer. 1994. Verb Semantics and Lexical Selection. In *32nd Annual Meeting of the ACL*, pages 133–138, New Mexico State University, Las Cruces, New Mexico.

# Comparison of Similarity Models for the Relation Discovery Task

**Ben Hachey**
School of Informatics
University of Edinburgh
2 Buccleuch Place, Edinburgh EH8 9LW
bhachey@inf.ed.ac.uk

## Abstract

We present results on the relation discovery task, which addresses some of the shortcomings of supervised relation extraction by applying minimally supervised methods. We describe a detailed experimental design that compares various configurations of conceptual representations and similarity measures across six different subsets of the ACE relation extraction data. Previous work on relation discovery used a semantic space based on a term-by-document matrix. We find that representations based on term co-occurrence perform significantly better. We also observe further improvements when reducing the dimensionality of the term co-occurrence matrix using probabilistic topic models, though these are not significant.

## 1 Introduction

This paper describes work that aims to improve upon previous approaches to identifying relationships between named objects in text (e.g., people, organisations, locations). Figure 1 contains several example sentences from the ACE 2005 corpus that contain relations and Figure 2 summarises the relations occurring in these sentences. So, for example, sentence 1 contains an *employment* relation between Lebron James and Nike, sentence 2 contains a *sports-affiliation* relation between Stig Toefting and Bolton and sentence 4 contains a *business* relation between Martha Stewart (she) and the board of directors (of Martha Stewart Living Omnimedia).

Possible applications include identifying companies taking part in mergers/acquisitions from business newswire, which could be inserted into a corporate intelligence database. In the biomedical domain, we may want to identify relationships between genes and proteins from biomedical publications, e.g. Hirschman et al. (2004), to help scientists keep up-to-date on the literature. Or, we may want to identify disease and treatment relations in publications and textbooks, which can be used to help formalise medical knowledge and assist general practitioners in diagnosis, treatment and prognosis (Rosario and Hearst, 2004).

Another application scenario involves building networks of relationships from text collections that indicate the important entities in a domain and can be used to visualise interactions. The networks could provide an alternative to searching when interacting with a document collection. This could prove beneficial, for example, in investigative journalism. It might also be used for social science research using techniques from social network analysis (Marsden and Lin, 1982). In previ-

| | |
|---|---|
| 1 | As for that $90 million shoe contract with Nike, it may be a good deal for James. |
| 2 | Toefting transferred to Bolton in February 2002 from German club Hamburg. |
| 3 | Toyoda founded the automaker in 1937 ... . |
| 4 | In a statement, she says she's stepping aside in the best interest of the company, but she will stay on the board of directors. |

Figure 1: Example sentences from ACE 2005.

| Sent | $Entity_1$ | $Entity_2$ | Relation |
|---|---|---|---|
| 1 | Lebron James | Nike | Employ |
| 2 | Stig Toefting | Bolton | Sports-Aff |
| 2 | Stig Toefting | Hamburg | Sports-Aff |
| 3 | Kiichiro Toyoda | Toyota Corp | Founder |
| 4 | Martha Stewart | board | Business |

Figure 2: Example entity pairs and relation types.



*Proceedings of the Workshop on Linguistic Distances*, pages 25–34,
Sydney, July 2006. ©2006 Association for Computational Linguistics

ous work, relations have been used for automatic text summarisation as a conceptual representation of sentence content in a sentence extraction framework (Filatova and Hatzivassiloglou, 2004).

In the next section, we motivate and introduce the relation discovery task, which addresses some of the shortcomings of conventional approaches to relation extraction (i.e. supervised learning or rule engineering) by applying minimally supervised methods.[1] A critical part of the relation discovery task is grouping entity pairs by their relation type. This is a clustering task and requires a robust conceptual representation of relation semantics and a measure of similarity between relations. In previous work (Hasegawa et al., 2004; Chen et al., 2005), the conceptual representation has been limited to term-by-document (TxD) models of relation semantics. The current work introduces a term co-occurrence (TxT) representation for the relation discovery task and shows that it performs significantly better than the TxD representation. We also explore dimensionality reduction techniques, which show a further improvement.

Section 3 presents a parameterisation of similarity models for relation discovery. For the purposes of the current work, this consists of the semantic representation for terms (i.e. how a term's context is modelled), dimensionality reduction technique (e.g. singular value decomposition, latent Dirichlet allocation), and the measure used to compute similarity.

We also build on the evaluation paradigm for relation discovery with a detailed, controlled experimental setup. Section 4 describes the experiment design, which compares the various system configurations across six different subsets of the relation extraction data from the automatic content extraction (ACE) evaluation. Finally, Section 5 presents results and statistical analysis.

## 2 The Relation Discovery Task

Conventionally, relation extraction is considered to be part of information extraction and has been approached through supervised learning or rule engineering (e.g., Blaschke and Valencia (2002), Bunescu and Mooney (2005)). However, traditional approaches have several shortcomings. First and foremost, they are generally based on predefined templates of what types of relations exist in the data and thus only capture information whose importance was anticipated by the template designers. This poses reliability problems when predicting new data in the same domain as the training data will be from a certain epoch in the past. Due to language change and topical variation, as time passes, it is likely that the new data will deviate more and more from the trained models. Additionally, there are cost problems associated with the conventional supervised approach when updating templates or transferring to a new domain, both of which require substantial effort in re-engineering rules or re-annotating training data.

The goal of the relation discovery task is to identify the existence of associations between entities, to identify the kinds of relations that occur in a corpus and to annotate particular associations with relation types. These goals correspond to the three main steps in a generalised algorithm (Hasegawa et al., 2004):

1. Identify co-occurring pairs of named entities
2. Group entity pairs using the textual context
3. Label each cluster of entity pairs

The first step is the relation identification task. In the current work, this is assumed to have been done already. We use the gold standard relations in the ACE data in order to isolate the performance of the second step. The second step is a clustering task and as such it is necessary to compute similarity between the co-occurring pairs of named entities (relations). In order to do this, a model of relation similarity is required, which is the focus of the current work.

We also assume that it is possible to perform the third step.[2] The evaluation we present here looks just at the quality of the clustering and does not attempt to assess the labelling task.

## 3 Modelling Relation Similarity

The possible space of models for relation similarity can be explored in a principled manner by parameterisation. In this section, we discuss several

[1]The relation discovery task is minimally supervised in the sense that it relies on having certain resources such as named entity recognition. The focus of the current paper is the unsupervised task of clustering relations.

[2]Previous approaches select labels from the collection of context words for a relation cluster (Hasegawa et al., 2004; Zhang et al., 2005). Chen et al. (2005) use discriminative category matching to make sure that selected labels are also able to differentiate between clusters.

parameters including the term context representation, whether or not we apply dimensionality reduction, and what similarity measure we use.

### 3.1 Term Context

Representing texts in such a way that they can be compared is a familiar problem from the fields of information retrieval (IR), text mining (TM), textual data analysis (TDA) and natural language processing (NLP) (Lebart and Rajman, 2000). The traditional model for IR and TM is based on a term-by-document (TxD) vector representation. Previous approaches to relation discovery (Hasegawa et al., 2004; Chen et al., 2005) have been limited to TxD representations, using *tf*idf* weighting and the cosine similarity measure. In information retrieval, the weighted term representation works well as the comparison is generally between pieces of text with large context vectors. In the relation discovery task, though, the term contexts (as we will define them in Section 4) can be very small, often consisting of only one or two words. This means that a term-based similarity matrix between entity pairs is very sparse, which may pose problems for performing reliable clustering.

An alternative method widely used in NLP and cognitive science is to represent a term context by its neighbouring words as opposed to the documents in which it occurs. This term co-occurrence (TxT) model is based on the intuition that two words are semantically similar if they appear in a similar set of contexts (see e.g. Pado and Lapata (2003)). The current work explores such a term co-occurrence (TxT) representation based on the hypothesis that it will provide a more robust representation of relation contexts and help overcome the sparsity problems associated with weighted term representations in the relation discovery task. This is compared to a baseline term-by-document (TxD) representation which is a re-implementation of the approach used by Hasegawa et al. (2004) and Chen et al. (2005).

### 3.2 Dimensionality Reduction

Dimensionality reduction techniques for document and corpus modelling aim to reduce description length and model a type of semantic similarity that is more linguistic in nature (e.g., see Landauer et al.'s (1998) discussion of LSA and synonym tests). In the current work, we explore singular value decomposition (Berry et al., 1994), a technique from linear algebra that has been applied to a number of tasks from NLP and cognitive modelling. We also explore latent Dirichlet allocation, a probabilistic technique analogous to singular value decomposition whose contribution to NLP has not been as thoroughly explored.

Singular value decomposition (SVD) has been used extensively for the analysis of lexical semantics under the name of latent semantic analysis (Landauer et al., 1998). Here, a rectangular matrix is decomposed into the product of three matrices ($X_{w \times p} = W_{w \times n} S_{n \times n} (P_{p \times n})^T$) with $n$ 'latent semantic' dimensions. The resulting decomposition can be viewed as a rotation of the $n$-dimensional axes such that the first axis runs along the direction of largest variation among the documents (Manning and Schütze, 1999). $W$ and $P$ represent terms and documents in the new space. And $S$ is a diagonal matrix of singular values in decreasing order.

Taking the product $W_{w \times k} S_{k \times k} (P_{p \times k})^T$ over the first $D$ columns gives the best least square approximation of the original matrix $X$ by a matrix of rank $D$, i.e. a reduction of the original matrix to $D$ dimensions. SVD can equally be applied to the word co-occurrence matrices obtained in the TxT representation presented in Section 2, in which case we can think of the original matrix as being a term $\times$ co-occurring term feature matrix.

While SVD has proved successful and has been adapted for tasks such as word sense discrimination (Schütze, 1998), its behaviour is not easy to interpret. Probabilistic LSA (pLSA) is a generative probabilistic version of LSA (Hofmann, 2001). This models each word in a document as a sample from a mixture model, but does not provide a probabilistic model at the document level. Latent Dirichlet Allocation (LDA) addresses this by representing documents as random mixtures over latent topics (Blei et al., 2003). Besides having a clear probabilistic interpretation, an additional advantage of these models is that they have intuitive graphical representations.

Figure 3 contains a graphical representation of the LDA model as applied to TxT word co-occurrence matrices in standard plate notation. This models the word features $f$ in the co-occurrence context (size $N$) of each word $w$ (where $w \in \mathcal{W}$ and $|\mathcal{W}| = W$) with a mixture of topics $z$. In its generative mode, the LDA model samples a topic from the word-specific multino-

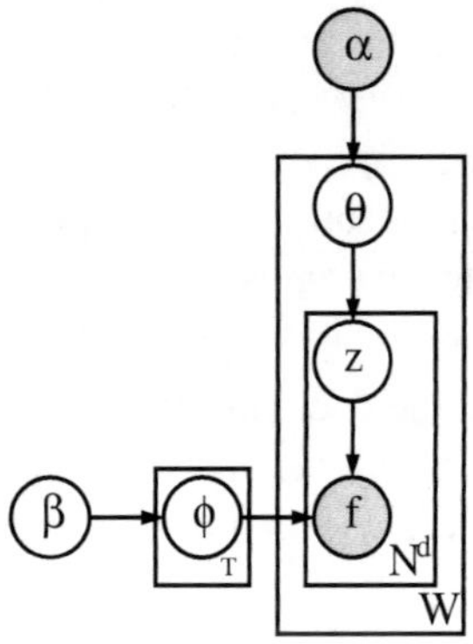


Figure 3: Graphical representation of LDA.

mial distribution $\theta$. Then, each context feature is generated by sampling from a topic-specific multinomial distribution $\phi_z$.[3] In a manner analogous to the SVD model, we use the distribution over topics for a word $w$ to represent its semantics and we use the average topic distribution over all context words to represent the conceptual content of an entity pair context.

### 3.3 Measuring Similarity

Cosine (Cos) is commonly used in the literature to compute similarities between *tf*idf* vectors:

$$Cos(p,q) = \frac{\sum_i p_i q_i}{\sqrt{\sum p^2}\sqrt{\sum q^2}}$$

In the current work, we use cosine over term and SVD representations of entity pair context. However, it is not clear which similarity measure should be used for the probabilistic topic models. Dagan et al. (1997) find that the symmetric information radius measure performs best on a pseudo-word sense disambiguation task, while Lee (1999) find that the asymmetric skew divergence – a generalisation of Kullback-Leibler divergence – performs best for improving probability estimates for unseen word co-occurrences.

In the current work, we compare KL divergence with two methods for deriving a symmetric measure. The KL divergence of two probability distributions ($p$ and $q$) over the same event space is defined as:

$$KL(p||q) = \sum_i p_i \log \frac{p_i}{q_i}$$

In information-theoretic terms, KL divergence is the average number of bits wasted by encoding events from a distribution $p$ with a code based on distribution $q$. The symmetric measures are defined as:

$$Sym(p,q) = \frac{1}{2}\left[KL(p||q) + KL(q||p)\right]$$

$$JS(p,q) = \frac{1}{2}\left[KL\left(p||\frac{p+q}{2}\right) + KL\left(q||\frac{p+q}{2}\right)\right]$$

The first is termed symmetrised KL divergence (Sym) and the second is termed Jensen-Shannon (JS) divergence. We explore KL divergence as well as the symmetric measures as it is not known in advance whether a domain is symmetric or not.

Technically, the divergence measures are dissimilarity measures as they calculate the difference between two distributions. However, they can be converted to increasing measures of similarity through various transformations. We treated this as a parameter to be tuned during development and considered two approaches. The first is from Dagan et al. (1997). For KL divergence, this function is defined as $Sim(p,q) = 10^{-\beta KL(p||q)}$, where $\beta$ is a free parameter, which is tuned on the development set (as described in Section 4.2). The same procedure is applied for symmetric KL divergence and JS divergence. The second approach is from Lee (1999). Here similarity for KL is defined as $Sim(p,q) = C - KL(p||q)$, where $C$ is a free parameter to be tuned.

## 4 Experimental Setup

### 4.1 Materials

Following Chen et al. (2005), we derive our relation discovery data from the automatic content extraction (ACE) 2004 and 2005 materials for evaluation of information extraction.[4] This is preferable to using the New York Times data used by Hasegawa et al. (2004) as it has gold standard annotation, which can be used for unbiased evaluation.

The relation clustering data is based on the gold standard relations in the information extraction

[3] The hyperparameters $\alpha$ and $\beta$ are Dirichlet priors on the multinomial distributions for word features ($\phi \sim Dir(\beta)$) and topics ($\theta \sim Dir(\alpha)$). The choice of the Dirichlet is explained by its conjugacy to the multinomial distribution, meaning that if the parameter (e.g. $\phi$, $\theta$) for a multinomial distribution is endowed with a Dirichlet prior then the posterior will also be a Dirichlet. Intuitively, it is a distribution over distributions used to encode prior knowledge about the parameters ($\phi$ and $\theta$) of the multinomial distributions for word features and topics. Practically, it allows efficient estimation of the joint distribution over word features and topics $P(\vec{f}, \vec{z})$ by integrating out $\phi$ and $\theta$.

[4] http://www.nist.gov/speech/tests/ace/

data. We only consider data from newswire or broadcast news sources. We constructed six data subsets from the ACE corpus based on four of the ACE entities: persons (PER), organisations (ORG), geographical/social/political entities (GPE) and facilities (FAC). The six data subsets were chosen during development based on a lower limit of 50 for the data subset size (i.e. the number of entity pairs in the domain), ensuring that there is a reasonable amount of data. We also set a lower limit of 3 for the number of classes (relation types) in a data subset, ensuring that the clustering task is not too simple.

The entity pair instances for clustering were chosen based on several criteria. First, we do not use ACE's *discourse* relations, which are relations in which the entity referred to is not an official entity according to world knowledge. Second, we only use pairs with one or more non-stop words in the intervening context, that is the context between the two entity heads.[5] Finally, we only keep relation classes with 3 or more members. Table 4.1 contains the full list of relation types from the subsets of ACE that we used. (Refer to Table 4.2 for definition of the relation type abbreviations.)

We use the Infomap tool[6] for singular value decomposition of TxT matrices and compute the conceptual content of an entity pair context as the average over the reduced $D$-dimensional representation of the co-occurrence vector of the terms in the relation context. For LDA, we use Steyvers and Griffiths' Topic Modeling Toolbox[7]). The input is produced by a version of Infomap which was modified to output the TxT matrix. Again, we compute the conceptual content of an entity pair as the average over the topic vectors for the context words. As documents are explicitly modelled in the LDA model, we input a matrix with raw frequencies. In the TxD, unreduced TxT and SVD models we use *tf*idf* term weighting.

We use the same preprocessing when preparing the text for building the SVD and probabilistic topic models as we use for processing the intervening context of entity pairs. This consisted of Mx-Terminator (Reynar and Ratnaparkhi., 1997) for sentence boundary detection, the Penn Treebank sed script[8] for tokenisation, and the Infomap stop word list. We also use an implementation of the Porter algorithm (Porter, 1980) for stemming.[9]

### 4.2 Model Selection

We used the ACE 2004 relation data to perform model selection. Firstly, dimensionality ($D$) needs to be optimised for SVD and LDA. SVD was found to perform best with the number of dimensions set to 10. For LDA, dimensionality interacts with the divergence-to-similarity conversion so they were tuned jointly. The optimal configuration varies by the divergence measure with $D = 50$ and $C = 14$ for KL divergence, $D = 200$ and $C = 4$ for symmetrised KL, and $D = 150$ and $C = 2$ for JS divergence. For all divergence measures, Lee's (1999) method outperformed Dagan et al.'s (1997) method. Also for all divergence measures, the model hyper-parameter $\beta$ was found to be optimal at 0.0001. The $\alpha$ hyper-parameter was always set to $50/T$ following Griffiths and Steyvers (2004).

Clustering is performed with the CLUTO software[10] and the technique used is identical across models. Agglomerative clustering is used for comparability with the original relation discovery work of Hasegawa et al. (2004). This choice was motivated because as it is not known in advance how many clusters there should be in a new domain.

One way to view the clustering problem is as an optimisation process where an optimal clustering is chosen with respect to a criterion function over the entire solution. The criterion function used here was chosen based on performance on the development data. We compared a number of criterion functions including single link, complete link, group average, $\mathcal{I}_1$, $\mathcal{I}_2$, $\mathcal{E}_1$ and $\mathcal{H}_1$. $\mathcal{I}_1$ is a criterion function that maximises sum of pairwise similarities between relation instances assigned to each cluster, $\mathcal{I}_2$ is an internal criterion function that maximises the similarity between each relation instance and the centroid of the cluster it is assigned to, $\mathcal{E}_1$ is an external criterion function that minimises the similarity between the centroid vector of each cluster and the centroid vector of the

[5]Following results reported by Chen et al. (2005), who tried unsuccessfully to incorporate words from the surrounding context to represent a relation's semantics, we use only intervening words.

[6]http://infomap.stanford.edu/

[7]http://psiexp.ss.uci.edu/research/programs_data/toolbox.htm

[8]http://www.cis.upenn.edu/~treebank/tokenizer.sed

[9]http://www.ldc.usb.ve/~vdaniel/porter.pm

[10]http://glaros.dtc.umn.edu/gkhome/cluto/cluto/overview

| ORG-GPE | | ORG-ORG | | PER-FAC | | PER-GPE | | PER-ORG | | PER-PER | |
|---|---|---|---|---|---|---|---|---|---|---|---|
| basedin | 54 | subsidiary | 36 | located | 127 | located | 222 | staff | 121 | business | 81 |
| subsidiary | 27 | emporgothr | 14 | owner | 14 | resident | 79 | executive | 100 | family | 20 |
| located | 15 | partner | 8 | near | 4 | executive | 42 | member | 44 | persocothr | 16 |
| gpeaffothr | 3 | member | 6 | | | staff | 30 | emporgothr | 27 | perorgothr | 9 |
| | | | | | | employgen | 7 | employgen | 9 | near | 7 |
| | | | | | | | | located | 4 | ethnic | 5 |
| | | | | | | | | | | executive | 3 |
| | | | | | | | | | | ideology | 3 |
| | | | | | | | | | | member | 3 |
| *Total* | 99 | *Total* | 64 | *Total* | 145 | *Total* | 380 | *Total* | 305 | *Total* | 147 |

Table 1: Relation distributions for entity pair domains.

| Type | Subtype | Abbr |
|---|---|---|
| AGENT-ARTIFACT | User-or-Owner | owner |
| EMPLOY/MEMBER | Employ-Executive | executive |
| | Employ-Staff | staff |
| | Employ-Undet'd | employgen |
| | Member-of-Group | member |
| | Other | artothr |
| | Partner | partner |
| | Subsidiary | subsidiary |
| GPE AFFILIATION | Based-In | basedin |
| | Citizen-or-Resdent | resident |
| | Other | gpeaffothr |
| PER/ORG AFFIL'N | Ethnic | ethnic |
| | Ideology | ideology |
| | Other | perorgothr |
| PERSONAL-SOC'L | Business | business |
| | Family | family |
| | Other | persocothr |
| PHYSICAL | Located | located |
| | Near | near |

Table 2: Overview of ACE relations with abbreviations used here.

entire collection, and $\mathcal{H}_1$ is a combined criterion function that consists of the ration of $\mathcal{I}_1$ over $\mathcal{E}_1$.

The $\mathcal{I}_2$, $\mathcal{H}_1$ and $\mathcal{H}_2$ criterion functions outperformed single link, complete link and group average on the development data. We use $\mathcal{I}_2$, which performed as well as $\mathcal{H}_1$ and $\mathcal{H}_2$ and is superior in terms of computational complexity (Zhao and Karypis, 2004).

## 5 Experiment

### 5.1 Method

This section describes experimental setup, which uses relation extraction data from ACE 2005 to answer four questions concerning the effectiveness of similarity models based on term co-occurrence and dimensionality reduction for the relation discovery task:

1. Do term co-occurrence models provide a better representation of relation semantics than standard term-by-document vector space?
2. Do textual dimensionality reduction techniques provide any further improvements?
3. How do probabilistic topic models perform with respect to SVD on the relation discovery task?
4. Does one similarity measure (for probability distributions) outperform the others on the relation discovery task?

System configurations are compared across six different data subsets (entity type pairs, i.e., *organisation-geopolitical entity*, *organisation-organisation*, *person-facility*, *person-geopolitical entity*, *person-organisation*, *person-person*) and evaluated following suggestions by Demšar (2006) for statistical comparison of classifiers over multiple data sets.

The dependent variable is the clustering performance as measured by the F-score. F-score accounts for both the amount of predictions made that are true (*P*recision) and the amount of true classes that are predicted (*R*ecall). We use the CLUTO implementation of this measure for evaluating hierarchical clustering. Based on (Larsen and Aone, 1999), this is a balanced F-score ($F = \frac{2RP}{R+P}$) that computes the maximum per-class score over all possible alignments of gold standard classes with nodes in the hierarchical tree. The average F-score for the entire hierarchical tree is a micro-average over the class-specific scores weighted according to the relative size of the class.

### 5.2 Results

Table 3 contains F-score performance on the test set (ACE 2005). The columns contain results from the different system configurations. The column labels in the top row indicate the different representations of relation similarity. The column labels in the second row indicate the dimensional-

| Sem Space | TxD | TxT | TxT | TxT | TxT | TxT |
|---|---|---|---|---|---|---|
| Dim Red'n | None | None | SVD | LDA | LDA | LDA |
| Similarity | Cos | Cos | Cos | KL | Sym | JS |
| ORG-GPE | 0.644 | 0.673 | 0.645 | 0.680 | 0.670 | 0.673 |
| ORG-ORG | 0.879 | 0.922 | 0.879 | 0.904 | 0.900 | 0.904 |
| PER-FAC | 0.811 | 0.827 | 0.831 | 0.832 | 0.826 | 0.820 |
| PER-GPE | 0.595 | 0.637 | 0.627 | 0.664 | 0.642 | 0.670 |
| PER-ORG | 0.520 | 0.551 | 0.532 | 0.569 | 0.552 | 0.569 |
| PER-PER | 0.534 | 0.572 | 0.593 | 0.633 | 0.553 | 0.618 |
| Micro Ave | 0.627 | 0.661 | 0.652 | 0.683 | 0.658 | 0.681 |
| Macro Ave | 0.664 | 0.697 | 0.684 | 0.714 | 0.689 | 0.709 |
| RankAve | 5.917 | 3.083 | 4.250 | 1.500 | 4.000 | 2.250 |

Table 3: F-score performance on the test data (ACE 2005) using agglomerative clustering with the $\mathcal{I}_2$ criterion function.

ity reduction technique used. The column labels in the third row indicated the similarity measure used, i.e. cosine (Cos) and KL (KL), symmetrised KL (Sym) and JS (JS) divergence. The rows contain results for the different data subsets. While we do not use them for analysis of statistical significance, we include micro and macro averages over the data subsets.[11] We also include the average ranks, which show that the LDA system using KL divergence performed best.

Initial inspection of the table shows that all systems that use the term co-occurrence semantic space outperform the baseline system that uses the term-by-document semantic space. To test for statistical significance, we use non-parametric tests proposed by Demšar (2006) for comparing classifiers across multiple data sets. The use of non-parametric tests is safer here as they do not assume normality and outliers have less effect. The first test we perform is a Friedman test (Friedman, 1940), a multiple comparisons technique which is the non-parametric equivalent of the repeated-measures ANOVA. The null hypothesis is that all models perform the same and observed differences are random. With a Friedman statistic ($\chi^2_F$ ) of $21.238$, we reject the null hypothesis at $p < 0.01$.

The first question we wanted to address is whether term co-occurrence models outperform the term-by-document representation of relation semantics. To address this question, we continue with post-hoc analysis. The objective here is to compare several conditions to a control (i.e., compare the term co-occurrence systems to the term-by-document baseline) so we use a Bonferroni-Dunn test. At a significance level of $p < 0.05$, the critical difference for the Bonferroni-Dunn test for comparing 6 systems across 6 data sets is $2.782$. We conclude that the unreduced term co-occurrence system and the LDA systems with KL and JS divergence all perform significantly better than baseline, while the SVD system and the LDA system with symmetrised KL divergence do not.

The second question asks whether SVD and LDA dimensionality reduction techniques provide any further improvement. We observe that the systems using KL and JS divergence both outperform the unreduced term co-occurrence system, though the difference is not significant.

The third question asks how the probabilistic topic models perform with respect to the SVD models. Here, Holm-correct Wilcoxon signed-ranks tests show that the KL divergence system performs significantly better than SVD while the symmetrised KL divergence and JS divergence systems do not.

The final question is whether one of the divergence measures (KL, symmetrised KL or JS) outperforms the others. With a statistic of $\chi^2_F = 9.336$, we reject the null hypothesis that all systems are the same at $p < 0.01$. Post-hoc analysis with Holm-corrected Wilcoxon signed-ranks tests show that the KL divergence system and the JS divergence system both perform significantly better than the symmetrised KL system at $p < 0.05$, while there is no significant difference between the KL and JS systems.

[11] Averages over data sets are unreliable where it is not clear whether the domains are commensurable (Webb, 2000). We present averages in our results but avoid drawing conclusions based on them.

## 6 Discussion

An interesting aspect of using the ACE corpus is the wealth of linguistic knowledge encoded. With respect to named entities, this includes class information describing the kind of reference the entity makes to something in the world (i.e., *specific referential*, *generic referential*, *under-specified referential*) and it includes mention type information (i.e., *names*, *quantified nominal constructions*, *pronouns*). It also includes information describing the lexical condition of a relation (i.e., *possessive*, *preposition*, *pre-modifier*, *formulaic*, , *verbal*). Based on a mapping between gold standard and predicted clusters, we assigned each case a value of 1 or 0 to indicate whether it is a correct or incorrect classification. We then carried out detailed statistical analysis[12] to test for effects of the entity and relation information described above on each system in each domain.

Overall, the effects were fairly small and do not generalise across domains or systems very well. However, there were some observable tendencies. With respect to entity class, relations with *specific referential* entities tend to correlate positively with correct classifications while *under-specified referential* entities tend to correlate negatively with correct classifications. With respect to entity mention type, relations entities that consist of *names* tend to correlate positively with correct classifications while *pronouns* tend to correlate negatively with correct classifications. Though, this is only reliably observed in the PER-GPE domain. Finally, with respect to lexical condition, we observe that *possessive* conditioned relations tend to correlate negatively, especially in the PER-GPE and PER-ORG domains with the PER-PER domain also showing some effect. *Pre-modifier* conditioned relations also tend to correlate negatively in the PER-GPE domain. The effect with *verbally* conditioned relations is mixed. This is probably due to the fact that verbal relations tend to have more words occurring between the entity pair, which provides more context but can also be misleading when the key terms describing the relation do not occur between the entity pair (e.g., the first sentence in Figure 1).

It is also informative to look at overall properties of the entity pair domains and compare this to the system performance. Table 6 contains, for each domain, the F-score of the LDA+KL system, the type-to-token ratio, and the entropy of the relation type distribution for each domain. Type-to-token ratio (TTR) is the number of words divided by the number of word instances and indicates how much repetition there is in word use. Since TTR can vary depending on the size of the text, we compute it on a random sample of 75 tokens from each domain. Entropy can be interpreted as a measure of the uniformity of a distribution. Low entropy indicates a more spiked distribution while high entropy indicates a more uniform distribution. Though there is not enough data to make a reliable conclusion, it seems that the system does poorly on domains that have both a high type-to-token ratio and a high entropy (uniform relation type distribution), while it performs very well on domains that have low TTR or low entropy.

| Domain | Score | TTR | Entrpy |
|---|---|---|---|
| ORG-GPE | 0.680 | 0.893 | 1.554 |
| ORG-ORG | 0.904 | 0.720 | 1.642 |
| PER-FAC | 0.832 | 0.933 | 0.636 |
| PER-GPE | 0.664 | 0.933 | 1.671 |
| PER-ORG | 0.569 | 0.973 | 2.001 |
| PER-PER | 0.633 | 0.867 | 2.179 |

Table 4: System score, type-to-token ratio (TTR) and relation type entropy (Entrpy) for entity pair domains.

## 7 Conclusions and Future Work

This paper presented work on the relation discovery task. We tested several systems for the clustering subtask that use different models of the conceptual/semantic similarity of relations. These models included a baseline system based on a term-by-document representation of term context, which is equivalent to the representation used in previous work by Hasegawa et al. (Hasegawa et al., 2004) and Chen et al. (Chen et al., 2005). We hypothesised that this representation suffers from a sparsity problem and showed that models that use a term co-occurrence representation perform significantly better.

Furthermore, we investigated the use of singular value decomposition and latent Dirichlet allocation for dimensionality reduction. It has been suggested that representations using these techniques are able to model a similarity that is less reliant on

[12] For this analysis, we used the Phi coefficient, which is a measure of relatedness for binomial variables that is interpreted like correlation.

specific word forms and therefore more semantic in nature. Our experiments showed an improvement over a term co-occurrence baseline when using LDA with KL and JS divergence, though it was not significant. We also found that LDA with KL divergence performs significantly better than SVD.

Comparing the different divergence measures for LDA, we found that KL and JS perform significantly better than symmetrised KL divergence. Interestingly, the performance of the asymmetric KL divergence and the symmetric JS divergence is very close, which makes it difficult to conclude whether the relation discovery domain is a symmetric domain or an asymmetric domain like Lee's (1999) task of improving probability estimates for unseen word co-occurrences.

A shortcoming of all the models we will describe here is that they are derived from the basic bag-of-words models and as such do not account for word order or other notions of syntax. Related work on relation discovery by Zhang et al. (2005) addresses this shortcoming by using tree kernels to compute similarity between entity pairs. In future work we will extend our experiment to explore the use of syntactic and semantic features following the frame work of Pado and Lapata (2003). We are also planning to look at non-parametric versions of LDA that address the model order selection problem and perform an extrinsic evaluation of the relation discovery task.

## Acknowledgements

This work was supported by Scottish Enterprise Edinburgh-Stanford Link grant R37588 as part of the EASIE project. I would like to thank Claire Grover, Mirella Lapata, Gabriel Murray and Sebastian Riedell for very useful comments and discussion on this work. I would also like to thank the anonymous reviewers for their comments.

## References

Michael W. Berry, Susan T. Dumais, and Gavin W. O'Brien. 1994. Using linear algebra for intelligent information retrieval. *SIAM Review*, 37(4):573–595.

Christian Blaschke and Alfonso Valencia. 2002. The frame-based module of the suiseki information extraction system. *IEEE Intelligent Systems*, 17:14–20.

David Blei, Andrew Y. Ng, and Michael I. Jordan. 2003. Latent dirichlet allocation. *Journal of Machine Learning Research*, 3.

Razvan C. Bunescu and Raymond J. Mooney. 2005. Subsequence kernels for relation extraction. In *Proceedings of the 19th Conference on Neural Information Processing Systems*, Vancouver, BC, Canada.

Jinxiu Chen, Donghong Ji, Chew Lim Tan, and Zhengyu Niu. 2005. Automatic relation extraction with model order selection and discriminative label identification. In *Proceedings of the 2nd International Joint Conference on Natural Language Processing*.

Ido Dagan, Lillian Lee, and Fernando Pereira. 1997. Similarity-based methods for word sense disambiguation. In *Proceedings of the 35th Annual Meeting of the Association for Computational Linguistics*, Madrid, Spain.

Janez Demšar. 2006. Statistical comparisons of classifiers over multiple data sets. *Journal of Machine Learning Research*, 7:1–30, Jan.

Elena Filatova and Vasileios Hatzivassiloglou. 2004. Event-based extractive summarization. In *Proceedings of the ACL-2004 Text Summarization Branches Out Workshop*, Barcelona, Spain.

Milton Friedman. 1940. A comparison of alternative tests of significance for the problem of m rankings. *The Annals of Mathematical Statistics*, 11:86–92.

Thomas L. Griffiths and Mark Steyvers. 2004. Finding scientific topics. *Proceedings of the National Academy of Sciences*, 101:5228–5235.

Takaaki Hasegawa, Satoshi Sekine, and Ralph Grishman. 2004. Discovering relations among named entities from large corpora. In *Proceedings of the 42nd Annual Meeting of Association of Computational Linguistics*.

Lynette Hirschman, Alexander Yeh, Christian Blaschke, and Alfonso Valencia. 2004. Overview of BioCreAtIvE: Critical assessment of information extraction for biology. In *Proceedings of Critical Assessment of Information Extraction Systems in Biology Workshop (BioCreAtIvE)*, Granada, Spain.

Thomas Hofmann. 2001. Unsupervised learning by probabilistic latent semantic analysis. *Machine Learning*, 42:177–196.

Thomas K. Landauer, Peter W. Foltz, and Darrell Laham. 1998. An introduction to latent semantic analysis. *Discourse Processes*, 25:259–284.

Buornar Larsen and Chinatsu Aone. 1999. Fast and effective text mining using linear-time document clustering. In *Proceedings of the 5th ACM SIGKDD International Conference on Knowledge Discovery and Data Mining*, San Diego, CA, USA.

Ludovic Lebart and Martin Rajman. 2000. Computing similarity. In Robert Dale, Hermann Moisl, and Harold Somers, editors, *Handbook of Natural Language Processing*, pages 477–505. Marcel Dekker, New York.

Lillian Lee. 1999. Measures of distributional similarity. In *Proceedings of the 37th Annual Meeting of the Association for Computational Linguistics*, College Park, MD, USA.

Christopher D. Manning and Hinrich Schütze. 1999. *Foundations of Statistical Natural Language Processing*. MIT Press.

Peter V. Marsden and Nan Lin, editors. 1982. *Social Structure and Network Analysis*. Sage, Beverly Hills.

Sebastian Pado and Mirella Lapata. 2003. Constructing semantic space models from parsed corpora. In *Proceedings of the 41st Annual Meeting of the Association for Computational Linguistics*, Sapporo, Japan.

Martin F. Porter. 1980. An algorithm for suffix stripping. *Program*, 14(3):130–137.

Jeffrey C. Reynar and Adwait Ratnaparkhi. 1997. A maximum entropy approach to identifying sentence boundaries. In *Proceedings of the 5th Conference on Applied Natural Language Processing*, Washington, D.C., USA.

Barbara Rosario and Marti Hearst. 2004. Classifying semantic relations in bioscience text. In *Proceedings of the 42nd Annual Meeting of the Association for Computational Linguistics*, Barcelona, Spain.

Hinrich Schütze. 1998. Automatic word sense discrimination. *Computational Linguistics*, 24(1):91–124.

Geoffrey I. Webb. 2000. Multiboosting: A technique for combining boosting and wagging. *Machine Learning*, 40(2):159–196.

Min Zhang, Jian Su, Danmei Wang, Guodong Zhou, and Chew Lim Tan. 2005. Discovering relations from a large raw corpus using tree similarity-based clustering. In *Proceedings of the 2nd International Joint Conference on Natural Language Processing*.

Ying Zhao and George Karypis. 2004. Empirical and theoretical comparisons of selected criterion functions for document clustering. *Machine Learning*, 55:311–331.

# Sentence Comparison using Robust Minimal Recursion Semantics and an Ontology

**Rebecca Dridan**◇ **and Francis Bond**♠
◇ rdrid@csse.unimelb.edu.au ♠ bond@cslab.kecl.ntt.co.jp
◇ The University of Melbourne
♠ NTT Communication Science Laboratories,
Nippon Telegraph and Telephone Corporation

## Abstract

We design and test a sentence comparison method using the framework of Robust Minimal Recursion Semantics which allows us to utilise the deep parse information produced by Jacy, a Japanese HPSG based parser and the lexical information available in our ontology. Our method was used for both paraphrase detection and also for answer sentence selection for question answering. In both tasks, results showed an improvement over Bag-of-Words, as well as providing extra information useful to the applications.

## 1 Introduction

Comparison between sentences is required for many NLP applications, including question answering, paraphrasing, text summarization and entailment tasks. In this paper we show an RMRS (Robust Minimal Recursion Semantics, see Section 1.1) comparison algorithm that can be used to compare sentences in any language that has RMRS generating tools available. Lexical resources of any language can be plugged in to give a more accurate and informative comparison.

The simplest and most commonly used methods of judging sentence similarity use word overlap – either looking for matching word sequences, or comparing a Bag-of-Words representation of each sentence. Bag-of-Words discards word order, and any structure designated by such, so that *the cat snored and the dog slept* is equivalent to *the dog snored and the cat slept*. Sequence matching on the other hand requires exact word order matching and hence *the game began quietly* and *the game quietly began* are not considered a match. Neither method allows for synonym matching.

Hirao et al. (2004) showed that they could get a much more robust comparison using dependency information rather than Bag-of-Words, since they could abstract away from word order but still compare the important elements of a sentence. Using deep parsing information, such as dependencies, but also deep lexical resources where available, enables a much more informative and robust comparison, which goes beyond lexical similarity. We use the RMRS framework as our comparison format because it has the descriptive power to encode the full semantics, including argument structure. It also enables easy combination of deep and shallow information and, due to its flat structure, is easy to manage computationally.

### 1.1 Robust Minimal Recursion Semantics

Robust Minimal Recursion Semantics (RMRS) is a form of flat semantics which is designed to allow deep and shallow processing to use a compatible semantic representation, while being rich enough to support generalized quantifiers (Frank, 2004). The main component of an RMRS representation is a bag of elementary predicates and their arguments.

An elementary predicate always has a unique label, a relation type, a relation name and an ARG0 feature. The example in Figure 1 has a label of *h5* which uniquely identifies this predicate. Relation types can either be REALPRED for a predicate that relates directly to a content word from the input text, or GPRED for grammatical predicates which may not have a direct referent in the text. For examples in this paper, a REALPRED is distinguished by an underscore (_) before the relation name.

The GPRED relation names come from a



*Proceedings of the Workshop on Linguistic Distances*, pages 35–42,
Sydney, July 2006. 

| | |
|---|---|
| _unten_s | |
| LBL | *h5* |
| ARG0 | *e6* |

Figure 1: Elementary predicate for 運転 *unten* "drive"

closed-set which specify common grammatical relations, but the REALPRED names are formed from the word in the text they relate to and this is one way in which RMRS allows underspecification. A full relation name is of the form lemma_pos_sense, where the pos (part of speech) is drawn from a small set of general types including **n**oun, **v**erb and **s**ahen (verbal noun). The sense is a number that identifies the sense of the word within a particular grammar being used. The POS and sense information are only used when available and hence the _unten_s_1 is more specific but compatible with _unten_s or even _unten.

The ARG0 feature (*e6* in Figure 1) is the referential index of the predicate. Predicates with the same ARG0 are said to be referentially co-indexed and therefore have the same referent in the text.

A shallow parse might provide only the features shown in Figure 1, but a deep parse can also give information about other arguments as well as scoping constraints. The features ARG1..ARG4 specify the indices of the semantic arguments of the relevant predicate, similar to PropBank's argument annotation (Kingsbury et al., 2002). While the RMRS specification does not define semantic roles for the ARGn features, in practice ARG1 is generally used for the AGENT and ARG2 for the PATIENT. Features ARG3 and ARG4 have less consistency in their roles.

We will use (1) and (2) as examples of similar sentences. They are definition sentences for one sense of ドライバー *doraiba-* "driver", taken from two different lexicons.

(1)

| 自動車 | を | 運転 | する | 人 |
|---|---|---|---|---|
| *jidōsha* | *wo* | *unten* | *suru* | *hito* |
| car | ACC | drive | do | person |

"a person who drives a car"

(2)

| 自動車 | など | の | 運転 | 者 |
|---|---|---|---|---|
| *jidōsha* | *nado* | *no* | *unten* | *sha* |
| car | etc. | ADN | drive | -er |

"a driver of cars etc."

Examples of deep and shallow RMRS results for (1) are given in Figure 2. Deep results for (2) are given in Figure 3.

## 2 Algorithm

The matching algorithm is loosely based on RMRS comparison code included in the LKB (Copestake, 2002: ⟨http://www.delph-in.net/lkb/⟩), which was used in Ritchie (2004), however that code used no outside lexical resources and we have substantially changed the matching algorithm.

The comparison algorithm is language independent and can be used for any RMRS structures. It first compares all elementary predicates from the RMRSs to construct a list of match records and then examines, and potentially alters, the list of match records according to constraints encoded in the ARGn variables. Using the list of scored matches, the lowest scoring possible match set is found and, after further processing on that set, a similarity score is returned. The threshold for deciding whether a pair of sentences should be considered similar or not can be determined separately for different applications.

### 2.1 Matching Predicates

The elementary predicates (EPs) of our RMRS structures are divided into two groups - those that have a referent in the text, hereafter known as content EPs, and those that don't. There are three kinds of content EP: REALPREDs, which correspond to content bearing words that the grammar knows; GPREDs with a CARG (Constant ARGument) feature, which are used to represent proper names and numbers; and GPREDs with a predicate name starting with generic such as generic_verb which are used for unknown words that have only been identified by their part of speech. All other EPs have no referent and are used to provide information about the content EPs or about the structure of the sentence as a whole. These non-content EPs can provide some useful information, but generally only in relation to other content EPs.

Each content EP of the first RMRS is compared to all content EPs in the second RMRS, as shown in Figure 4.

Matches are categorised as EXACT, SYNONYM, HYPERNYM, HYPONYM or NO MATCH and a numerical score is assigned. The nu-

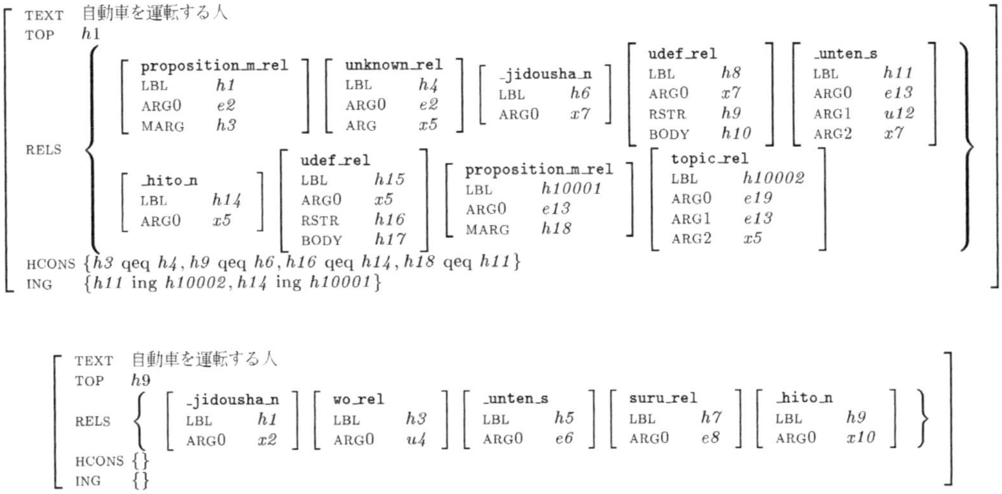


Figure 2: Deep (top) and shallow (bottom) RMRS results for 自動車 を 運転 する 人

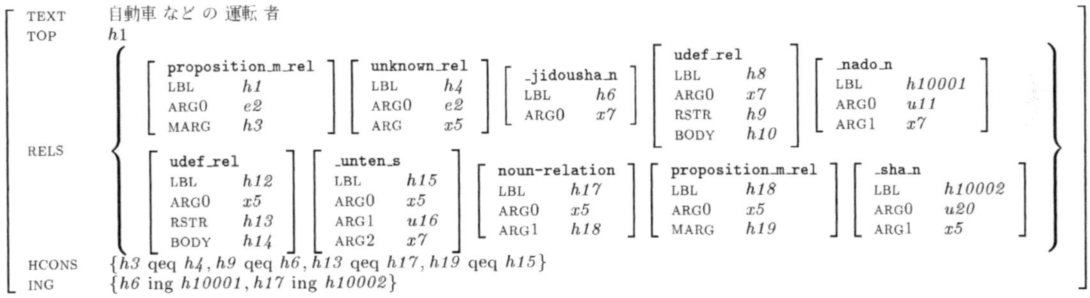


Figure 3: RMRS representation for 自動車 など の 運転 者

```
foreach ep1 in contentEPs1
 foreach ep2 in contentEPs2
  (score, match) = match_EPs(ep1, ep2)
  if match != NO_MATCH
    add_to_matches(ep1, ep2, score, match)
  endif
 done
done
```

Figure 4: Predicate match pseudo-code

merical score represents the distance between the two EPs, and hence an EXACT match is assigned a score of zero.

The level of matching possible depends on the lexical resources available. With no extra resources, or only a dictionary to pick up orthographic variants, the only match types possible are EXACT and NO MATCH. By adding a thesaurus, an ontology or a gazetteer, it is then possible to return SYNONYM, HYPERNYM and HYPONYM match relations. In our experiments we used the ontology described in Section 3.2.2, which provides all three extra match types. Adding a thesaurus only would enable SYNONYM matching, while a gazetteer could be added to give, for example, `Tokyo` is a HYPONYM of `city`.

```
Matches:
   hito_n    - sha_n    : HYPERNYM (2)
   jidosha_n - jidosha_n: EXACT (0)
   unten_s_2 - unten_s_2: EXACT (0)
```

Figure 5: First pass match list for (1) and (2)

At the end of the first pass, a list of match records shows all EP matches with their match type and score. Each EP can have multiple possible matches. The output of comparing (1) and (2), with the RMRSes in Figures 2 and 3, is shown in Figure 5. This shows `hito_n` (人 *hito* "person") tagged as a HYPERNYM of

```
foreach match in matches
 gpreds1 = get_gpreds_arg0(ep1{arg0})
 gpreds2 = get_gpreds_arg0(ep2{arg0})
 totalgpreds = len gpreds1 + len gpreds2
 foreach ep1 in gpreds1
  foreach ep2 in gpreds2
   if(match_gram_eps(ep1, ep2)
    remove(ep1, gpreds1)
    remove(ep2, gpreds2)
   endif
  done
 done
 gpreds_left = len gpreds1 + len gpreds2
 left = gpreds_left/totalgpreds
 match{score}+= left*gpredWeight
done
```

Figure 6: Matching ARG0s

`sha_n` (者 *sha* "-er" is a suffix indicating a person, normally the agent of a verb: it is more restrictive than English *-er*, in that it only refers to people).

### 2.2 Constraints Pass

For each possible match, all the non-content EPs that have the same ARG0 value as the content EPs in the match are examined, since these have the same referent. If each non-content EP related to the content EP on one side of the match can be matched to the non-content EPs related to the other content EP, no change is made. If not, however, a penalty is added to the match score, as shown in Figure 6. In our example, `unten_s_2` from the first sentence has a `proposition_m_rel` referentially co-indexed, while the second `unten_s_2` has a `proposition_m_rel`, a `noun-relation` and a `udef_rel`, and so a small penalty is added as shown in Figure 7.

The second check in the constraint match pass examines the arguments (ARG1, ARG2, ARG3, ARG4) of each of the matches. It looks for possible matches found between the EPs listed as ARGn for each match. This check can result in three separate results: both EPs have an ARGn but there is no potential match found between the respective ARGn EPs, a potential match has been found between the ARGn EPs, or only one of the EPs in the match has an ARGn feature.

Where both EPs have an ARGn feature, the score (distance) of the match is decreased or increased depending on whether a match between the ARGn variables was found. Given that the RMRS definition does not specify a

```
Matches:
   hito_n     - sha_n      : HYPERNYM (2.1)
   jidosha_n - jidosha_n: EXACT (0)
   unten_s_2 - unten_s_2: EXACT (0.05)
```

Figure 7: Match list
Slight penalty added to `unten_s_2` and `hito_n` for non-matching non-content EPs

'meaning' for the ARGn variables, comparing, for example, ARG1 variables from two different predicates may not necessarily be comparing the same semantic roles. However, because of the consistency found in ARG1 and ARG2 meaning this is still a useful check. Of course, if we are comparing the same relation, the ARGs will all have the same meaning. The comparison method allows for different penalties for each of ARG1 to ARG4, and also includes a scaling factor so that mismatches in ARGs when comparing EXACT EP matches will have more effect on the score than in non EXACT matches. If one EP does not have the ARGn feature, no change is made to the score. This allows for the use of underspecified RMRSs, in the case where the parse fails.

At the end of this pass, the scores of the matches in the match list may have changed but the number of matches is still the same.

### 2.3 Constructing the Sets

Match sets are constructed by using a branch-and-bound decision tree. Each match is considered in order, and the tree is branched if the next match is possible, given the proceeding decisions. Any branch which is more than two decisions away from the best score so far is pruned. At the end of this stage, the lowest scoring match set is returned and then this is further processed.

If no matches were found, processing stops and a sentinel value is returned. Otherwise, the non matching predicates are grouped together by their ARG0 value. Scoping constraints are checked and if any non matching predicate outscopes a content predicate it is added to that grouping. Hence if it outscopes a matching EP it becomes part of the match, otherwise it becomes part of a non-matching EP group.

Any group of grammatical EPs that shares an ARG0 but does not contain a content predicate is matched against any similar groupings

```
Best score is 0.799 for the match set:
MATCHES:
 hito_n-sha_n: HYPERNYM:2.1
 jidousha_n-jidousha_n:EXACT:0
 unten_s_2-unten_s_2:EXACT:0.05
 proposition_m_rel-proposition_m_rel:EXACT:0
UNMATCHED1:
UNMATCHED2:
 u11: h10001:nado_n
```

Figure 8: Verbose comparison output

in the other RMRS. This type of match can only be EXACT or NO MATCH and will make only a small difference in the final score.

Content predicates that have not been matched by this stage are not processed any further, although this is an area for further investigation. Potentially negation and other modifiers could be processed at this point.

### 2.4 Output

The output of the comparison algorithm is a numeric score and also a representation of the final best match found.

The numerical score, using the default scoring parameters, ranges between 0 (perfect match) and 3. As well as the no match score (-5), sentinel values are used to indicate missing input data so it is possible to fall back to a shallow parse if the deep parse failed.

Details of the match set are also returned for further processing or examination if the application requires. This shows which predicates were deemed to match, and with what score, and also shows the unmatched predicates. Figure 8 shows the output of our example comparison.

## 3 Resources

While the comparison method is language independent, the resources required are language specific. The resources fall in to two different categories: parsing and morphological analysis tools that produce the RMRSs, and lexical resources such as ontologies, dictionaries and gazetteers for evaluating matches.

### 3.1 Parsing

Japanese language processing tools are freely available. We used the Japanese grammar Jacy (Siegel and Bender, 2002), a deep parsing HPSG grammar that produces RMRSs for our primary input source.

When parsing with Jacy failed, comparisons could still be made with RMRS produced from shallow tools such as ChaSen (Matsumoto et al., 2000), a morphological analyser or CaboCha (Kudo and Matsumoto, 2002), a Japanese dependency parser. Tools have been built to produced RMRS from the standard output of both those tools.

The CaboCha output supplies similar dependency information to that of the Basic Elements (BE) tool used by Hovy et al. (2005b) for multi-document summarization. Even this intermediate level of parsing gives better comparisons than either word or sequence overlap, since it is easier to compare meaningful elements (Hovy et al., 2005a).

### 3.2 Lexical Resources

Whilst deep lexical resources are not available for every language, where they are available, they should be used to make comparisons more informative. The comparison framework allows for different lexical resources to be added to a pipeline. The pipeline starts with a simple relation name match, but this could be followed by a dictionary to extract orthographic variants and then by ontologies such as WordNet (Fellbaum, 1998) or GoiTaikei (Ikehara et al., 1997), gazetteers or named entity recognisers to recognise names of people and places. The sections below detail the lexical resources we used within our experiments.

#### 3.2.1 The Lexeed Semantic Database

The Lexeed Semantic Database of Japanese is a machine readable dictionary that covers the most familiar words in Japanese, based on a series of psycholinguistic tests (Kasahara et al., 2004). Lexeed has 28,000 words divided into 46,000 senses and defined with 75,000 definition sentences. Each entry includes a list of orthographic variants, and the pronunciation, in addition to the definitions.

#### 3.2.2 Ontology

The lexicon has been sense-tagged and parsed to give an ontology linking senses with various relations, principally **hypernym** and **synonym** (Nichols et al., 2005). For example, ⟨HYPERNYM, ドライバー *doraibā* "driver", クラブ *kurabu* "club"⟩. The ontology entries for nouns have been hand checked and corrected, including adding hypernyms for words where the genus term in the definition was very general, e.g "a word used to refer insultingly to men" where *man* is a more useful hypernym than *word* for the defined term *yarou*.

## 4 Evaluation

We evaluated the performance of the RMRS comparison method in two tasks. First it was used to indicate whether two sentences were possible paraphrases. In the second task, we used the comparison scores to select the most likely sentence to contain the answer to a question.

### 4.1 Paraphrasing

In this task we compared definitions sentences for the same head word from two different Japanese dictionaries - the Lexeed dictionary (§3.2.1) and the Iwanami Kokugo Jiten (Iwanami: Nishio et al., 1994), the Japanese dictionary used in the SENSEVAL-2 Japanese lexical task (Shirai, 2002).

There are 60,321 headwords and 85,870 word senses in Iwanami. Each sense in the dictionary consists of a sense ID and morphological information (word segmentation, POS tag, base form and reading, all manually post-edited).

The definitions in Lexeed and Iwanami were linked by headword and three Japanese native speakers assessed each potential pair of sense definitions for the same head word to judge which definitions were describing the same sense. This annotation not only described which sense from each dictionary matched, but also whether the definitions were equal, equivalent, or subsuming.

The examples (1) and (2) are the definitions of sense 2 of ドライバー *doraibā* "driver" from Lexeed and Iwanami respectively. They were judged to be equivalent definitions by all three annotators.

#### 4.1.1 Method

Test sets were built consisting of the Lexeed and Iwanami definition pairs that had been annotated in the gold standard to be either non-matching, equal or equivalent. Leaving out those pairs annotated as having a subsumption relation made it a clearer task judging between paraphrase or not, rather than examining partial meaning overlap. Ten sets of 5,845 definition pairs were created, with each set being equally split between matching and non-matching pairs. This gives data that is to some extent semantically equivalent (the same word sense is being defined), but with no guarantee of syntactic equivalence.

Comparisons were made between the first sentence of each definition with both a Bag-of-Words comparison method and our RMRS based method. If RMRS output was not available from Jacy (due to a failed parse), RMRS from CaboCha was used as a fall back shallow parse result.

Scores were output and then the best threshold score for each method was calculated on one of the 10 sets. Using the calculated threshold score, pairs were classified as either matching or non-matching. Pairs classified as matching were evaluated as correct if the gold standard annotation was either equal or equivalent.

#### 4.1.2 Results

The Bag-of-Words comparison got an average accuracy over all sets of 73.9% with 100% coverage. A break down of the results shows that this method was more accurate (78%) in correctly classifying non-matches than matches (70%). This is to be expected since it won't pick up equivalences where a word has been changed for its synonym.

The RMRS comparison had an accuracy was 78.4% with almost 100% coverage, an improvement over the Bag-of-Words. The RMRS based method was also more accurate over non matches (79.9%) than matches (76.6%), although the difference is not as large. Considering only those sentences with a parse from JACY gave an accuracy of 81.1% but with a coverage of only 46.1%. This shows that deep parsing improves precision, but must be used in conjunction with a shallower fallback.

To explore what effect the ontology was having on the results, another evaluation was performed without the ontology matching. This had an accuracy of 77.3% (78.1% using Jacy, 46.1% coverage). This shows that the information available in the ontology definitely improves scores, but that even without that sort of deep lexical resource, the RMRS matching can still improve on Bag-of-Words using just surface form abstraction and argument matching.

### 4.2 Answer Sentence Selection

To emulate a part of the question answering pipeline, we used a freely available set of 2000 Japanese questions, annotated with, among other things, answer and answer document ID (Sekine et al., 2002). The document IDs for the answer containing documents refer to the Mainichi Newspaper 1995 corpus which has been used as part of the document collection for NTCIR's Question Answering Challenges. The documents range in length from 2 to 83 sentences.

#### 4.2.1 Method

For every question, we compared it to each sentence in the answer document. The sentence that has the best similarity to the question is returned as the most likely to contain the answer. For this sort of comparison, an *entails* option was added that changes the similarity scoring method slightly so that only non-matches in the first sentence increase the score. The rationale being that in Question Answering (and also in entailment), everything present in the question (or hypothesis) should be matched by something in the answer, but having extra, unmatched information in the answer should not be penalised.

The task is evaluated by checking if the answer does exist in the sentence selected. This means that more than one sentence can be the correct answer for any question (if the answer is mentioned multiple times in the article).

#### 4.2.2 Results

The Bag-of-Words comparison correctly found a sentence containing the answer for 62.5% of the 2000 questions. The RMRS comparison method gave a small improvement, with a result of 64.3%. Examining the data showed this to be much harder than the paraphrase task because of the language level involved. In the paraphrasing task, the sentences averaged around 10 predicates each, while the questions and sentences in this task averaged over 3 times longer, with about 34 predicates. The words used were also less likely to be in the lexical resources both because more formal, less familiar words were used, and also because of the preponderance of named entities. Adding name lists of people, places and organisations would greatly improve the matching in this instance.

## 5 Future Directions

### 5.1 Applications

Since the comparison method was written to be language independent, the next stage of evaluation would be to use it in a non-Japanese task. The PASCAL Recognising Textual Entailment (RTE) Challenge (Dagan et al., 2005) is one recent English task where participants used sentence comparison extensively. While the task appears to call for inference and reasoning, the top 5 participating groups used statistical methods and word overlap only. Vanderwende et al. (2005) did a manual evaluation of the test data and found that 37% could be decided on syntactic information alone, while adding a thesaurus could increase that coverage to 49%. This means that RMRS comparison has the potential to perform well. Not only does it improve on basic word overlap, but it allows for easy addition of a thesaurus or dictionary. Further, because of the detailed match output available, the method could be extended in post processing to encompass some basic inference methods.

Aside from comparing sentences, the RMRS comparison can be used to compare the RMRS output of different tools for the same sentence so that the compatibility of the outputs can be evaluated and improved.

### 5.2 Extensions

One immediate future improvement planned is to add named entity lists to the lexical resources so that names of people and places could be looked up. This would allow partial matches between, e.g., `Clinton` is a HYPONYM of `person`, which would be particularly useful for Question Answering.

Another idea is to add a bilingual dictionary and try cross-lingual comparisons. As the RMRS abstracts away much of the surface specific details, this might be useful for sentence alignment.

To go beyond sentence by sentence comparison, we have plans to implement a method for multi-sentence comparisons by either combining the RMRS structures before comparison, or post-processing the sentence comparison outputs. This could be particularly interesting for text summarization.

## 6 Conclusions

Deep parsing information is useful for comparing sentences and RMRS gives us a useful framework for utilising this information when it is available. Our RMRS comparison was more accurate then basic word overlap similarity measurement particularly in the paraphrase task where synonyms were often used. Even when the ontology was not used, abstracting away from surface form, and matching arguments did give an improvement. Falling back to shallow parse methods increases the robustness which is often an issue for tools that use deep processing, while still allowing the use of the most accurate information available.

The comparison method is language agnostic and can be used for any language that has RMRS generating tools. The output is much more informative than Bag-of-Words, making it useful in many applications that need to know exactly how a sentence matched or aligned.

### Acknowledgements

This work was started when the first author was a visitor at the NTT Communication Science Laboratories, Nippon Telegraph and Telephone Corporation. The first author was also supported by the Pam Todd scholarship from St Hilda's College. We would like to thank the NTT Natural Language Research Group and two anonymous reviewers for their valuable input.

## References

Ann Copestake. 2002. *Implementing Typed Feature Structure Grammars*. CSLI Publications.

Ido Dagan, Oren Glickman, and Bernado Magnini. 2005. The PASCAL recognising textual entailment challenge. In *Proceedings of the PASCAL Challenges Workshop on Recognising Textual Entailment*.

Christine Fellbaum. 1998. A semantic network of English verbs. In Christine Fellbaum, editor, *WordNet: An Electronic Lexical Database*, chapter 3, pages 70–104. MIT Press.

Anette Frank. 2004. Constraint-based RMRS construction from shallow grammars. In *20th International Conference on Computational Linguistics: COLING-2004*, pages 1269–1272. Geneva.

Tsutomu Hirao, Jun Suzuki, Hideki Isozaki, and Eisaku Maeda. 2004. Dependency-based sentence alignment for multiple document summarization. In *Proceedings of the COLING*.

Eduard Hovy, Junichi Fukumoto, Chin-Yew Lin, and Liang Zhao. 2005a. Basic elements. (`http://www.isi.edu/~cyl/BE`).

Eduard Hovy, Chin-Yew Lin, and Liang Zhao. 2005b. A BE-based multi-document summarizer with sentence compression. In *Proceedings of Multilingual Summarization Evaluation*.

Satoru Ikehara, Masahiro Miyazaki, Satoshi Shirai, Akio Yokoo, Hiromi Nakaiwa, Kentaro Ogura, Yoshifumi Ooyama, and Yoshihiko Hayashi. 1997. *Goi-Taikei A Japanese Lexicon*. Iwanami Shoten, Tokyo. 5 volumes/CDROM.

Kaname Kasahara, Hiroshi Sato, Francis Bond, Takaaki Tanaka, Sanae Fujita, Tomoko Kanasugi, and Shigeaki Amano. 2004. Construction of a Japanese semantic lexicon: Lexeed. SIG NLC-159, IPSJ, Tokyo. (in Japanese).

Paul Kingsbury, Martha Palmer, and Mitch Marcus. 2002. Adding semantic annotation to the penn treebank. In *Proceedings of the Human Language Technology 2002 Conference*.

Taku Kudo and Yuji Matsumoto. 2002. Japanese dependency analysis using cascaded chunking. In *CoNLL 2002: Proceedings of the 6th Conference on Natural Language Learning 2002 (COLING 2002 Post-Conference Workshops)*, pages 63–69. Taipei.

Yuji Matsumoto, Kitauchi, Yamashita, Hirano, Matsuda, and Asahara. 2000. *Nihongo Keitaiso Kaiseki System: Chasen*, version 2.2.1 manual edition. `http://chasen.aist-nara.ac.jp`.

Eric Nichols, Francis Bond, and Daniel Flickinger. 2005. Robust ontology acquisition from machine-readable dictionaries. In *Proceedings of the International Joint Conference on Artificial Intelligence IJCAI-2005*, pages 1111–1116. Edinburgh.

Minoru Nishio, Etsutaro Iwabuchi, and Shizuo Mizutani. 1994. *Iwanami Kokugo Jiten Dai Go Han [Iwanami Japanese Dictionary Edition 5]*. Iwanami Shoten, Tokyo. (in Japanese).

Anna Ritchie. 2004. Compatible RMRS representations from RASP and the ERG. Technical Report UCAM-CL-TR-661.

Satoshi Sekine, Kiyoshi Sudo, Yusuke Shinyama, Chikashi Nobata, Kiyotaka Uchimoto, and Hitoshi Isahara. 2002. NYU/CRL QA system, QAC question analysis and CRL QA data. In *Working Notes of NTCIR Workshop 3*.

Kiyoaki Shirai. 2002. Construction of a word sense tagged corpus for SENSEVAL-2 Japanese dictionary task. In *Third International Conference on Language Resources and Evaluation (LREC-2002)*, pages 605–608.

Melanie Siegel and Emily M. Bender. 2002. Efficient deep processing of Japanese. In *Proceedings of the 3rd Workshop on Asian Language Resources and International Standardization at the 19th International Conference on Computational Linguistics*. Taipei.

Lucy Vanderwende, Deborah Coughlin, and Bill Dolan. 2005. What syntax can contribute in entailment task. In *Proceedings of the PASCAL Challenges Workshop on Recognising Textual Entailment*.

# Evaluation of Several Phonetic Similarity Algorithms on the Task of Cognate Identification

**Grzegorz Kondrak** and **Tarek Sherif**
Department of Computing Science
University of Alberta
Edmonton, Alberta, Canada T6G 2E8
{kondrak,tarek}@cs.ualberta.ca

## Abstract

We investigate the problem of measuring phonetic similarity, focusing on the identification of cognates, words of the same origin in different languages. We compare representatives of two principal approaches to computing phonetic similarity: manually-designed metrics, and learning algorithms. In particular, we consider a stochastic transducer, a Pair HMM, several DBN models, and two constructed schemes. We test those approaches on the task of identifying cognates among Indoeuropean languages, both in the supervised and unsupervised context. Our results suggest that the averaged context DBN model and the Pair HMM achieve the highest accuracy given a large training set of positive examples.

## 1 Introduction

The problem of measuring phonetic similarity between words arises in various contexts, including speech processing, spelling correction, commercial trademarks, dialectometry, and cross-language information retrieval (Kessler, 2005). A number of different schemes for computing word similarity have been proposed. Most of those methods are derived from the notion of edit distance. In its simplest form, edit distance is the minimum number of edit operations required to transform one word into the other. The set of edit operations typically includes substitutions, insertions, and deletions, and may incorporate more complex transformations.

By assigning variable weights to various edit operations depending on the characters involved in the operations, one can design similarity schemes that are more sensitive to a given task. Such variable weight schemes can be divided into two main groups. One approach is to manually design edit operation weights on the basis of linguistic intuition and/or physical measurements. Another approach is to use machine learning techniques to derive the weights automatically from training data composed of a set of word pairs that are considered similar. The manually-designed schemes tend to be somewhat arbitrary, but can be readily applied to diverse tasks. The learning approaches are also easily adaptable to various tasks, but they crucially require training data sets of reasonable size. In general, the more complex the underlying model, the larger the data sets needed for parameter estimation.

In this paper, we focus on a few representatives of both approaches, and compare their performance on the specific task of cognate identification. Cognate identification is a problem of finding, in distinct languages, words that can be traced back to a common word in a proto-language. Beyond historical linguistics, cognate identification has applications in other areas of computational linguistics (Mackay and Kondrak, 2005). Because the likelihood that two words across different languages are cognates is highly correlated with their phonetic similarity, cognate identification provides an objective test of the quality of phonetic similarity schemes.

The remainder of this paper is organized as fol-



*Proceedings of the Workshop on Linguistic Distances*, pages 43–50,
Sydney, July 2006. ©2006 Association for Computational Linguistics

lows. Section 2 discusses the two manually designed schemes: the ALINE algorithm and a linguistically-motivated metric. Section 3 discusses various learning approaches. In Section 4, we describe Dynamic Bayesian Nets. Finally, in Section 5, we discuss the results of our experiments.

## 2 Two manually constructed schemes

In this section, we first describe two different constructed schemes and then compare their properties.

### 2.1 ALINE

The ALINE algorithm (Kondrak, 2000) assigns a similarity score to pairs of phonetically-transcribed words on the basis of the decomposition of phonemes into elementary phonetic features. The algorithm was originally designed to identify and align cognates in vocabularies of related languages. Nevertheless, thanks to its grounding in universal phonetic principles, the algorithm can be used for estimating the similarity of any pair of words.

The principal component of ALINE is a function that calculates the similarity of two phonemes that are expressed in terms of about a dozen multi-valued phonetic features (*Place*, *Manner*, *Voice*, etc.). The phonetic features are assigned *salience* weights that express their relative importance. Feature values are encoded as floating-point numbers in the range $[0,1]$. For example, the feature *Manner* can take any of the following seven values: *stop* = 1.0, *affricate* = 0.9, *fricative* = 0.8, *approximant* = 0.6, *high vowel* = 0.4, *mid vowel* = 0.2, and *low vowel* = 0.0. The numerical values reflect the distances between vocal organs during speech production.

The overall similarity score is the sum of individual similarity scores between pairs of phonemes in an optimal alignment of two words, which is computed by a dynamic programming algorithm (Wagner and Fischer, 1974). A constant insertion/deletion penalty is applied for each unaligned phoneme. Another constant penalty is set to reduce relative importance of vowel—as opposed to consonant—phoneme matches. The similarity value is normalized by the length of the longer word.

ALINE's behavior is controlled by a number of parameters: the maximum phonemic score, the insertion/deletion penalty, the vowel penalty, and the feature salience weights. The parameters have default settings for the cognate matching task, but these settings can be optimized (tuned) on a development set that includes both positive and negative examples of similar words.

### 2.2 A linguistically-motivated metric

Phonetically natural classes such as /p b m/ are much more common among world's languages than unnatural classes such as /o z g/. In order to show that the bias towards phonetically natural patterns of phonological classes can be modeled without stipulating phonological features, Mielke (2005) developed a phonetic distance metric based on acoustic and articulatory measures. Mielke's metric encompasses 63 phonetic segments that are found in the inventories of multiple languages. Each phonetic segment is represented by a 7-dimensional vector that contains three acoustic dimensions and four articulatory dimensions (perceptual dimensions were left out because of the difficulties involved in comparing almost two thousand different sound pairs). The phonetic distance between any two phonetic segments were then computed as the Euclidean distance between the corresponding vectors.

For determining the acoustic vectors, the recordings of 63 sounds were first transformed into waveform matrices. Next, distances between pairs of matrices were calculated using the Dynamic Time Warping technique. These acoustic distances were subsequently mapped to three acoustic dimensions using multidimensional scaling. The three dimensions can be interpreted roughly as (a) sonorous vs. sibilant, (b) grave vs. acute, and (c) low vs. high formant density.

The articulatory dimensions were based on ultrasound images of the tongue and palate, video images of the face, and oral and nasal airflow measurements. The four articulatory dimensions were: oral constriction location, oral constriction size, lip constriction size, and nasal/oral airflow ratio.

### 2.3 Comparison

When ALINE was initially designed, there did not exist any concrete linguistically-motivated similarity scheme to which it could be compared. Therefore, it is interesting to perform such a comparison with the recently proposed metric.

The principal difficulty in employing the metric for computing word similarity is the limited size of the phonetic segment set, which was dictated by practical considerations. The underlying database of phonological inventories representing 610 languages contains more than 900 distinct phonetic segments, of which almost half occur in only one language. However, because a number of complex measurements have to be performed for each sound, only 63 phonetic segments were analyzed, which is a set large enough to cover only about 20% of languages in the database. The set does not include such common phones as dental fricatives (which occur in English and Spanish), and front rounded vowels (which occur in French and German). It is not at all clear how one to derive pairwise distances involving sounds that are not in the set.

In contrast, ALINE produces a similarity score for any two phonetic segment so long as they can be expressed using the program's set of phonetic features. The feature set can in turn be easily extended to include additional phonetic features required for expressing unusual sounds. In practice, any IPA symbol can be encoded as a vector of universal phonetic features.

Another criticism that could be raised against Mielke's metric is that it has no obvious reference point. The choice of the particular suite of acoustic and articulatory measurements that underlie the metric is not explicitly justified. It is not obvious how one would decide between different metrics for modeling phonetic generalizations if more than one were available.

On the other hand, ALINE was designed with a specific reference in mind, namely cognate identification. The "goodness" of alternative similarity schemes can be objectively measured on a test set containing both cognates and unrelated pairs from various languages.

A perusal of individual distances in Mielke's metric reveals that some of them seem quite unintuitive. For example, [t] is closer to [j] than it is to [ʦ], [ə] is closer to [n] than to [i], [ʒ] is closer to [e] than to [g], etc. This may be caused either by the omission of perceptual features from the underlying set of features, or by the assignment of uniform weights to different features (Mielke, *personal communication*).

It is difficult to objectively measure which phonetic similarity scheme produces more "intuitive" values. In order to approximate a human evaluation, we performed a comparison with the perceptual judgments of Laver (1994), who assigned numerical values to pairwise comparisons of 22 English consonantal phonemes on the basis of "subjective auditory impressions". We counted the number of perceptual conflicts with respect to Laver's judgments for both Mielke's metric and ALINE's similarity values. For example, the triple ([ʃ], [j], [k]) is an example of a conflict because [ʃ] is considered closer to [j] than to [k] in Mielke's matrix but the order is the opposite in Laver's matrix. The program identified 1246 conflicts with Mielke's metric, compared to 1058 conflicts with ALINE's scheme, out of 4620 triples. We conclude that in spite of the fact that ALINE is designed for identifying cognates, rather than directly for phonetic similarity, it is more in agreement with human perceptual judgments than Mielke's metric which was explicitly designed for quantifying phonetic similarity.

## 3 Learning algorithms

In this section, we briefly describe several machine learning algorithms that automatically derive weights or probabilities for different edit operations.

### 3.1 Stochastic transducer

Ristad and Yianilos (1998) attempt to model edit distance more robustly by using Expectation Maximization to learn probabilities for each of the possible edit operations. These probabilities are then used to create a stochastic transducer, which scores a pair of words based on either the most probable sequence of operations that could produce the two words (Viterbi scoring), or the sum of the scores of all possible paths that could have produced the two words (stochastic scoring). The score of an individual path here is simply the product of the probabilities of the edit operations in the path. The algorithm was evaluated on the task of matching surface pronunciations in the Switchboard data to their canonical pronunciations in a lexicon, yielding a significant improvement in accuracy over Levenshtein distance.

### 3.2 Levenshtein with learned weights

Mann and Yarowsky (2001) applied the stochastic transducer of Ristad and Yianilos (1998) for inducing translation lexicons between two languages, but found that in some cases it offered no improvement over Levenshtein distance. In order to remedy this problem, they they proposed to filter the probabilities learned by EM into a few discrete cost classes, which are then used in the standard edit distance algorithm. The LLW approach yielded improvement over both regular Levenshtein and the stochastic transducer.

### 3.3 CORDI

CORDI (Kondrak, 2002) is a program for detecting recurrent sound correspondences in bilingual wordlists. The idea is to relate recurrent sound correspondences in wordlists to translational equivalences in bitexts. A *translation model* is induced between phonemes in two wordlists by combining the maximum similarity alignment with the competitive linking algorithm of Melamed (2000). Melamed's approach is based on the *one-to-one* assumption, which implies that every word in the bitext is aligned with at most one word on the other side of the bitext. In the context of the bilingual wordlists, the correspondences determined under the *one-to-one* assumption are restricted to link single phonemes to single phonemes. Nevertheless, the method is powerful enough to determine valid correspondences in wordlists in which the fraction of cognate pairs is well below 50%.

The discovered phoneme correspondences can be used to compute a correspondence-based similarity score between two words. Each valid correspondence is counted as a link and contributes a constant positive score (no crossing links are allowed). Each unlinked segment, with the exception of the segments beyond the rightmost link, is assigned a smaller negative score. The alignment with the highest score is found using dynamic programming (Wagner and Fischer, 1974). If more than one best alignment exists, links are assigned the weight averaged over the entire set of best alignments. Finally, the score is normalized by dividing it by the average of the lengths of the two words.

### 3.4 Pair HMM

Mackay and Kondrak (2005) propose to computing similarity between pairs of words with a technique adapted from the field of bioinformatics. A Pair Hidden Markov Model differs form a standard HMM by producing two output streams in parallel, each corresponding to a word that is being aligned. The model has three states that correspond to the basic edit operations: substitution, insertion, and deletion. The parameters of the model are automatically learned from training data that consists of word pairs that are known to be similar. The model is trained using the Baum-Welch algorithm (Baum et al., 1970).

## 4 Dynamic Bayesian Nets

A Bayesian Net is a directed acyclic graph in which each of the nodes represents a random variable. The random variable can be either deterministic, in which case the node can only take on one value for a given configuration of its parents, or stochastic, in which case the configuration of the parents determines the probability distribution of the node. Arcs in the net represent dependency relationships.

Filali and Bilmes (2005) proposed to use Dynamic Bayesian Nets (DBNs) for computing word similarity. A DBN is a Bayesian Net where a set of arcs and nodes are maintained for each point in time in a dynamic process. This involves set of prologue frames denoting the beginning of the process, chunk frames which are repeated for the middle of the process, and epilogue frames to end the process. The conditional probability relationships are time-independent. DBNs can encode quite complex interdependencies between states.

We tested four different DBN models on the task of cognate identification. In the following description of the models, $Z$ denotes the current edit operation, which can be either a substitution, an insertion, or a deletion.

**MCI** The *memoriless context-independent model* (Figure 1) is the most basic model, which is meant to be equivalent to the stochastic transducer of Ristad and Yianilos (1998). Its lack of memory signifies that the probability of $Z$ taking on a given value does not depend in any way on what previous values of $Z$ have been. The context-independence refers to the fact that

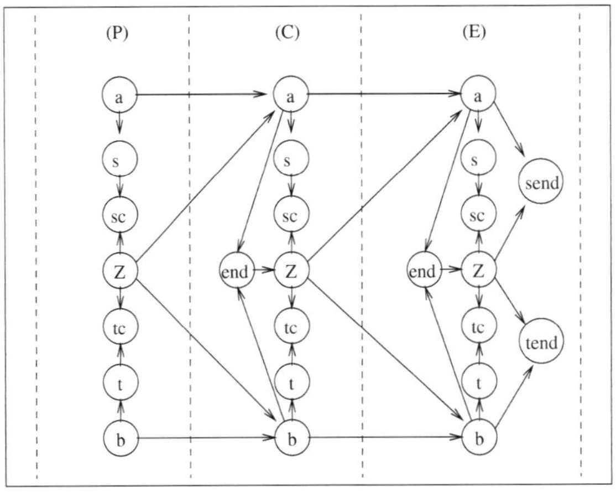


Figure 1: The MCI model.

the probability of $Z$ taking on a certain value does not depend on the letters of the source or target word. The $a$ and $b$ nodes in Figure 1 represent the current position in the source and target words, respectively. The $s$ and $t$ nodes represent the current letter in the source and target words. The *end* node is a switching parent of $Z$ and is triggered when the values of the $a$ and $b$ nodes move past the end of both the source and target words. The $sc$ and $tc$ nodes are consistency nodes which ensure that the current edit operation is consistent with the current letters in the source and target words. Consistency here means that the source side of the edit operation must either match the current source letter or be $\varepsilon$, and that the same be true for the target side. Finally, the *send* and *tend* nodes appear only in the last frame of the model, and are only given a positive probability if both words have already been completely processed, or if the final edit operation will conclude both words. The following models all use the MCI model as a basic framework, while adding new dependencies to $Z$.

**MEM** In the *memory model*, the probability of the current operation being performed depends on what the previous operation was.

**CON** In the *context-dependent model*, the probability that $Z$ takes on certain values is dependent on letters in the source word or target word. The model that we test in Section 5, takes into account the context of two letters in the source word: the current one and the immediately preceding one. We experimented with several other variations of context sets, but they either performed poorly on the development set, or required inordinate amounts of memory.

**LEN** The *length model* learns the probability distribution of the number of edit operations to be performed, which is the incorporated into the similarity score. This model represents an attempt to counterbalance the effect of longer words being assigned lower probabilities.

The models were implemented with the GMTK toolkit (Bilmes and Zweig, 2002). A more detailed description of the models can be found in (Filali and Bilmes, 2005).

## 5 Experiments

### 5.1 Setup

We evaluated various methods for computing word similarity on the task of the identification of cognates. The input consists of pairs of words that have the same meaning in distinct languages. For each pair, the system produces a score representing the likelihood that the words are cognate. Ideally, the scores for true cognate pairs should always be higher than scores assigned to unrelated pairs. For binary classification, a specific score threshold could be applied, but we defer the decision on the precision-recall trade-off to downstream applications. Instead, we order the candidate pairs by their scores, and evaluate the ranking using *11-point interpolated average precision* (Manning and Schutze, 2001). Scores are normalized by the length of the longer word in the pair.

Word similarity is not always a perfect indicator of cognation because it can also result from lexical borrowing and random chance. It is also possible that two words are cognates and yet exhibit little surface similarity. Therefore, the upper bound for average precision is likely to be substantially lower than 100%.

| Languages | | Proportion of cognates | EDIT | MIEL | ALINE | R&Y | LLW | PHMM | DBN |
|---|---|---|---|---|---|---|---|---|---|
| English | German | 0.590 | 0.906 | 0.909 | 0.912 | 0.894 | 0.918 | 0.930 | 0.927 |
| French | Latin | 0.560 | 0.828 | 0.819 | 0.862 | 0.889 | 0.922 | 0.934 | 0.923 |
| English | Latin | 0.290 | 0.619 | 0.664 | 0.732 | 0.728 | 0.725 | 0.803 | 0.822 |
| German | Latin | 0.290 | 0.558 | 0.623 | 0.705 | 0.642 | 0.645 | 0.730 | 0.772 |
| English | French | 0.275 | 0.624 | 0.623 | 0.623 | 0.684 | 0.720 | 0.812 | 0.802 |
| French | German | 0.245 | 0.501 | 0.510 | 0.534 | 0.475 | 0.569 | 0.734 | 0.645 |
| Albanian | Latin | 0.195 | 0.597 | 0.617 | 0.630 | 0.568 | 0.602 | 0.680 | 0.676 |
| Albanian | French | 0.165 | 0.643 | 0.575 | 0.610 | 0.446 | 0.545 | 0.653 | 0.658 |
| Albanian | German | 0.125 | 0.298 | 0.340 | 0.369 | 0.376 | 0.345 | 0.379 | 0.420 |
| Albanian | English | 0.100 | 0.184 | 0.287 | 0.302 | 0.312 | 0.378 | 0.382 | 0.446 |
| AVERAGE | | 0.2835 | **0.576** | **0.597** | **0.628** | **0.601** | **0.637** | **0.704** | **0.709** |

Table 1: 11-point average cognate identification precision for various methods.

### 5.2 Data

The training data for our cognate identification experiments comes from the Comparative Indoeuropean Data Corpus (Dyen et al., 1992). The data contains word lists of 200 basic meanings representing 95 speech varieties from the Indoeuropean family of languages. Each word is represented in an orthographic form without diacritics using the 26 letters of the Roman alphabet. Approximately 180,000 cognate pairs were extracted from the corpus.

The development set was composed of three language pairs: Italian-Croatian, Spanish-Romanian, and Polish-Russian. We chose these three language pairs because they represent very different levels of relatedness: 25.3%, 58.5%, and 73.5% of the word pairs are cognates, respectively. The percentage of cognates within the data is important, as it provides a simple baseline from which to compare the success of our algorithms. If our cognate identification process were random, we would expect to get roughly these percentages for our recognition precision (on average).

The test set consisted of five 200-word lists representing English, German, French, Latin, and Albanian, compiled by Kessler (2001). The lists for these languages were removed from the training data (except Latin, which was not part of the training set), in order to keep the testing and training data as separate as possible. For the supervised experiments, we converted the test data to have the same orthographic representation as the training data.

The training process for the DBN models consisted of three iterations of Expectation Maximization, which was determined to be optimal on the development data. Each pair was used twice, once in each source-target direction, to enforce the symmetry of the scoring, One of the models, the context-dependent model, remained asymmetrical despite to two-way training. In order to remove the undesirable asymmetry, we averaged the scores in both directions for each word pair.

### 5.3 Results

Table 1 shows the average cognate identification precision on the test set for a number of methods. EDIT is a baseline edit distance with uniform costs. MIEL refers to edit distance with weights computed using the approach outlined in (Mielke, 2005). ALINE denotes the algorithm for aligning phonetic sequences (Kondrak, 2000) described in Section 2.1. R&Y is the stochastic transducer of Ristad and Yianilos (1998). LLW stands for *Levenshtein with learned weights*, which is a modification of R&Y proposed by Mann and Yarowsky (2001). The PHMM column provides the results reported in (Mackay and Kondrak, 2005) for the best Pair HMM model, which uses log odds scoring. Finally, DBN stands for our best results obtained with a DBN model, in this case the averaged context model.

Table 2 show the aggregate results for various DBN models. Two different results are given for each model: the raw score, and the score normal-

| Model | Raw Score | Normalized |
|---|---|---|
| MCI | 0.515 | 0.601 |
| MEM | 0.563 | 0.595 |
| LEN | 0.516 | 0.587 |
| CON-FOR | 0.582 | 0.599 |
| CON-REV | 0.624 | 0.619 |
| CON-AVE | 0.629 | 0.709 |

Table 2: Average cognate identification precision for various DBN models.

ized by the length of the longer word. The models are the memoriless context-independent model (MCI), memory model (MEM), length model (LEN) and context model (CON). The context model results are split as follows: results in the original direction (FOR), results with all word pairs reversed (REV), and the results of averaging the scores for each word pair in the forward and reverse directions (AVE).

Table 3 shows the aggregate results for the unsupervised approaches. In the unsupervised tests, the training set was not used, as the models were trained directly on the testing data without access to the cognation information. For the unsupervised tests, the original, the test set was in its original phonetic form. The table compares the results obtained with various DBN models and with the CORDI algorithm described in Section 3.3.

### 5.4 Discussion

The results in Table 1 strongly suggest that the learning approaches are more effective than the manually-designed schemes for cognate identification. However, it has to be remembered that the learning process was conducted on a relatively large set of Indoeuropean cognates. Even though there was no overlap between the training and the test set, the latter also contained cognate pairs from the same language family. For each of the removed languages, there are other closely related languages that are retained in the training set, which may exhibit similar or even identical regular correspondences.

The manually-designed schemes have the advantage of not requiring any training sets after they have been developed. Nevertheless, Mielke's metric appears to produce only small improvement over

| Model | Raw Score | Normalized |
|---|---|---|
| MCI | 0.462 | 0.430 |
| MEM | 0.351 | 0.308 |
| LEN | 0.464 | 0.395 |
| CON-AVE | 0.433 | 0.414 |
| CORDI | — | 0.629 |

Table 3: Phonetic test results.

simple edit distance. ALINE outperforms Mielke's metric, which is not surprising considering that ALINE was developed specifically for identifying cognates, and Mielke's substitution matrix lacks several phonemes that occur in the test set.

Among the DBN models, the average context model performs the best. The averaged context model is clearly better than either of the unidirectional models on which it is based. It is likely that the averaging allows the scoring to take contextual information from both words into account, instead of just one or the other. The averaged context DBN model performs about as well as on average as the Pair HMM approach, but substantially better than the R&Y approach and its modification, LLW.

In the unsupervised context, all DBN models fail to perform meaningfully, regardless of whether the scores are normalized or not. In view of this, it is remarkable that CORDI achieves a respectable performance just by utilizing discovered correspondences, having no knowledge of phonetics nor identity of phonemes. The precision of CORDI is at the same level as the phonetically-based ALINE. In fact, a method that combines ALINE and CORDI achieves the average precision of 0.681 on the same test set (Kondrak, *in preparation*).

In comparison with the results of Filali and Bilmes (2005), certain differences are apparent. The memory and length models, which performed better than the memoriless context-independent model on the pronunciation task, perform worse overall here. This is especially notable in the case of the length model which was the best overall performer on their task. The context-dependent model, however, performed well on both tasks.

As mentioned in (Mann and Yarowsky, 2001), it appears that there are significant differences between the pronunciation task and the cognate identification task. They offer some hypotheses as to why this may be the case, such as noise in the data and the size of the training sets, but these issues are not apparent in the task presented here. The training set was quite large and consisted only of known cognates. The two tasks are inherently different, in that scoring in the pronunciation task involves finding the best match of a surface pronunciation with pronunciations in a lexicon, while the cognate task involves the ordering of scores relative to each other. Certain issues, such as length of words, may become more prominent in this setup. We countered this by normalizing all scores, which was not done in (Filali and Bilmes, 2005). As can be seen in Table 2, the normalization by length appears to improve the results on average. It notable that normalization even helps the length model on this task, despite the fact that it was designed to take word length into account.

## 6 Conclusion

We have compared the effectiveness of a number of different methods, including the DBN models, on the task of cognate identification. The results suggest that some of the learning methods, namely the Pair HMMs and the averaged context DBN model, outperform the manually designed methods, provided that large training sets are available.

In the future, we would like to apply DBNs to other tasks involving computing word similarity and/or alignment. An interesting next step would be to use them for tasks involving generation, for example the task of machine transliteration.

## Acknowledgments

We would like to thank Karim Filali for the DBN scripts, and for advice about how to use them. Thanks to Jeff Mielke for making his phoneme similarity matrix available for our experiments, and for commenting on the results. This research was supported by the Natural Sciences and Engineering Research Council of Canada.

## References

Leonard E. Baum, Ted Petrie, George Soules, and Norman Weiss. 1970. A maximization technique occurring in the statistical analysis of probabilistic function of Markov chains. *The Annals of Mathematical Statistics*, 41(1):164–171.

Jeff Bilmes and Geoffrey Zweig. 2002. The graphical models toolkit: An open source software system for speech and time-series processing. In *Proc. IEEE Intl. Conf. on Acoustics, Speech, and Signal Processing*.

Isidore Dyen, Joseph B. Kruskal, and Paul Black. 1992. An Indoeuropean classification: A lexicostatistical experiment. *Transactions of the American Philosophical Society*, 82(5).

Karim Filali and Jeff Bilmes. 2005. A dynamic Bayesian framework to model context and memory in edit distance learning: An application to pronunciation classification. In *Proceedings of ACL 2005*, pages 338–345.

Brett Kessler. 2001. *The Significance of Word Lists*. Stanford: CSLI Publications, Stanford, California.

Brett Kessler. 2005. Phonetic comparison algorithms. *Transactions of the Philological Society*, 103(2):243–260.

Grzegorz Kondrak. 2000. A new algorithm for the alignment of phonetic sequences. In *Proceedings of NAACL 2000*, pages 288–295.

Grzegorz Kondrak. 2002. Determining recurrent sound correspondences by inducing translation models. In *Proceedings of COLING 2002*, pages 488–494.

John Laver. 1994. *Principles of Phonetics*. Cambridge University Press.

Wesley Mackay and Grzegorz Kondrak. 2005. Computing word similarity and identifying cognates with Pair Hidden Markov Models. In *Proceedings of the 9th Conference on Computational Natural Language Learning (CoNLL)*, pages 40–47.

Gideon S. Mann and David Yarowsky. 2001. Multipath translation lexicon induction via bridge languages. In *Proceedings of NAACL 2001*, pages 151–158.

Christopher D. Manning and Hinrich Schutze. 2001. *Foundations of Statistical Natural Language Processing*. The MIT Press.

I. Dan Melamed. 2000. Models of translational equivalence among words. *Computational Linguistics*, 26(2):221–249.

Jeff Mielke. 2005. Modeling distinctive feature emergence. In *Proceedings of the 24th West Cost Conference on Formal Linguistics*, pages 281–289.

Eric Sven Ristad and Peter N. Yianilos. 1998. Learning string-edit distance. *IEEE Transactions on Pattern Analysis and Machine Intelligence*, 20(5):522–532.

Robert A. Wagner and Michael J. Fischer. 1974. The string-to-string correction problem. *Journal of the ACM*, 21(1):168–173.

# Evaluation of String Distance Algorithms for Dialectology

**Wilbert Heeringa, Peter Kleiweg, Charlotte Gooskens & John Nerbonne**
Humanities Computing, University of Groningen
{W.J.Heeringa, P.C.J.Kleiweg, C.S.Gooskens, J.Nerbonne}@rug.nl

## Abstract

We examine various string distance measures for suitability in modeling dialect distance, especially its perception. We find measures superior which do *not* normalize for word length, but which *are* are sensitive to order. We likewise find evidence for the superiority of measures which incorporate a sensitivity to phonological context, realized in the form of $n$-grams—although we cannot identify which form of context (bigram, trigram, etc.) is best. However, we find no clear benefit in using gradual as opposed to binary segmental difference when calculating sequence distances.

## 1 Introduction

We compare string distance measures for their value in modeling dialect distances. Traditional dialectology relies on identifying language features which are common to one dialect area while distinguishing it from others. It has difficulty in dealing with partial matches of linguistic features and with non-overlapping language patterns. Therefore Seguy (1973) and Goebl (1982; 1984) advocate using aggregates of linguistic features to analyze dialectal patterns, effectively introducing the perspective of DIALECTOMETRY.

Kessler (1995) introduced the use of string edit distance measure as a means of calculating the distance between the pronunciations of corresponding words in different dialects. Following Seguy's and Goebl's lead, he calculated this distance for pairs of pronunciations of many words in many Irish-speaking towns. String edit distance is sensitive to the degrees of overlap of strings and allows one to process large amounts of pronunciation data, including that which does not follow other isoglosses neatly. Heeringa (2004) examines several variants of edit distance applied to Norwegian and Dutch data, focusing on measures which involve a length normalization, and which ignore phonological context, and demonstrating that measures using binary segment differences are no worse than those using feature-based measures of segment difference.

This paper inspects a range of further refinements in measuring pronunciation differences. First, we inspect the role of normalization by length, showing that it actually worsens non-normalized measures. Second, we compare edit distance measures to simpler measures which ignore linear order, and show that order-sensitivity is important. Third, we inspect measures which are sensitive to phonetic context, and show that these, too, tend to be superior. Fourth, we compare versions of string edit distance which are constrained to respect syllable structure (always matching vowels with vowels, etc.), and conclude that this is mildly advantageous. Finally we compare binary (i.e., same/different) treatments of the segments in edit distance to gradual treatments of segment differentiation, and find no indication of the superiority of the gradual measures.

The quality of the measures is assayed primarily through their agreement with the judgments of dialect speakers about which varieties are perceived as more similar (or dissimilar) to their own. In addition we inspect a validation technique which purports to show how successfully a dialect measure uncovers the geographic structure in the data (Nerbonne and Kleiweg, 2006), but this technique yields unstable results when applied to our data. We have perception data only for Norwegian, so



*Proceedings of the Workshop on Linguistic Distances*, pages 51–62,
Sydney, July 2006. 

that data figures prominently in our argument, and we evaluate both Norwegian and German data geographically.

The results differ, and the perceptual results (concerning Norwegian) are most easily interpretable. There we find, as noted above, that non-normalized measures are superior to normalized ones, that both order and context sensitivity are worthwhile, as is the vowel/consonant distinction. The (geographic) results for German are more complicated, but also less stable. We include them for the sake of completeness.

In addition we note two minor contributions. First, although some literature ends up evaluating both distance and similarity measures, because these are not consistently each others' inverses under some normalizations (Kondrak, 2005; Inkpen et al., 2005), we suggest a normalization based on alignment length which guarantees that similarity is exactly the inverse of distance, allowing us to concentrate on distance.

Second, we note that there is no great problem in applying edit distance to bigrams and trigrams, even though recent literature has been sceptical about the feasibility of this step. For example Kessler (2005) writes:

> [...] one major shortcoming [in applying edit distance to linguistic data, WH et al] that is rarely discussed is that the phonetic environment of the sounds in question cannot be taken into account, while still making use of the efficient dynamic programming algorithm (p. 253).

Somewhat further Kessler writes: "Currently, the predominant solution to this problem is to ignore context entirely." In fact Kondrak (2005) applies edit distance straightforwardly using $n$-gram as basic elements. Our findings accord with Kondrak's, who also found no problem in applying edit distance using $n$-grams, but we evaluate the technique in its application to dialectology.

### 1.1 Background

Heeringa (2004) demonstrates that edit distance applied to comparable words (see below for examples) is a superior measure of dialect distance when compared to unigram corpus frequency and also that it is superior to both the frequency of phonetic features in corpora (a technique which Hoppenbrouwers & Hoppenbrouwers (2001) had advocated) and to the frequency of phonetic features taken one word at a time. Heeringa compares these techniques using the results of a perception experiment we also employ below. Heeringa shows that word-based techniques are superior to corpus-based techniques, and moreover, that most word-based techniques perform about the same. We therefore ignore measures which view corpora as undifferentiated collections below and study only word-based techniques.

A further question was whether to compare words based on a binary difference between segments or whether to use instead phonetic features to derive a more sensitive measure of segment distance. It turned out that measures using binary segment distinctions outperform the feature-based methods (see Heeringa, pp. 184–186), even though a number of feature systems and comparisons of feature vectors were experimented with. We likewise accept these results (at least for present purposes) and focus exclusively on measures using the binary segment distinctions below.

Kondrak (2005) and Inkpen et al. (2005) present several methods for measuring string similarity and distance which complement Heeringa's results nicely. We should note, however, that these papers focus on other areas of application, viz., the problems of identifying (i) technical names which might be confused, (ii) linguistic cognates (words from the same root), and (iii) translational cognates (words which may be used as translational equivalences). Inkpen et al. consider 12 different orthographic similarity measures, including some in which the order of segments does not play a role (e.g., DICE), and others which use order in alignment (e.g. edit distance). They further consider comparison on the basis of unigrams, bigrams, trigrams and "xbigrams," which are trigrams without the middle element. Some methods are similarity measures, others are distance measures. We return to this in Section 2.

### 1.2 This paper

In this paper we apply string distance measures to Norwegian and German dialect data. As noted above, we focus on word-based methods in which segments are compared at a binary (same/different) level. The methods we consider will be explained in Section 2. Section 3 describes the Norwegian and German data to which the methods are applied. In Section 4 we describe how we evaluate the methods, namely by comparing the algorithmic results to the distances as perceived by the dialect speakers themselves. We likewise aimed to evaluate by calculating the degree to which a measure uncovers geographic cohesion in dialect data, but as we shall see, this means of validation yields rather unstable results. In Section 5 we present results for the different methods and finally, in Section 6, we draw some conclusions.

## 2 String Comparison Algorithms

In this section we describe a number of string comparison algorithms largely following Inkpen et al. (2005). The methods can be classified according to different factors: representation (unigram, bigram, trigram, xbigram), comparison of $n$-grams (binary or gradual), status of order (with or without alignment), and type of alignment (free or forced alignment with respect to the vowel/consonant distinction). We illustrate the methods with examples, in which we compare German and Dutch dialect pronunciations of the word *milk*.[1]

### 2.1 Contextual sensitivity

In the German dialect of Reelkirchen *milk* is pronounced as [mɛlkə]. The bigram notation is [–m mɛ ɛl lk kə ə–] and the trigram notation is [—m –mɛ mɛl ɛlk lkə kə– ə—]. The same word is pronounced as [mɛləç] in the German dialect of Tann. The bigram and trigram representations are [–m mɛ ɛl lə əç ç–] and [—m –mɛ mɛl ɛlə ləç əç– ç—] respectively.

In the simplest method we present in this paper, the distance is found by calculating 1 minus twice the number of shared segment $n$-grams divided by the total number of $n$-grams in both words. Inkpen et al. mention a bigram-based, a trigram-based and a xbigram-based procedure, which they call DICE, TRIGRAM and XDICE respectively. We also consider an unigram-based procedure which we call UNIGRAM. The two pronunciations share four unigrams: [m, ɛ, l] and [ə]. There are $5+5 = 10$ unigram tokens in total in the two words, so the unigram similarity is $(2 \times 4)/10 = 0.8$, and the distance $1 - 0.8 = 0.2$. The two pronunciations share three bigrams: [–m, mɛ] and [ɛl]. There are $6 + 6 = 12$ bigram tokens in the two strings, so bigram similarity is $(2 \times 3)/12 = 0.5$, and the distance $1 - 0.5 = 0.5$. Finally, the two pronunciations have three trigrams in common: [—m, –mɛ] and [mɛl] among $7+7 = 14$ in total, yielding a trigram similarity of $(2 \times 3)/14 = 0.4$ and distance $1 - 0.4 = 0.6$.

Our interest in this issue is linguistic: longer $n$-grams allow comparison on the basis of phonic context, and unigram comparisons have correctly been criticized for ignoring this (Kessler, 2005).

### 2.2 Order of segments

When comparing the German dialect pronunciation of Reelkirchen [mɛlkə] with the Dutch dialect pronunciation of Haarlem [mɛlək], the unigram procedure presented above will detect no difference. One might argue that we are dealing with a swap, but this is effectively an appeal to order. The example is not convincing for $n$-gram measures, $n \geq 2$, but we should prefer to separate issues of order from issues of context sensitivity. We use edit distance (aka Levenshtein distance) for this purpose, and we assume familiarity with this (Kruskal, 1999). In our use of edit distance all operations have a cost of 1.

### 2.3 Normalization by length

When the edit distance is divided by the length of the longer string, Inkpen et al. call it normalized edit distance (NED). In our approach we divide "raw edit distance" by alignment length. The same minimum distance found by the edit distance algorithm may be obtained on the basis of several alignments which may have different lengths. We found that the longest alignment has the greatest number of matches. Therefore we normalize by dividing the edit distance by the length of the longest alignment.

We have normally employed a length normalization in earlier work (Heeringa, 2004), reasoning that words are such fundamental linguistic units that dialect perception was likely to be word-based. We shall test this premise in this paper.

Marzal & Vidal (1993) show that the normalized edit distance between two strings cannot be obtained via "post-normalization", i.e., by first computing the (unnormalized) edit distance and then normalizing this by the length of the corresponding editing path. Unnormalized edit distance satisfies the triangle inequality, which is axiomatic for distances, but the quantities obtained via post-normalization need not satisfy this axiom. Marzdal & Vidal provide an alternative procedure which is guaranteed to produce genuine

[1]Our transcriptions omit diacritics for simplicity's sake.

distances, satisfying all of the relevant axioms. In their modified algorithm, one computes one minimum weight for *each* of the possible lengths of editing paths at each point in the computational lattice. Once all these weights are calculated, they are divided by their corresponding path lengths, and the minimum quotient represents the normalized edit distance.

The basic idea behind edit distance is to find the minimum cost of changing one string into another. Length normalization represents a deviation from this basic idea. If a higher cost corresponds with a longer path length so that quotient of the edit costs divided by the path length is minimal, then Marzal & Vidal's procedure opts for the minimal normalized length, while post-normalization seeks what one might call "the normalized minimal length" (see Marzal & Vidal's example 3.1 and Figure 2, p. 928).

Marzal & Vidal's examples of normalized minimal distances which are not also minimal normalized distances all involve operation costs we normally do not employ. In particular they allow INDELS (insertions and deletions) to be associated with much lower costs than substitutions, so that the longer paths associated with derivations involving indels is more than compensated by the length normalization. Our costs are never structured in this way, so we conjecture that our post-normalizations do not genuinely run the risk of violating the distance axioms. We use 0 for the cost of mapping a symbol to itself, 1 to map it to a different symbol, including the empty symbol (covering the costs of indels), and $\infty$ for non-allowed mappings[2] We maintain therefore that (unnormalized) costs higher than the minimum will never correspond to longer alignment lengths. If this is so, then the minimal edit cost divided by alignment length will also be the minimal normalized cost. If the unnormalized edit distance is minimal, we claim that the post-normalized edit distance must therefore be minimal as well.

We inspect an example to illustrate these issues. We compare the Frisian (Grouw), [mɔlkə], with the Haarlem pronunciation [mɛlək]. The Levenshtein algorithm may align the pronunciations as follows:

| 1 | 2 | 3 | 4 | 5 | 6 |
|---|---|---|---|---|---|
| m | ɔ | l | | k | ə |
| m | ɛ | l | ə | k | |
| | 1 | | 1 | | 1 |

The one pronunciation is transformed into the other by substituting [ɛ] for [ɔ], by deleting [ə] after [l], and by inserting [ə] after [k]. Since each operation has a cost of 1, and the alignment is 6 elements long, the normalized distance is $(1 + 1 + 1)/6 = 0.5$. The Levenshtein distance will also find an alignment in which the [ə]'s are matched, while the [k]'s are inserted and deleted. That alignment gives the same (normalized) distance. Levenshtein distance will not find an alignment any longer than the one shown here, since longer alignments will not yield the minimum cost. This also holds for the examples shown below.

### 2.4 $n$-gram weights

In the dialect of the German dialect of Frohnhausen *milk* is pronounced as [mɪljə], and in the German of Großwechsungen as [mɛlɪç]. If we compare these using the techniques of Section 2.2, using bigrams, we obtain the following:

| 1 | 2 | 3 | 4 | 5 | 6 |
|---|---|---|---|---|---|
| -m | mɪ | ɪl | lj | jə | ə- |
| -m | mɛ | ɛl | lɪ | ɪk | k- |
| | 1 | 1 | 1 | 1 | 1 |

Since $n$-grams are compared in a binary way, the normalized distance is equal to $(1+1+1+1+1)/6 = 0.83$. But [mɪ] and [mɛ] (second position) are clearly more similar to each other than [jə] and [ɪk] (fifth position). Inkpen et al. suggest weighting $n$-gram differences using segment overlap. They provide a formula for measuring gradual similarity of $n$-grams to be used in BI-DIST and TRI-DIST. Since we measure distances rather than similarity, we calculate $n$-gram distance as follows:

$$s(x_1...x_n, y_1...y_n) = \frac{1}{n}\sum_{i=1}^{n} d(x_i, y_i)$$

where $d(a, b)$ returns 1 if $a$ and $b$ are different, and 0 otherwise. We apply this to our example:

| 1 | 2 | 3 | 4 | 5 | 6 |
|---|---|---|---|---|---|
| -m | mɪ | ɪl | lj | jə | ə- |
| -m | mɛ | ɛl | lɪ | ɪk | k- |
| | 0.5 | 0.5 | 0.5 | 1 | 0.5 |

obtaining $(0.5+0.5+0.5+1+0.5)/6 = 3.0/6 = 0.5$ distance after normalization.

[2]For example, in some versions of edit distance, the value $\infty$ is assigned to the replacement of a vowel by a consonant in order to avoid alignments which violate syllabic structure.

## 2.5 Linguistic Alignment

When comparing the Frisian (Grouw) dialect pronunciation, [mɔlkə], with that of German Großwechsungen, [mɛlɪç], using unigrams, we obtain:

| 1 | 2 | 3 | 4 | 5 |
|---|---|---|---|---|
| m | ɔ | l | k | ə |
| m | ɛ | l | ɪ | ç |
| | 1 | | 1 | 1 |

The normalized distance is then $(1+1+1)/5 = 0.6$. But this is linguistically an implausible alignment: syllables do not align when e.g. [k] aligns with [ɪ], etc. We may remedy this by requiring the Levenshtein algorithm to respect the distinction between vowels and consonants, requiring that the alignments respect this distinction with only three exceptions, in particular that semivowels [j, w] may match vowels (or consonants), that the maximally high vowels [i, u] match consonants (or vowels), and that [ə] match sonorant consonants (nasals and liquids) in addition to vowels. Disallowed matches are weighted so heavily (via the cost of the substitution operation) that the algorithm always will use alternative alignments, effectively preferring insertions and deletions (indels) instead. Applying these restrictions, we obtain the following, with normalized distance $(1+1+1+1)/6 = 0.67$:

| 1 | 2 | 3 | 4 | 5 | 6 |
|---|---|---|---|---|---|
| m | ɔ | l | | k | ə |
| m | ɛ | l | ɪ | ç | |
| | 1 | | 1 | 1 | 1 |

In comparisons based on bigrams, we allow two bigrams to match when at least one segment pair matches, the first, the second, or both. Two trigrams match when at least the middle pair matches. Comparing the same pronunciations as above using bigrams without linguistic conditions, we obtain the following alignment:

| 1 | 2 | 3 | 4 | 5 | 6 |
|---|---|---|---|---|---|
| -m | mɔ | ɔl | lk | kə | ə- |
| -m | mɛ | ɛl | lɪ | ɪç | ç- |
| | 1 | 1 | 1 | 1 | 1 |
| | 0.5 | 0.5 | 0.5 | 1 | 0.5 |

The normalized distance is $(1+1+1+1+1)/6 = 0.83$ using binary bigram weights (costs), and $(0.5+0.5+0.5+1+0.5)/6 = 0.5$ using gradual weights. But the above alignment does *not* respect the vowel/consonant distinction at the fifth position, where neither [k] vs. [ɪ] nor [ə] vs. [ç] is allowed. We correct this at once:

| 1 | 2 | 3 | 4 | 5 | 6 | 7 |
|---|---|---|---|---|---|---|
| -m | mɔ | ɔl | lk | | kə | ə- |
| -m | mɛ | ɛl | lɪ | ɪç | ç- | |
| | 1 | 1 | 1 | 1 | 1 | 1 |
| | 0.33 | 0.33 | 0.67 | 1 | 1 | 1 |

Using binary bigram weights, the normalized distance is $(1+1+1+1+1+1)/7 = 0.86$.

The calculation based on gradual weights is a bit more complex. Two bigrams may match even when a non-allowed pair occurs in one of the two positions, e.g., [k] vs. [ɪ] at the fourth position in the alignment immediately above. The cost of this match should be higher (via weights) than that of an allowed pair with different elements—e.g., the pair [ɔ] versus [ɛ] at the second or third position—but not so high that the match cannot occur.

We settle on the following scheme. Two $n$-grams $[x_1...x_n]$ and $[y_1...y_n]$ can only match if at least one pair $(x_i, y_i)$ matches linguistically. We weight linguistically mismatching pairs $(x_j, y_j)$ twice as high as matching (but non-identical) pairs. Since we have at most $n-1$ matching pairs, and at least 1 mismatching pair, we set the most expensive match of two $n$-grams to 1, and we assign the weight of $2/(2n-1)$ to a mismatching pair, and $1/(n-1)$ to a matching (but non-identical) one. Indels cost the same as the most costly (matching) $n$-grams, in this case 1.

In our bigram-based example, we obtain a weight of $2/(2 \times 2 - 1) = 0.67$ at position 4, since the pair [k] vs. [ɪ] is a linguistic mismatch. At positions 2 and 3 we obtain weights of $1/(2 \times 2 - 1) = 0.33$ since [ɔ] and [ɛ] are (non-identical) matches. Note that a segment (vowel or consonant) versus '-' (boundary) is processed as a mismatch. Therefore the weight at position 6 is equal to 0.33 ([k] vs. [ç]) +0.67 ([ə] versus [-]), summing to 1.

## 2.6 Similarity vs. distance

Theoretically, similarity and distance should be each others' inverses. Thus in Section 2.1 we suggested that similarity should always be (1 − distance). This is not always straightforward when we normalize.

Inkpen et al. use both similarity and distance measures. Similarity measures are LCSR (Longest Common Subsequence Ratio), BI-SIM and TRI-SIM (LCSR generalized to bigrams and trigrams), and the corresponding distance measures are NED, BI-DIST and TRI-DIST. The measures are further distinguished in the way $n$-gram weights are compared: as binary weights in the similarity measures, and as gradual weights in the distance measures. When comparing the pronunciations of Frisian Hindelopen [mɔəlkə] with German Großwechsungen, [mɛlɪç], and respecting the linguistic alignment conditions (Section 2.5) we obtain:

| m | ɔ | ə | l | | k | ə |
|---|---|---|---|---|---|---|
| m | ɛ | | l | ɪ | ç | |
| 0 | 1 | 1 | 0 | 1 | 1 | 1 |

The non-normalized similarity is equal to 2, and the non-normalized distance is equal to 5. Inkpen et al. normalize "by dividing the total edit cost by the length of the longer string" which is 6 in our example. Other possibilities are dividing by the length of the shorter string (5), the average length of the two strings (5.5) or the length of the alignment (7). Summarizing:

| | shorter string | longer string | average string | alignment |
|---|---|---|---|---|
| sim. | 0.4 | 0.33 | 0.36 | 0.29 |
| dist. | 1.0 | 0.83 | 0.91 | 0.71 |
| total | 1.4 | 1.17 | 1.27 | 1.00 |

Only the normalization via alignment length respects the wish that we regard similarity and distance as each others' inverses. [3] We can enforce this requirement in other approaches by first normalizing and then taking the inverse, but we take the result above to indicate that normalization via alignment length is the most natural procedure.

## 3 Data Sources

The methods presented in Section 2 are applied to Norwegian and German dialect data described in this section. We emphasize that we measured distances only at the level of the segmental base, ignoring stress and tone marks, suprasegmentals and diacritics. We in fact examined measurements which included the effects of segmental diacritics, which, however resulted in decreased consistency and no apparent increase in quality.

### 3.1 Norwegian

The Norwegian data comes from a database comprising more than 50 dialect sites, compiled by Jørn Almberg and Kristian Skarbø of the Department of Linguistics of the University of Trondheim.[4] The database includes recordings *and* transcriptions of the fable 'The North Wind and the Sun' in various Norwegian dialects. The Norwegian text consists of 58 different words, some of which occur more than once, in which case we seek a least expensive pairing of the different elements (Nerbonne and Kleiweg, 2003, p. 349).

On the basis of the recordings, Gooskens carried out a perception experiment which we describe in Section 4.1. The experiment is based on 15 dialects, the total number of dialects available at that time (spring, 2000). Since we want to use the results of the experiment for validating our methods, we used the same set of 15 Norwegian dialects. It is important to note that Gooskens presented the recordings holistically, including differences in syntax, intonation and morphology. Our methods are restricted to words.

### 3.2 German

The German data comes from the *Phonetischer Atlas Deutschlands* and includes 186 dialect locations. For each location 201 words were recorded and transcribed. The data are available at the *Forschungsinstitut für deutsche Sprache - Deutscher Sprachatlas* in Marburg. The material is from translations of *Wenker-Sätze*, taken from the famous survey by Georg Wenker in the 1879–1887 among teachers from $\approx$ 40.000 locations in Germany. The transcriptions are made on the basis of recordings made under the direction of Joachim Göschel in the 1960's and 1970's in West Germany (Göschel 1992, pp. 64–70). After the German reunification similar surveys were conducted in former East Germany.

The data were transcribed by four transcribers, and each item was transcribed independently by at least two phoneticians who subsequently consulted to come to an agreement. In 2002 the data was digitized at the University of Groningen.

## 4 Validation Methods

When we apply a measurement technique to a specific problem we are interested both in the consistency of the measure and in its validity. The consistency of the measurement reflects the degree to which the independent elements in the sample sample tend to provide the same signal. Nunnally (1978, p.211) recommends the generalized

[3] We have no proof that normalization by alignment length always allows this simple relation to similarity, but we have examined a large number of calculations in which this always seems to hold.

[4] The database is available at `http://www.ling.hf.ntnu.no/nos/`.

form of the Spearman-Brown formula for this purpose, which has come to be known as the CRONBACH'S $\alpha$ value. It is determined by the inter-item correlation, i.e. the average correlation coefficient for all of the pairs of items in the test, and the test size. The Cronbach's $\alpha$ measure rises with the sample size, and it is therefore normally used to determine whether samples are large enough to provide reliable signals.

The validity of a measure, or more precisely, the application of a measure to a particular problem is much more difficult and controversial issue (Nunnally, 1978, Chap. 3), but the basic issue is whether the procedures in fact measure what they purport to measure, in our case the sort of pronunciation similarity which is important in distinguishing similar language varieties. In examining our measures for their validity in identifying the sort of pronunciation similarity which plays a role in dialectology we compare the measures to other indications we have that pronunciations are dialectally similar. We discuss these below in more detail. We consider the correlation with distances as perceived by the dialect speakers themselves (see Section 4.1) and the local (geographic) incoherence of dialect distances (see Section 4.2).

### 4.1 Perception

The best opportunity for examining the quality of the measurements presents itself in the case of Norwegian, for which we were able to obtain the results of a perception experiment (Gooskens and Heeringa, 2004). For each of 15 varieties a recording of the fable 'The North Wind and the Sun' was presented to 15 groups of Norwegian high school pupils, one group from each of the 15 dialects sites represented in the material. All pupils were familiar with their own dialect and had lived most of their lives in the place in question (on average 16.7 years). Each group consisted of 16 to 27 listeners. The mean age of the listeners was 17.8 years, 52 percent were female and 48 percent male.

The 15 dialects were presented in a randomized order, and each session was preceded by a (short) practice run. While listening to the dialects the listeners were asked to judge each of the 15 dialects on a scale from 1 (similar to native dialect) to 10 (not similar to native dialect). This means that each group of listeners judged the linguistic distances between their own dialect and the 15 dialects, including their own dialect. In this way we get a matrix with $15 \times 15$ perceived linguistic distances. This matrix is not completely symmetric. For example, the distance which the listeners from Bergen perceived between their own dialect and the dialect of Trondheim (8.55) is different from the distance as perceived by the listeners from Trondheim to Bergen (7.84).

In order to use this material to calibrate the different computational measurements, we examine the correlations between the $15 \times 15$ computational matrices with the $15 \times 15$ perceptual matrix. In calculating correlations we excluded the distances of dialects with respect to themselves, i.e. the distance of Bergen to Bergen, of Bjugn to Bjugn, etc. In computational matrices these values are always zero, in the perceptual matrix they vary, but are normally greater than zero. This may be due to non-geographic (social or individual) variation, but it distorts results in a non-random way (diagonal distances can only be too high, never too low), we exclude them when calculating the correlation coefficient.

We calculated the standard Pearson product-moment correlation coefficient, but we interpret its significance cautiously, using the Mantel test (Bonnet and Van de Peer, 2002). In classical tests the assumption is made that the observations are independent, which observations in distance matrices emphatically are not. This is certainly true for calculations of geographic distances, which are minimally constrained to satisfy the standard distance axioms (non-negativity, symmetry, and the triangle inequality). We have argued above (§ 2.2) that the edit distances we employ are likewise genuine distances, which means that sums of edit distances are likewise constrained, and therefore should not be regarded as independent observations (in the sense need for hypothesis testing).

The Mantel test raises the standards of significance a good deal— so much that it will turn out that our small ($15 \times 15$) matrices would need to differ by more than 0.1 in correlation coefficient in order to demonstrate significance. We will nonetheless urge that the results should be taken seriously as the data needed is difficult to obtain, and the indications are fairly clear (see below).

### 4.2 Local Incoherence

It is fundamental to dialectology that geographically closer varieties are, in general, linguistically more similar. Nerbonne and Kleiweg (2006) use this fact to select more probative measurements, namely those measurements which maximize the degree to which geographically close elements are likewise seen to be linguistically similar. Given our emphasis on distance it is slightly more convenient to formulate a measure of LOCAL INCOHERENCE and then to examine the degree to which various string distance measures minimize it. The basic idea is that we begin with each measurement site $s$, and inspect the $n$ linguistically most similar sites in order of decreasing linguistic similarity to $s$. We then measure how far away these linguistically most similar sites are geographically, for example, in kilometers. *Good* measurements show that linguistically similar sites are geographically close better than *poor* measurements do.

The details of the formulation reflect the results of dialectometry that dialect distances certainly increase with geographic distance, leveling off, however, so that geographically more remote variety-pairs tend to have more nearly the same linguistic distances to each other. We sort variety pairs in order of decreasing linguistic similarity and weight more similar ones exponentially more than less similar ones. Given this disproportionate weighting of the most similar varieties, it also quickly becomes uninteresting to incorporate the effects of more than a small number of geographically closest varieties. We restrict our attention to the eight most similar linguistic varieties in calculating local incoherence.

$$
\begin{aligned}
\mathrm{I}_l &= \frac{1}{n}\sum_{i=1}^{n}\frac{D_i^L - D_i^G}{D_i^G} \\
D_i^L &= \sum_{j=1}^{k} d_{i,j}^L \cdot 2^{-0.5j} \\
D_i^G &= \sum_{j=1}^{k} d_{i,j}^G \cdot 2^{-0.5j}
\end{aligned}
$$

$d_{i,j}^L, d_{i,j}^G$ : geo. dist. between $i$ en $j$

$d_{i,1\cdots n-1}^L$ : geo. dist. sorted by increasing ling. diff.

$d_{i,1\cdots n-1}^G$ : geo. dist, sorted by increasing geo. dist.

Several remarks may be helpful in understanding the proposed measurement. First, all of the $d_{i,j}$ concern *geographic* distances. $d_{i,1\cdots n-1}^L$ (summed in $D_i^L$) range over the geographic distances, arranged, however, in increasing order of *linguistic* distance, while $d_{i,1\cdots n-1}^G$ (summed in $D_i^G$) ranges over the geographic distances among the sites in the sample, arranged in increasing order of *geographic* distance. We examine the latter as an ideal case. If a given measurement technique always demonstrated that the neighbors of a given site used the most similar varieties, then $D_i^L$ would be the same $D_i^G$, and $I_l$ would be 0. Second, we have argued above that it is appropriate to count most similar varieties much more heavily in $I_l$, and this is reflected in the exponential decay in the weighting, i.e., $2^{-0.5j}$ where $j$ ranges over the increasingly less similar sites. Given this weighting of most similar varieties, we are also justified in restricting the sum in $D_i^L = \sum_{j=1}^{k}[\ldots]$ to $k = 8$, and all of the results below use this limitation, which likewise improves efficiency.

We suppress further discussion of the calculation in the interest of saving space here, noting, however, that we used two different notions of geographic distance. When examining measurements of the German data, we measured geographic distance "as the crow flies", but since Norway is very mountainous, we used (19th century) travel distances (Gooskens, ).

## 5 Experiments and Results

In this section we present results based on the Norwegian and German data sources in 5.1 and Sections 5.3.

For each data source we consider 40 string comparison algorithms. We distinguish between methods with a binary comparison of $n$-grams and those with a gradual comparison of $n$-grams (see Section 2.4). Within the category of binary methods, we distinguish between three groups. In the first group, strings are compared just by counting the number of common $n$-grams, ignoring the order of elements, see Section 2.1). In the second group the $n$-grams are aligned (see Section 2.2). We call this 'free alignment'. In the third group we insist on the linguistically informed alignment of $n$-grams (see Section 2.5), dubbing this 'forced alignment'. Within the category of gradual methods, we distinguish between 'free alignment' (see Section 2.6) and 'forced alignment'. Finally, for each of these methods, we consider both an unnormalized version of the measure as well as one normalized by length (see Section 2.3).

A measure can only be valid when it is consistent, but it may be consistent without being valid. Since consistency is a necessary condi-

| | binary | | | gradual | |
|---|---|---|---|---|---|
| | no alignment | free alignment | forc. alignment | free alignment | forc. alignment |
| uni | 0.69 | 0.66 | 0.66 | 0.66 | 0.66 |
| bi | 0.70 | 0.69 | 0.69 | 0.66 | 0.68 |
| tri | 0.71 | 0.70 | 0.72 | 0.66 | 0.73 |
| xbi | 0.70 | 0.69 | 0.72 | 0.67 | 0.73 |

Table 1: Correlations between perceptual distances and *unnormalized* string edit distance measurements among 15 Norwegian dialects. Higher coefficients indicate better results.

| | binary | | | gradual | |
|---|---|---|---|---|---|
| | no alignment | free alignment | forc. alignment | free alignment | forc. alignment |
| uni | 0.66 | 0.66 | 0.66 | 0.66 | 0.66 |
| bi | 0.67 | 0.67 | 0.67 | 0.66 | 0.66 |
| tri | 0.68 | 0.68 | 0.70 | 0.66 | 0.70 |
| xbi | 0.68 | 0.68 | 0.70 | 0.69 | 0.70 |

Table 2: Correlations between perceptual distances and different *normalized* string edit distance measurements among 15 Norwegian dialects. Higher coefficients indicate better results.

tion for validity, we check the consistency of phonetic distance methods. For each of the methods we calculated Cronbach's $\alpha$ values, which is based on the average inter-correlation among the words (Heeringa, 2004, pp. 170–173). A widely-accepted threshold in social science for an acceptable $\alpha$ is 0.70 (Nunnally, 1978). After the consistency check, we discuss validation results.

### 5.1 Norwegian Perception

In this section we first discuss results of unnormalized string edit distance measures, and will compare them with their normalized counterparts farther onwards in this section.

The Cronbach's $\alpha$ values of the unnormalized measurements vary from 0.84 to 0.87. The Cronbach's $\alpha$ values of the methods with 'forced alignment' are a bit lower than the $\alpha$ values of the other methods. An outlier arises when using the 'forced alignment' and gradual bigram distances: $\alpha$=0.78, but these all indicate that the measurements are quite consistent.

We calculated correlations to the perceptual distances which are described in Section 4.1. Results are given in Table 1. Let's note that the effect size, i.e., the $r$ value itself, is quite high, $0.66 < r < 0.73$, meaning that the various distance measure are accounting for 43.6–53.3% of the variance in the perception measurements. All of the correlation coefficients are massively significant ($p < 0.001$), but given the stringency of the Mantel test, they do not differ significantly from one another.

The correlations are quite similar. The maximal difference we found was 0.07, so that we conclude that none of the methods is strikingly better or worse in operationalizing the level of pronunciation difference that dialect speakers are sensitive to.

The small flood of numbers in Table 1 may seem confusing. Therefore we calculated averages per factor which are presented in Table 4. We invite the reader to refer to both Table 1 and Tablee 4 in following the discussion below. Table 4 shows systematic differences. For example, contextually sensitive measures (bigrams, trigrams, and xbigrams) are usually better (and never worse) than unigram measures. The differences among the different means of operationalizing context (bigrams, trigrams and xbigrams) seem unremarkable, however. Third, measures which are sensitive to linear order are slightly worse than those which are not (variants of DICE) on average[5]. But when comparing the first column in Table 1 with the others, we see that the highest correlations (0.73) are found among the order sensitive methods. Fourth, forcing alignment to respect vowel/consonant differences yields a modest improvement in scores. Fifth, we see no clear advantage in measurements which weight $n$-grams more sensitively to those binary comparison methods which distinguish only same and different.

Sixth, and most surprisingly, we can compare Table 1 which provides the correlation of edit distances which were *not* normalized for length, with Table 2, which provides the results of the measurements which *were* normalized. For some normalized measurements the Cronbach's $\alpha$ value are minimally higher (0.01). But comparison of the correlation coefficients shows that normalization never improves measurements, and often leads to a deterioration. In Table 4 averages for the normalized measurements are given. Normalized mea-

[5]When using the unnormalized versions of the 'DICE' family, the distance is just equal to the number of non-shared $n$-grams.

| | binary | | | gradual | |
|---|---|---|---|---|---|
| | no alignment | free alignment | forc. alignment | free alignment | forc. alignment |
| uni | 0.41 | 0.37 | 0.37 | 0.37 | 0.37 |
| bi | 0.37 | 0.35 | 0.37 | 0.36 | 0.35 |
| tri | 0.37 | 0.33 | 0.35 | 0.36 | 0.35 |
| xbi | 0.36 | 0.35 | 0.35 | 0.37 | 0.35 |

Table 3: Local incoherence values based on travel distances for the *unnormalized* string edit distance measurements between 15 Norwegian dialects. The lower the local incoherence value, the better the measurement technique.

surements display the same systematic differences that unnormalized measurements show, except for the differences between methods which consider the order of segments and methods which do not. Measures which are sensitive to linear order are slightly better than those which are not (variants of DICE).

### 5.2 Norwegian Geographic Sensitivity

As we mentioned in Section 4.2, Norway is very rugged. Therefore we based our local incoherence values on travel distances rather than on geographic distances "as the crow flies". We computed local incoherence values for both unnormalized and normalized string edit distance measurements. The comparison confirms the findings of Section 5.1: unnormalized methods always perform better than normalized ones. The unnormalized results are presented in Table 3.

Recall that lower local incoherence values should reflect better measurement techniques. When we examine the table as a whole, we note again that the various techniques are not hugely different—they perform with similar degrees of success.

In Table 4, we find average local incoherence values for the factors under investigation. We find first that contextually sensitive measures (bigrams, trigrams, and xbigrams) are again superior to unigram methods, and second, measures which are sensitive to linear order are superior to the DICE-like methods (unnormalized versions). Third, linguistically informed alignments, which respect the vowel/consonant distinction, perform better than uninformed ("free") alignment (for the normalized versions). Fourth, the average values do not suggest any benefit to the gradual weighting of $n$-grams in comparison with the binary weighting. Most surprisingly, normalization again appears to have a deleterious effect on the probity of the measurements.

We must stress again that these finer interpretations results require confirmation with a larger set of sites.

### 5.3 German Geographic Sensitivity

When checking the consistency of the German measurements we find Cronbach's $\alpha$ values of 0.95 and 0.96 for all methods without alignment or with 'free alignment' and for all unigram based methods. The higher Cronbach's $\alpha$ levels for this data set reflect the fact that it is larger. We find lower $\alpha$ values of 0.83–0.85 for the methods with 'forced alignment'. This accords with the consistency results for the Norwegian measurements.

When using bigrams, $\alpha$ is equal to $0.80$ (binary, normalized), $0.51$ (gradual, normalized), $0.74$ (binary, unnormalized) and $0.45$ (gradual, unnormalized). These low values are striking, and we found no explanation for them, but they suggest that we should not attach much significance to this combination of measurement properties. On average, the unnormalized $\alpha$'s are the same as the normalized $\alpha$'s.

Since consistency values are higher than $0.70$ (with one exception), we validated the methods by calculating the geographic local incoherence values. We would have preferred to use perceptions, but we have no such data in the German case.

Since we found unnormalized string edit distance measurements superior to normalized ones in the Sections 5.1 and 5.2, we focus in this section on the unnormalized methods. Unnormalized results are shown in Table 5.

Recall that the lower the local incoherence value, the better the measurement technique. We include this table for the sake of completeness, but it is clear that the results do not jibe with the results obtained from the Norwegian data. Unigram-based processing appears to be superior, and context inferior; order-sensitive processing is inferior to order-insensitive processing, and linguistically informed ("forced") alignment appears to offer no advantage.

We leave the contrast between the Norwegian and German results as a puzzle to be addressed in future work, but it should be clear that we have

| Factor | Correlation with perception | | Local incoherence | | Number of measurements |
|---|---|---|---|---|---|
| | raw | normalized | raw | normalized | |
| no order | 0.70 | 0.67 | 0.38 | 0.45 | 4 |
| order | 0.69 | 0.68 | 0.36 | 0.46 | 16 |
| unnormalized | 0.69 | | 0.36 | | 20 |
| normalized | | 0.68 | | 0.43 | 20 |
| binary | 0.69 | 0.68 | 0.36 | 0.43 | 8 |
| gradual | 0.68 | 0.67 | 0.36 | 0.43 | 8 |
| free | 0.67 | 0.67 | 0.36 | 0.43 | 8 |
| forced | 0.70 | 0.68 | 0.36 | 0.42 | 8 |
| unigram | 0.67 | 0.66 | 0.38 | 0.45 | 5 |
| bigram | 0.68 | 0.67 | 0.36 | 0.45 | 5 |
| trigram | 0.70 | 0.68 | 0.35 | 0.42 | 5 |
| xbigram | 0.70 | 0.69 | 0.36 | 0.41 | 5 |

Table 4: Average correlations between perceptual distances and *raw,* i.e., *unnormalized* string edit distance measurements among 15 Norwegian dialects. Higher coefficients and lower local incoherence values indicate better results.

| | binary | | | gradual | |
|---|---|---|---|---|---|
| | no alignment | free alignment | forc. alignment | free alignment | forc. alignment |
| uni | 0.94 | 0.88 | 0.87 | 0.88 | 0.87 |
| bi | 1.00 | 0.98 | 2.09 | 0.92 | 5.71 |
| tri | 1.09 | 1.05 | 2.45 | 0.93 | 2.09 |
| xbi | 0.96 | 0.95 | 2.45 | 0.98 | 2.45 |

Table 5: Local incoherence values based on geographic distances for for the *unnormalized* string edit distance measurements 186 German dialects. The lower the local incoherence value, the better the measurement technique.

rather more confidence in the Norwegian than in the German results. This is due on the one had to the availability of independently behavioral data we can use to independently validate our computations, but also to the more stable set of values we see in the case of the Norwegian data. Exactly *why* the German data is so much more variable is also a question we must postpone to future work.

## 6 Conclusions and Prospects

In this paper we examined a range of string comparison algorithms by applying them to Norwegian and German dialect comparison. The Norwegian results suggest that sensitivity to linguistic context in the form of $n$-grams, and to linguistic structure in alignment improves measurement techniques, but they do not confirm the value of differential weighting for $n$-grams. The results mostly suggest that sensitivity to order of segments improves the measurements.

The larger German data likewise is unfortunately more recalcitrant (as are other data sets we have examined, but in which we have less confidence). A disadvantage of the German data may be that several transcribers were involved, working over a period of twenty years, and that two types of surveys were used, having different orders of sentences. There may be subtle differences in pronunciation as a result of subjects' becoming more relaxed or more impatient in the course of a survey interview.

On the other hand, the Norwegian data set is small (15 dialect sites). Our conclusions rely on assumptions of its quality and transcriber consistency, but this warrants further examination. We also cannot exclude the possibility that optimal measurements depend on features of the language and/or data set.

It is tempting to wish to redo this study using a large, antiseptically clean data set, transcribed reliably by a minimal number of phoneticians, but the more important practical direction may be to try to understand which properties of data sets are important in selecting variants of pronunciation distance measures. Atlases of material on language varieties simply are not always clean and reliable, and if we wish to contribute to their analysis, we must keep this in mind.

## Acknowledgments

We are grateful to Therese Leinonen, Jens Moberg and Jelena Prokič for comments on this work, and in particular for their suggestion that one should also examine the length normalization. We also thank the workshop reviewers, in particularly one who was productively harsh about the treatment of normalization in an earlier version, and also pointed out literature we had insufficiently taken note of. Finally, we are indebted to the Netherlands Organization for Scientific Research, NWO, for support (project "Determinants of Dialect Variation, 360-70-120, P.I. J. Nerbonne)

## References

Eric Bonnet and Yves Van de Peer. 2002. zt: A software tool for simple and partial Mantel tests. *Journal of Statistical Software*, 7(10):1–12. Available via: `http://www.jstatsoft.org/`.

Hans Goebl. 1982. *Dialektometrie: Prinzipien und Methoden des Einsatzes der Numerischen Taxonomie im Bereich der Dialektgeographie*. Österreichische Akademie der Wissenschaften, Wien.

Hans Goebl. 1984. *Dialektometrische Studien: Anhand italoromanischer, rätoromanischer und galloromanischer Sprachmaterialien aus AIS und ALF. 3 Vol.* Max Niemeyer, Tübingen.

Charlotte Gooskens. Traveling time as a predictor of linguistic distance. *Dialectologia et Geolinguistica*. submitted, 3/2004.

Charlotte Gooskens and Wilbert Heeringa. 2004. Perceptual evaluation of Levenshtein dialect distance measurements using Norwegian dialect data. *Language Variation and Change*, 16(3):189–207.

Joachim Göschel. 1992. Das Forschungsinstitut für Deutsche Sprache "Deutscher Sprachatlas. Wissenschaftlicher Bericht, Das Forschungsinstitut für Deutsche Sprache, Marburg.

Wilbert Heeringa. 2004. *Measuring Dialect Pronunciation Differences using Levenshtein Distance*. Ph.D. thesis, Rijksuniversiteit Groningen.

Cor Hoppenbrouwers and Geer Hoppenbrouwers. 2001. *De indeling van de Nederlandse streektalen: Dialecten van 156 steden en dorpen geklasseerd volgens de FFM (feature frequentie methode)*. Koninklijke Van Gorcum, Assen.

Diana Inkpen, O. Frunza, and Grzegorz Kondrak. 2005. Automatic Identification of Cognates and False Friends in French and English. In Galia Angelova, Kalina Bontcheva, Ruslan Mitkov, Nicolas Nicolov, and Nicolai Nicolov, editors, *International Conference Recent Advances in Natural Language Processing*, pages 251–257, Borovets.

Brett Kessler. 1995. Computational dialectology in Irish Gaelic. In *Proc. of the European ACL*, pages 60–67, Dublin.

Brett Kessler. 2005. Phonetic comparision algorithms. *Transactions of the Philological Society*, 103(2):243–260.

Grzegorz Kondrak. 2005. N-gram similarity and distance. In *Proceedings of the Twelfth International Conference on String Processing and Information Retrieval (SPIRE 2005)*, pages 115–126, Buenos Aires, Argentina.

Joseph Kruskal. 1999. An overview of sequence comparison. In David Sankoff and Joseph Kruskal, editors, *Time Warps, String Edits and Macromolecules: The Theory and Practice of Sequence Comparison*, pages 1–44. CSLI, Stanford. [1]1983.

Andrés Marzal and Enrique Vidal. 1993. Computation of normalized edit distance and applications. *IEEE Transactions on Pattern Analysis and Machine Intelligence*, 15(9):926–932.

John Nerbonne and Peter Kleiweg. 2003. Lexical variation in LAMSAS. *Computers and the Humanities*, 37(3):339–357. Special Iss. on Computational Methods in Dialectometry ed. by John Nerbonne and William Kretzschmar, Jr.

John Nerbonne and Peter Kleiweg. 2006. Toward a dialectological yardstick. *Quantitative Linguistics*, 13. accepted.

Jum C. Nunnally. 1978. *Psychometric Theory*. McGraw-Hill, New York.

Jean Séguy. 1973. La dialectometrie dans l'atlas linguistique de gascogne. *Revue de Linguistique Romane*, 37:1–24.

# Study of Some Distance Measures for Language and Encoding Identification

**Anil Kumar Singh**
Language Technologies Research Centre
International Institute of Information Technology
Hyderabad, India
anil@research.iiit.net

## Abstract

To determine how close two language models (e.g., $n$-grams models) are, we can use several distance measures. If we can represent the models as distributions, then the similarity is basically the similarity of distributions. And a number of measures are based on information theoretic approach. In this paper we present some experiments on using such similarity measures for an old Natural Language Processing (NLP) problem. One of the measures considered is perhaps a novel one, which we have called *mutual cross entropy*. Other measures are either well known or based on well known measures, but the results obtained with them *vis-a-vis* one-another might help in gaining an insight into how similarity measures work in practice.

The first step in processing a text is to identify the language and encoding of its contents. This is a practical problem since for many languages, there are no universally followed text encoding standards. The method we have used in this paper for language and encoding identification uses pruned character $n$-grams, alone as well augmented with word $n$-grams. This method seems to give results comparable to other methods.

## 1 Introduction

Many kinds of models in NLP can be seen as distributions of a variable. For various NLP problems, we need to calculate the similarity of such models or distributions. One common example of this is the $n$-grams model. We might have several reference data sets and then we may want to find out which of those matches most closely with a test data set. The problem of language and encoding identification can be represented in these terms. One of the most important questions then is which similarity measure to use. We can expect that the performance obtained with the similarity measure will vary with the specific problem and the kind of model used or some other problem specific details. Still, it will be useful to explore how these measures relate to each other.

The measures we are going to focus on in this paper are all very simple ones and they all try to find the similarity of two models or distributions in a (more or less) information theoretic way, except the *out of rank* measure proposed by Cavnar and Trenkle (Cavnar and Trenkle, 1994).

This work had started simply as an effort to build a language and encoding identification tool specifically for South Asian languages. During the course of this work, we experimented with various similarity measures and some of the results we obtained were at least a bit surprising. One of the measures we used was something we have called *mutual cross entropy* and its performance for the current problem was better than other measures.

Before the content of a Web page or of any kind of text can be processed for computation, its language and encoding has to be known. In many cases this language-encoding is not known beforehand and has to be determined automatically. For languages like Hindi, there is no standard encoding followed by everyone. There are many well known web sites using their own proprietary encoding. This is one of the biggest problems in actually using the Web as a multilingual corpus and for enabling a crawler to search the text in lan-



*Proceedings of the Workshop on Linguistic Distances*, pages 63–72,
Sydney, July 2006. 

guages like Hindi. This means that the content in these languages, limited as it is, is invisible not just to people (which could be just due to lack of display support or unavailability of fonts for a particular encoding) but even to crawlers.

The problem of language identification is similar to some other problems in different fields and the techniques used for one such problem have been found to be effective for other problems too. Some of these problems are text categorization (Cavnar and Trenkle, 1994), cryptanalysis (Beesley, 1988) and even species identification (Dunning, 1994) from genetic sequences. This means that if something works for one of these problems, it is likely to work for these other problems.

It should be noted here that the identification problem here is that of identifying both language and encoding. This is because (especially for South Asian languages) the same encoding can be used for more than one languages (ISCII for all Indian languages which use Brahmi-origin scripts) and one language can have many encodings (ISCII, Unicode, ISFOC, typewriter, phonetic, and many other proprietary encodings for Hindi).

In this paper we describe a method based mainly on character *n*-grams for identifying the language-encoding pair of a text. The method requires some training text for each language-encoding, but this text need not have the same content. A few pages (2500-10000 words) of text in a particular language-encoding is enough. A pruned character based *n*-grams model is created for each language-encoding. A similar model is created for the test data too and is compared to the training models. The best match is found using a similarity measure. A few (5-15) words of test data seems to be enough for identification in most cases.

The method has been evaluated using various similarity measures and for different test sizes. We also consider two cases, one in which the pruned character *n*-grams model is used alone, and the other in which it is augmented with a word *n*-gram model.

## 2 Previous Work

Language identification was one of the first natural language processing (NLP) problems for which a statistical approach was used.

Ingle (Ingle, 1976) used a list of short words in various languages and matched the words in the test data with this list. Such methods based on lists of words or letters (unique strings) were meant for human translators and couldn't be used directly for automatic language identification. They ignored the text encoding, since they assumed printed text. Even if adapted for automatic identification, they were not very effective or scalable.

However, the earliest approaches used for automatic language identification were based on the above idea and could be called 'translator approaches'. Newman (Newman, 1987), among others, used lists of letters, especially accented letters for various languages and identification was done by matching the letters in the test data to these lists.

Beesley's (Beesley, 1988) automatic language identifier for online texts was based on mathematical language models developed for breaking ciphers. These models basically had characteristic letter sequences and frequencies ('orthographical features') for each language, making them similar to *n*-grams models. The insights on which they are based, as Beesley points out, have been known at least since the time of Ibn ad-Duraihim who lived in the 14th century. Beesley's method needed 6-64 K of training data and 10-12 words of test data. It treats language and encoding pair as one entity.

Adams and Resnik (Adams and Resnik, 1997) describe a client-server system using Dunning's *n*-grams based algorithm (Dunning, 1994) for a variety of tradeoffs available to NLP applications like between the labelling accuracy and the size and completeness of language models. Their system dynamically adds language models. The system uses other tools to identify the text encoding. They use 5-grams with add-*k* smoothing. Training size was 1-50 K and test size above 50 characters. Some pruning is done, like for frequencies up to 3.

Some methods for language identification use techniques similar to *n*-gram based text categorization (Cavnar and Trenkle, 1994) which calculates and compares profiles of *n*-gram frequencies. This is the approach nearest to ours. Such methods differ in the way they calculate the likelihood that the test data matches with one of the profiles. Beesley's method simply uses word-wise probabilities of 'digram' sequences by multiplying the probabilities of sequences in the test string. Others use some distance measure between training and test profiles to find the best match.

Cavnar also mentions that top 300 or so $n$-grams are almost always highly correlated with the language, while the lower ranked $n$-grams give more specific indication about the text, namely the topic. The distance measure used by Cavnar is called 'out-of-rank' measure and it sums up the differences in rankings of the $n$-grams found in the test data as compared to the training data. This is among the measures we have tested.

The language model used by Combrinck and Botha (Combrinck and Botha, 1994) is also based on bigram or trigram frequencies (they call them 'transition vectors'). They select the most distinctive transition vectors by using as measure the ratio of the maximum percentage of occurrences to the total percentage of occurrences of a transition vector. These distinctive vectors then form the model.

Dunning (Dunning, 1994) also used an $n$-grams based method where the model selected is the one which is most likely to have generated the test string. Giguet (Giguet, 1995b; Giguet, 1995a) relied upon grammatically correct words instead of the most common words. He also used the knowledge about the alphabet and the word morphology via *syllabation*. Giguet tried this method for tagging sentences in a document with the language name, i.e., dealing with multilingual documents.

Another method (Stephen, 1993) was based on 'common words' which are characteristic of each language. This methods assumes unique words for each language. One major problem with this method was that the test string might not contain any unique words.

Cavnar's method, combined with some heuristics, was used by Kikui (Kikui, 1996) to identify languages as well as encodings for a multilingual text. He relied on known mappings between languages and encodings and treated East Asian languages differently from West European languages.

Kranig (Muthusamy et al., 1994) and (Simon, 2005) have reviewed and evaluated some of the well known language identification methods. Martins and Silva (Martins and Silva, 2005) describe a method similar to Cavnar's but which uses a different similarity measure proposed by Jiang and Conrath (Jiang and Conrath, 1997). Some heuristics are also employed.

Poutsma's (Poutsma, 2001) method is based on Monte Carlo sampling of $n$-grams from the beginning of the document instead of building a complete model of the whole document. Sibun and Reynar (Sibun and Reynar, 1996) use mutual information statistics or relative entropy, also called Kullback-Leibler distance for language identification. Souter et al.(Souter et al., 1994) compared unique character string, common word and 'trigraph' based approaches and found the last to be the best.

Compression based approaches have also been used for language identification. One example of such an approach is called Prediction by Partial Matching (PPM) proposed by Teahan (Teahan and Harper, 2001). This approach uses cross entropy of the test data with a language model and predicts a character given the context.

## 3 Pruned Character $N$-grams

Like in Cavnar's method, we used pruned $n$-grams models of the reference or training as well as test data. For each language-encoding pair, some training data is provided. A character based $n$-gram model is prepared from this data. $N$-grams of all orders are combined and ranked according to frequency. A certain number of them (say 1000) with highest frequencies are retained and the rest are dropped. This gives us the pruned character $n$-grams model, which is used for language-encoding identification.

As an attempt to increase the performance, we also tried to augment the pruned character $n$-grams model with a word $n$-gram model.

## 4 Distance Measures

Some of the measures we have experimented with have already been mentioned in the section on previous work. The measures considered in this work range from something as simple as log probability difference to the one based on Jiang and Conrath (Jiang and Conrath, 1997) measure.

Assuming that we have two models or distributions $P$ and $Q$ over a variable $X$, the measures (*sim*) are defined as below ($p$ and $q$ being probabilities and $r$ and $s$ being ranks in models $P$ and $Q$:

1. Log probability difference:

$$sim = \sum_{x} (log\, p(x) - log\, q(x)) \tag{1}$$

2. Absolute log probability difference:

$$sim = \sum_{x} (abs(log\, p(x)) - abs(log\, q(x))) \tag{2}$$

3. Cross entropy:

$$sim = \sum_x (p(x) * log\, q(x)) \quad (3)$$

4. RE measure (based on relative entropy or Kullback-Leibler distance – see note below):

$$sim = \sum_x p(x) \frac{log\, p(x)}{log\, q(x)} \quad (4)$$

5. JC measure (based on Jiang and Conrath's measure) (Jiang and Conrath, 1997):

$$sim = A - B \quad (5)$$

where,

$$A = 2 * \sum_x (log\, p(x) + log\, q(x)) \quad (6)$$

and,

$$B = \sum_x log\, p(x) + \sum_x log\, q(x) \quad (7)$$

6. Out of rank measure (Cavnar and Trenkle, 1994):

$$sim = \sum_x abs(r(x) - s(x)) \quad (8)$$

7. MRE measure (based on mutual or symmetric relative entropy, the original definition of KL-distance given by Kullback and Leibler):

$$sim = \sum_x p(x) \frac{log\, p(x)}{log\, q(x)} + \sum_x q(x) \frac{log\, q(x)}{log\, p(x)} \quad (9)$$

8. Mutual (or symmetric) cross entropy:

$$sim = \sum_x (p(x) * log\, q(x) + q(x) * log\, p(x)) \quad (10)$$

As can be noticed, all these measures, in a way, seem to be information theoretic in nature. However, our focus in this work is more on the presenting empirical evidence rather than discussing mathematical foundation of these measures. The latter will of course be interesting to look into.

NOTE:

We had initiallly experimented with relative entropy or KL-distance as defined below (instead of the RE measure mentioned above):

$$sim = \sum_x p(x)\, log \frac{p(x)}{q(x)} \quad (11)$$

Another measure we tried was DL measure (based on Dekang Lin's measure, on which the JC measure is based):

$$sim = \frac{A}{B} \quad (12)$$

where $A$ and $B$ are as given above.

The results for the latter measure were not very good (below 50% in all cases) and the RE measure defined above performed better than relative entropy. These results have not been reported in this paper.

## 5 Mutual Cross Entropy

Cross entropy is a well known distance measure used for various problems. *Mutual cross entropy* can be seen as bidirectional or symmetric cross entropy. It is defined simply as the sum of the cross entropies of two distributions with each other.

Our motivation for using 'mutual' cross entropy was that many similarity measures like cross entropy and relative entropy measure how similar one distribution is to the other. This will not necessary mean the same thing as measuring how similar two distributions are to each other. Mutual information measures this bidirectional similarity, but it needs joint probabilities, which means that it can only be applied to measure similarity of terms within one distribution. Relative entropy or Kullback-Leibler measure is applicable, but as the results show, it doesn't work as well as expected.

Note that some authors treat relative entropy and mutual information interchangeably. They are very similar in nature except that one is applicable for one variable in two distributions and the other for two variables in one distribution.

Our guess was that symmetric measures may give better results as both the models give some information about each other. This seems to be supported by the results for cross entropy, but (asymmetric) cross entropy and RE measures also gave good results.

## 6 The Algorithm

The foundation of the algorithm for identifying the language and encoding of a text or string has already been explained earlier. Here we give a summary of the algorithm we have used. The parameters for the algorithm and their values used in our experiments reported here have also been listed. These parameters allow the algorithm to be tuned

Table 1: DESCRIPTION OF DATA SETS

| | Names | Total Count |
|---|---|---|
| **Languages** | Afrikaans (1), Assamese (1), Bengali (2), Bulgarian (1), Catalan (1)<br>Czech (1), Danish (1), Dutch (1), English (1), Esperanto (1)<br>Finnish (1), French (1), German (1), Gujarati (2), Hindi (8)<br>Icelandic (1), Iloko (1), Iroquoian (1), Italian (1), Kannada (1)<br>Khasi (1), Latin (1), Malayalam (1), Marathi (5), Modern Greek (1)<br>Nahuatl (1), Norwegian (1), Oriya (2), Polish (1), Portugues (1)<br>Punjabi (1), Romanian (1), Russian (1), Serbian (1), Spanish (1)<br>Tagalog (1), Tamil (1), Telugu (1), Welsh (1) | 39 |
| **Encodings** | UTF8 (7), ISO-8859-1 (16), ISO-8859-2 (1), US-ASCII (4)<br>Windows-1251 (2), Windows-1250 (1), ISCII (10), ISFOCB (1)<br>ITrans (1), Shusha (1), Typewriter (1), WX (1), Gopika (1)<br>Govinda (1), Manjusha (1), Saamanaa (1), Subak (1)<br>Akruti Sarala (1), Webdunia (1) | 19 |

Counts in parenthesis represent the extra ambiguity for that language or encoding.
For example, Hindi (8) means that 8 different encodings were tested for Hindi.

**Language-Encoding Pairs:** 53

**Minimum training data size:** 16035 characters (2495 words)

**Maximum training data size:** 650292 characters (102377 words)

**Average training data size:** 166198 characters (22643 words)

**Confusable Languages:** Assamese/Bengali/Oriya, Dutch/Afrikaans, Norwegian/Danish, Spanish/Tagalog, Hindi/Marathi, Telugu/Kannada/Malayalam, Latin/Franch

Table 2: NUMBER OF TEST SETS

| Size | Number |
|---|---|
| 100 | 22083 |
| 200 | 10819 |
| 500 | 4091 |
| 1000 | 1867 |
| 2000 | 1524 |
| All test data | 840 |

or customized for best performance. Perhaps they can even be learned by using some approach as the EM algorithm.

1. Train the system by preparing character based and word based (optional) $n$-grams from the training data.

2. Combine $n$-grams of all orders ($O_c$ for characters and $O_w$ for words).

3. Sort them by rank.

4. Prune by selecting only the top $N_c$ character $n$-grams and $N_w$ word $n$-grams for each language-encoding pair.

5. For the given test data or string, calculate the character $n$-gram based score $sim_c$ with every model for which the system has been trained.

6. Select the $t$ most likely language-encoding pairs (training models) based on this character based $n$-gram score.

7. For each of the $t$ best training models, calculate the score with the test model. The score is calculated as:

$$score = sim_c + a * sim_w \quad (13)$$

where $c$ and $w$ represent character based and word based $n$-grams, respectively. And $a$ is the weight given to the word based $n$-grams. In our experiment, this weight was 1 for the case when word $n$-grams were considered and 0 when they were not.

8. Select the most likely language-encoding pair out of the $t$ ambiguous pairs, based on the combined score obtained from word and character based models.

Table 3: PRECISION FOR VARIOUS MEASURES AND TEST SIZES

| Test Size (characters) | | Precision LPD | ALPD | CE | RE | CT | JC | MRE | MCE |
|---|---|---|---|---|---|---|---|---|---|
| 100 | CN | 91.00 | 90.69 | 96.13 | 98.51 | 78.92 | 97.71 | 98.26 | 97.64 |
| | CWN | 94.31 | 94.15 | 97.50 | 75.54 | 81.63 | 98.35 | 94.16 | 98.38 |
| 200 | CN | 94.46 | 94.37 | 97.72 | 99.35 | 91.24 | 99.05 | 99.24 | 99.05 |
| | CWN | 96.52 | 96.52 | 98.85 | 90.54 | 92.79 | 99.21 | 91.13 | 99.39 |
| 500 | CN | 96.24 | 96.24 | 98.39 | 99.68 | 96.41 | 99.58 | 99.63 | 99.63 |
| | CWN | 98.19 | 97.80 | 99.46 | 94.65 | 96.82 | 99.63 | 98.78 | 99.85 |
| 1000 | CN | 97.18 | 96.81 | 98.81 | 99.78 | 97.73 | 99.89 | 99.73 | 99.95 |
| | CWN | 98.21 | 98.21 | 99.68 | 96.64 | 98.05 | 99.89 | 99.40 | 100.00 |
| 2000 | CN | 95.01 | 94.21 | 98.20 | 99.40 | 95.21 | 99.33 | 99.20 | 99.47 |
| | CWN | 96.74 | 97.14 | 99.47 | 94.01 | 95.81 | 99.40 | 96.67 | 99.60 |
| All available test data | CN | 82.50 | 88.57 | 98.33 | 99.88 | 94.76 | 99.88 | 99.76 | 100.00 |
| | CWN | 89.88 | 94.64 | 99.88 | 94.76 | 96.55 | 99.88 | 97.86 | 100.00 |

*CN:* Character $n$-grams only, *CWN:* Character $n$-grams plus word $n$-grams

To summarize, the parameters in the above method are:

1. Character based $n$-gram models $P_c$ and $Q_c$
2. Word based $n$-gram models $P_w$ and $Q_w$
3. Orders $O_c$ and $O_w$ of $n$-grams models
4. Number of retained top $n$-grams $N_c$ and $N_w$ (pruning ranks for character based and word based $n$-grams, respectively)
5. Number $t$ of character based models to be disambiguated by word based models
6. Weight $a$ of word based models

Parameters 3 to 6 can be used to tune the performace of the identification system. The results reported in this paper used the following values of these parameters:

1. $O_c = 4$
2. $O_w = 3$
3. $N_c = 1000$
4. $N_w = 500$
5. $t = 5$
6. $a = 1$

There is, of course, the type of similarity score, which can also be used to tune the performance. Since **MCE** gave the best overall performance in our experiments, we have selected it as the default score type.

## 7 Implementation

The language and encoding tool has been implemented as a small API in Java. This API uses another API to prepare pruned character and word $n$-grams which was developed as part of another project. A graphical user interface (GUI) has also been implemented for identifying the languages and encodings of texts, files, or batches of files. The GUI also allows a user to easily train the tool for a new language-encoding pair. The tool will be modified to work in client-server mode for documents from the Internet.

From implementation point of view, there are some issues which can significantly affect the performance of the system:

1. Whether the data should be read as text or as a binary file.
2. The assumed encoding used for reading the text, both for training and testing. For example, if we read UTF8 data as ISO-8859-1, there will be errors.
3. Whether the tranining models should be read every time they are needed or be kept in memory.
4. If training models are stored (even if they are only read at the beginning and then kept in memory), as will have to be done for practical applications, how should they be stored: as text or in binary files?

To take care of these issues, we adopted the following policy:

1. For preparing character based models, we read the data as binary files and the characters are read as bytes and stored as numbers. For word based models, the data is read as text and the encoding is assumed to be UTF8. This can cause errors, but it seems to be the best (easy) option as we don't know the actual encoding. A slightly more difficult option to implement would be to use character based models to guess the encoding and then build word based models using that as the assumed encoding. The problem with this method will be that no programming environment supports all possible encodings. Note that since we are reading the text as bytes rather than characters for preparing 'character based $n$-grams', technically we should say that we are using byte based $n$-grams models, but since we have not tested on multi-byte encodings, a byte in our experiments was almost always a character, except when the encoding was UTF8 and the byte represented some meta-data like the script code. So, for practical purposes, we can say that we are using character based $n$-grams.

2. Since after pruning, the size of the models (character as well as word) is of the order of 50K, we can afford to keep the training models in memory rather than reading them every time we have to identify the language and encoding of some data. This option is naturally faster. However, for some applications where language and encoding identification is to be done rarely or where there is a memory constraint, the other option can be used.

3. It seems to be better to store the training models in binary format since we don't know the actual encoding and the assumed encoding for storing may be wrong. We tried both options and the results were worse when we stored the models as text.

Our identification tool provides customizability with respect to all the parameters mentioned in this and the previous section.

## 8 Evaluation

Evaluation was performed for all the measures listed earlier. These are repeated here with a code for easy reference in table-3.

- **LPD**: Log probability difference
- **ALPD**: Absolute log probability difference
- **CE**: Cross entropy
- **RE**: RE measure based on relative entropy
- **JC**: JC measure (based on Jiang and Conrath's measure)
- **CT**: Cavnar and Trenkle's *out of rank* measure
- **MRE**: MRE measure based on mutual (symmetric) relative entropy
- **MCE**: Mutual (symmetric) cross entropy

We tested on six different sizes in terms of characters, namely 100, 200, 500, 1000, 2000, and all the available test data (which was not equal for various language-encoding pairs). The number of language-encoding pairs was 53 and the minimum number of test data sets was 840 when we used all available test data. In other cases, the number was naturally larger as the test files were split in fragments (see table-2).

The languages considered ranged from Esperanto and Modern Greek to Hindi and Telugu. For Indian languages, especially Hindi, several encodings were tested. Some of the pairs had UTF8 as the encoding, but the information from UTF8 byte format was not explicitly used for identification. The number of languages tested was 39 and number encodings was 19. Total number of language-encoding pairs was 53 (see table-1).

The test and training data for about half of the pairs was collected from web pages (such as Gutenberg). For Indian languages, most (but not all) data was from what is known as the CIIL corpus.

We didn't test on various training data sizes. The size of the training data ranged from 2495 to 102377 words, with more on the lower side than on the higher.

Note that we have considered the case where both the language and the encoding are unknown, not where one of them is known. In the latter case, the performance can only improve. Another point worth mentioning is that the training data was not very clean, i.e., it had noise (such as words or sentences from other languages). Error details have been given in table-4.

Table 4: Error Details

| **Language-Encoding** | **Identified As** |
|---|---|
| Afrikaans::ISO-8859-1 | Dutch::ISO-8859-1 (9) |
| Assamese::ISCII | Bengali::ISCII (6), Oriya::ISCII (113) |
| Bengali::ISCII | Hindi::ISCII (2), Oriya::ISCII (193) |
| Bulgarian::Windows-1251 | Marathi::ISCII (6) |
| Catalan::ISO-8859-1 | Latin::ISO-8859-1 (4) |
| Danish::ISO-8859-1 | Norwegian::ISO-8859-1 (7) |
| Dutch::ISO-8859-1 | Afrikaans::ISO-8859-1 (4) |
| English::ASCII | Icelandic::UTF8 (36) |
| Esperanto::UTF8 | Danish::ISO-8859-1 (5), Italian::ISO-8859-1 (1) |
| French::ISO-8859-1 | Catalan::ISO-8859-1 (6) |
| German::ISO-8859-1 | Dutch::ISO-8859-1 (4), Latin::ISO-8859-1 (3) |
| Hindi::ISCII | English::ASCII (14), Marathi::ISCII (20) |
| Hindi::Isfocb | Dutch::ISO-8859-1 (4), English::ASCII (6) |
| Hindi::Phonetic-Shusha | English::ASCII (14) |
| Hindi::Typewriter | English::ASCII (12) |
| Hindi::UTF8 | Marathi::UTF8 (82) |
| Hindi::WX | English::ASCII (8) |
| Hindi::Webdunia | French::ISO-8859-1 (2), Gujarati::Gopika (9) |
| Icelandic::UTF8 | Dutch::ISO-8859-1 (3), Latin::ISO-8859-1 (2) |
| Iloko::ISO-8859-1 | Tagalog::ISO-8859-1 (18) |
| Iroquoian::ISO-8859-1 | French::ISO-8859-1 (7) |
| Italian::ISO-8859-1 | Catalan::ISO-8859-1 (2) |
| Kannada::ISCII | Malayalam::ISCII (9) |
| Latin::ISO-8859-1 | Catalan::ISO-8859-1 (3), Dutch::ISO-8859-1 (85) French::ISO-8859-1 (28) |
| Malayalam::ISCII | Tamil::ISCII (3) |
| Marathi::ISCII | Hindi::ISCII (13) |
| Marathi::Manjusha | English::ASCII (1) |
| Marathi::UTF8 | Hindi::UTF8 (30) |
| Nahuatl::ISO-8859-1 | English::ASCII (2) |
| Norwegian::ISO-8859-1 | Danish::ISO-8859-1 (69) |
| Oriya::ISCII | Assamese::ISCII (5), Bengali::ISCII (70), Hindi::ISCII (7) |
| Portugues::ISO-8859-1 | Catalan::ISO-8859-1 (4) |
| Punjabi::ISCII | Assamese::ISCII (2), Hindi::ISCII (1) |
| Romanian::US-ASCII | Italian::ISO-8859-1 (2) |
| Russian::Windows-1251 | Portugues::ISO-8859-1 (12) |
| Spanish::ISO-8859-1 | Portugues::ISO-8859-1 (2), Tagalog::ISO-8859-1 (44) |
| Tagalog::ISO-8859-1 | English::ASCII (37), Khasi::US-ASCII (15) |
| Telugu::ISCII | Hindi::ISCII (15), Kannada::ISCII (21), Malayalam::ISCII (2) |

*These error were for* **MCE**, *both with and without word models for all the test data sizes from 200 to all available data. Most of the errors were for smaller sizes, i.e., 100 and 200 characters.*

## 9 Results

The results are presented in table-3. As can be seen almost the measures gave at least moderately good results. The best results on the whole were obtained with mutual cross entropy. The JC measure gave almost equally good results. Even a simple measure like log probability difference gave surprisingly good results.

It can also be observed from table-3 that the size of the test data is an important factor in performance. More test data gives better results. But this does not always happen, which too is surprising. It means some other factors also come into play. One of these factors seem to whether the training data for different models is of equal size or not. Another factor seems to be noise in the data. This seems to affect some measures more than the others. For example, **LPD** gave the worst performance when all the available test data was used. For smaller data sets, noise is likely to get isolated in some data sets, and therefore is less likely to affect the results.

Using word $n$-grams to augment character $n$-grams improved the performance in most of the cases, but for measures like **JC**, **RE**, **MRE** and **MCE**, there wasn't much scope for improvement. In fact, for smaller sizes (100 and 200 characters), word models actually reduced the performance for these better measures. This means either that word models are not very good for better measures, or we have not used them in the best possible way, even though intuitively they seem to offer scope for improvement when character based models don't perform perfectly.

## 10 Issues and Enhancements

Although the method works very well even on little test and training data, there are still some issues and possible enhancements. One major issue is that Web pages quite often contain text in more than one language-encoding. An ideal language-encoding identification tool should be able to mark which parts of the page are in which language-encoding.

Another possible enhancement is that in the case of Web pages, we can also take into account the language and encoding specified in the Web page (HTML). Although it may not be correct for non-standard encodings, it might still be useful for differentiating between very close encodings like ASCII and ISO-8859-1 which might seem identical to our tool.

If the text happens to be in Unicode, then it might be possible to identify at least the encoding (the same encoding might be used for more than one languages, e.g., Devanagari for Hindi, Sanskrit and Marathi) without using a statistical method. This might be used for validating the result from the statistical method.

Since every method, even the best one, has some limitations, it is obvious that for practical applications we will have to combine several approaches in such a way that as much of the available information is used as possible and the various approaches complement each other. What is left out by one approach should be taken care of by some other approach. There will be some issues in combining various approaches like the order in which they have to used, their respective priorities and their interaction (one doesn't nullify the gains from another).

It will be interesting to apply the same method or its variations on text categorization or topic identification and other related problems. The distance measures can also be tried for other problems.

## 11 Conclusion

We have presented the results about some distance measures which can be applied to NLP problems. We also described a method for automatically identifying the language and encoding of a text using several measures including one called 'mutual cross entropy'. All these measures are applied on character based pruned $n$-grams models created from the training and the test data. There is one such model for each of the known language-encoding pairs. The character based models may be augmented with word based models, which increases the performance for not so good measures, but doesn't seem to have much effect for better measures. Our method gives good performance on a few words of test data and a few pages of training data for each language-encoding pair. Out of the measures considered, mutual cross entropy gave the best results, but **RE**, **MRE** and **JC** measures also performed almost equally well.

## 12 Acknowledgement

The author wishes to thank Preeti Pradhan, Nandini Upasani and Anita Chaturvedi of Language

Technologies Research Centre, International Institute of Information Technology, Hyderabad, India for helping in preparing the data for some of the language-encoding pairs. The comments of reviewers also helped in improving the paper.

## References

Gary Adams and Philip Resnik. 1997. A language identification application built on the Java client-server platform. In Jill Burstein and Claudia Leacock, editors, *From Research to Commercial Applications: Making NLP Work in Practice*, pages 43–47. Association for Computational Linguistics.

K. Beesley. 1988. Language identifier: A computer program for automatic natural-language identification on on-line text.

William B. Cavnar and John M. Trenkle. 1994. N-gram-based text categorization. In *Proceedings of SDAIR-94, 3rd Annual Symposium on Document Analysis and Information Retrieval*, pages 161–175, Las Vegas, US.

H. Combrinck and E. Botha. 1994. Automatic language identification: Performance vs. complexity. In *Proceedings of the Sixth Annual South Africa Workshop on Pattern Recognition.*

Ted Dunning. 1994. Statistical identification of language. Technical Report CRL MCCS-94-273, Computing Research Lab, New Mexico State University, March.

E. Giguet. 1995a. Categorization according to language: A step toward combining linguistic knowledge and statistic learning.

Emmanuel Giguet. 1995b. Multilingual sentence categorisation according to language. In *Proceedings of the European Chapter of the Association for Computational Linguistics, SIGDAT Workshop, From Text to Tags: Issues in Multilingual Language Analysis, Dublin, Ireland.*

Norman C. Ingle. 1976. A language identification table. In *The Incorporated Linguist, 15(4).*

Jay J. Jiang and David W. Conrath. 1997. Semantic similarity based on corpus statistics and lexical taxonomy.

G. Kikui. 1996. Identifying the coding system and language of on-line documents on the internet. In *COLING*, pages 652–657.

Bruno Martins and Mario J. Silva. 2005. Language identification in web pages. In *Proceedings of ACM-SAC-DE, the Document Engeneering Track of the 20th ACM Symposium on Applied Computing.*

Y. K. Muthusamy, E. Barnard, and R. A. Cole. 1994. Reviewing automatic language identification. In *IEEE Signal Processing Magazine.*

Patricia Newman. 1987. Foreign language identification - first step in the translation process. In *Proceedings of the 28th Annual Conference of the American Translators Association.*, pages 509–516.

Arjen Poutsma. 2001. Applying monte carlo techniques to language identification. In *Proceedings of CLIN.*

P. Sibun and J. C. Reynar. 1996. Language identification: Examining the issues. In *In Proceedings of SDAIR-96, the 5th Symposium on Document Analysis and Information Retrieval.*, pages 125–135.

Kranig Simon. 2005. Evaluation of language identification methods. In *BA Thesis*. Universitt Tbingens.

C. Souter, G. Churcher, J. Hayes, J. Hughes, and S. Johnson. 1994. Natural language identification using corpus-based models. In *Hermes Journal of Linguistics.*, pages 183–203.

Johnson Stephen. 1993. Solving the problem of language recognition. In *Technical Report*. School of Computer Studies, University of Leeds.

W. J. Teahan and D. J. Harper. 2001. Using compression based language models for text categorization. In *J. Callan, B. Croft and J. Lafferty (eds.), Workshop on Language Modeling and Information Retrieval.*, pages 83–88. ARDA, Carnegie Mellon University.

# Towards Case-Based Parsing: Are Chunks Reliable Indicators for Syntax Trees?

**Sandra Kübler**
SfS-CL, University of Tübingen
Wilhelmstr. 19
72074 Tübingen, Germany
kuebler@sfs.uni-tuebingen.de

## Abstract

This paper presents an approach to the question whether it is possible to construct a parser based on ideas from case-based reasoning. Such a parser would employ a partial analysis of the input sentence to select a (nearly) complete syntax tree and then adapt this tree to the input sentence. The experiments performed on German data from the Tüba-D/Z treebank and the KaRoPars partial parser show that a wide range of levels of generality can be reached, depending on which types of information are used to determine the similarity between input sentence and training sentences. The results are such that it is possible to construct a case-based parser. The optimal setting out of those presented here need to be determined empirically.

## 1 Introduction

Linguistic similarity has often been used as a bias in machine learning approaches to Computational Linguistics problems. The success of applying memory-based learning to problems such as POS tagging, named-entity recognition, partial parsing, or word sense disambiguation (cf. (Daelemans et al., 1996; Daelemans et al., 1999; Mooney, 1996; Tjong Kim Sang, 2002; Veenstra et al., 2000)) shows that the bias of this similarity-based approach is suitable for processing natural language problems.

In (Kübler, 2004a; Kübler, 2004b), we extended the application of memory-based learning to full scale parsing, a problem which cannot easily be described as a classification problem. In this approach, the most similar sentence is found in the training data, and the respective syntax tree is then adapted to the input sentence. The parser was developed for parsing German dialog data, and it is based on the observation that dialogs tend to be repetitive in their structure. Thus, there is a higher than normal probability of finding the same or a very similar sentence in the training data.

The present paper examines the possibilities of extending the concepts in (Kübler, 2004a; Kübler, 2004b) to unrestricted newspaper text. Since in newspaper text, the probability of finding the same sentence or a very similar one is rather low, the parser needs to be extended to a more flexible approach which does not rely as much on identity between sentences as the original parser.

The paper is structured as follows: Section 2 explains the original parser in more detail, and section 3 describes the treebank used in the investigation. Section 4 investigates whether the chunk sequences used for selecting the most similar sentence in the training data give a reliable estimate of the syntax tree, section 5 investigates properties of tree sets associated with chunk sequences, and section 6 draws conclusions on the architecture of an extended case-based parser.

## 2 A Memory-Based Parser

The parser in (Kübler, 2004a; Kübler, 2004b) approaches parsing as the task of finding a complete syntax tree rather than incrementally building the tree by rule applications, as in standard PCFGs. Despite this holistic approach to selecting the most similar tree, the parser has a reasonable performance: the first column of Table 1 shows the parser's evaluation on German spontaneous speech dialog data. This approach profits from the fact that it has a more global view on parsing than a PCFG parser. In this respect, the memory-based



*Proceedings of the Workshop on Linguistic Distances*, pages 73–81,
Sydney, July 2006. 

| | memory-based parser | KaRoPars |
|---|---|---|
| labeled recall (syntactic categories) | 82.45% | 90.86% |
| labeled precision (syntactic categories) | 87.25% | 90.17% |
| $F_1$ | 84.78 | 90.51 |
| labeled recall (incl. gramm. functions) | 71.72% | |
| labeled precision (incl. gramm. functions) | 75.79% | |
| $F_1$ | 73.70 | |

Table 1: Results for the memory-based parser (Kübler, 2004a; Kübler, 2004b) and KaRoPars (Müller and Ule, 2002; Müller, 2005). The evaluation of KaRoPars is based on chunk annotations only.

parser employs a similar strategy to the one in *Data-Oriented Parsing* (DOP) (Bod, 1998; Scha et al., 1999). Both parsers use larger tree fragments than the standard trees. The two approaches differ mainly in two respects: 1) DOP allows different tree fragments to be extracted from one tree, thus making different combinations of fragments available for the assembly of a specific tree. Our parser, in contrast, allows only one clearly defined tree fragment for each tree, in which only the phrase-internal structure is variable. 2) Our parser does not use a probabilistic model, but a simple cost function instead. Both factors in combination result in a nearly deterministic, and thus highly efficient parsing strategy.

Since the complete tree structure in the memory-based parser is produced in two steps (retrieval of the syntax tree belonging to the most similar sentence and adaptation of this tree to the input sentence), the parser must rely on more information than the local information on which a PCFG parser suggests the next constituent. For this reason, we suggested a backing-off architecture, in which each modules used different types of easily obtainable linguistic information such as the sequence of words, the sequence of POS tags, and the sequence of chunks. Chunk parsing is a partial parsing approach (Abney, 1991), which is generally implemented as cascade of finite-state transducers. A chunk parser generally gives an analysis on the clause level and on the phrase level. However, it does not make any decisions concerning the attachment of locally ambiguous phrases. Thus, the German sentence in (1a) receives the chunk annotation in (1b).

(1) a. In der bewußten Wahrnehmung des
*In the conscious perception of the*
Lebens sieht der international
*life discerns the internationally*
angesehene Künstler den Ursprung aller
*distinguished artist the origin of all*
Kreativität.
*creativity.*

'The internationally recognized artist discerns the origin of all creativity in the conscious perception of life.'

b. [PC In der bewußten Wahrnehmung des Lebens] [VCL sieht] [NC der international angesehene Künstler] [NC den Ursprung] [NC aller Kreativität].

NCs are noun chunks, PC is a prepositional chunk, and VCL is the finite verb chunk. While for the chunks to the right of the verb chunk, no attachment decision could be made, the genitive noun phrase *des Lebens* could be grouped with the PC because of German word order regularities, which allow exactly one constituent in front of the finite verb.

It can be hypothesized that the selection of the most similar sentence based on sequences of words or POS tags works best for dialog data because of the repetitive nature of such dialogs. The strategy with the greatest potential for generalization to newspaper texts is thus the usage of chunk sequences. In the remainder of this paper, we will therefore concentrate on this approach.

The proposed parser is based on the following architecture: The parser needs a syntactically annotated treebank for training. In the learning phase, the training data are chunk parsed, the chunk sequences are extracted from the chunk parse and fitted to the syntax trees; then the trees are stored in memory. In the annotation phase, the new sentence is chunk parsed. Based on the sequence of chunks, the group of most similar sentences, which all share the same chunk analysis, is retrieved from memory. In a second step, the best sentence from this group needs to be selected, and the corresponding tree needs to be adapted to the input sentence.

The complexity of such a parser crucially depends on the question whether these chunk sequences are reliable indicators for the correct syntax trees. Basically, there exist two extreme possibilities: 1) most chunk sequences are associated with exactly one sentence, and 2) there is only a small number of different chunk sequences, which are each associated with many sentences. In the first case, the selection of the correct tree based on a chunk sequence is trivial but the coverage of the parser would be rather low. The parser would encounter many sentences with chunk sequences which are not present in the training data. In the second case, in contrast, the coverage of chunk sequences would be good, but then such a chunk sequence would correspond to many different trees. As a consequence, the tree selection process would have to be more elaborate. Both extremes would be extremely difficult for a parser to handle, so in the optimal case, we should have a good coverage of chunk sequences combined with a reasonable number of trees associated with a chunk sequence.

The investigation on the usefulness of chunk sequences was performed on the data of the German treebank TüBa-D/Z (Telljohann et al., 2004) and on output from KaRoPars, a partial parser for German (Müller and Ule, 2002). But in principle, the parsing approach is valid for languages ranging from a fixed to a more flexible word order. The German data will be described in more detail in the following section.

## 3 The German Data

### 3.1 The Treebank TüBa-D/Z

The TüBa-D/Z treebank is based on text from the German newspaper 'die tageszeitung', the present release comprises approx. 22 000 sentences. The treebank uses an annotation framework that is based on phrase structure grammar enhanced by a level of predicate-argument structure. The annotation scheme uses pure projective tree structures. In order to treat long-distance relationships, TüBa-D/Z utilizes a combination of topological fields (Höhle, 1986) and specific functional labels (cf. the tree in Figure 5, there the extraposed relative clause modifies the subject, which is annotated via the label *ON-MOD*). Topological fields described the main ordering principles in a German sentence: In a declarative sentence, the position of the finite verb as the second constituent and of the remaining verbal elements at the end of the clause is fixed. The finite verb constitutes the *left sentence bracket* (LK), and the remaining verbal elements the *right sentence bracket* (VC). The left bracket is preceded by the *initial field* (VF), between the two verbal fields, we have the unstructured *middle field* (MF). Extraposed constituents are in the *final field* (NF).

The tree for sentence (1a) is shown in Figure 1. The syntactic categories are shown in circular nodes, the function-argument structure as edge labels in square boxes. Inside a phrase, the function-argument annotation describes head/non-head relations; on the clause level, directly below the topological fields, grammatical functions are annotated. The prepositional phrase (PX) is marked as a verbal modifier (V-MOD), the noun phrase *der international angesehene Künstler* as subject (ON), and the complex noun phrase *den Ursprung aller Kreativität* as accusative object (OA). The topological fields are annotated directly below the clause node (SIMPX): the finite verb is placed in the left bracket, the prepositional phrase constitutes the initial field, and the two noun phrases the middle field.

### 3.2 Partially Parsed Data

KaRoPars (Müller and Ule, 2002) is a partial parser for German, based on the finite-state technology of the TTT suite of tools (Grover et al., 1999). It employs a mixed bottom-up top-down routine to parse German. Its actual performance is difficult to determine exactly because it employed manually written rules. The figures presented in Table 1 result from an evaluation (Müller, 2005) in which the parser output was compared with treebank structures. The figures in the Table are based on an evaluation of chunks only, i.e. the annotation of topological fields and clause boundaries was not taken into account.

The output of KaRoPars is a complex XML representation with more detailed information than is needed for the present investigation. For this reason, we show a condensed version of the parser output for sentence (1a) in Figure 2. The figure shows only the relevant chunks and POS tags, the complete output contains more embedded chunks, the n-best POS tags from different taggers, morphological information, and lemmas. As can be seen from this example, chunk boundaries often do not coincide with phrase boundaries. In the present case, it is clear from the word ordering constraints in German that the noun phrase *des*

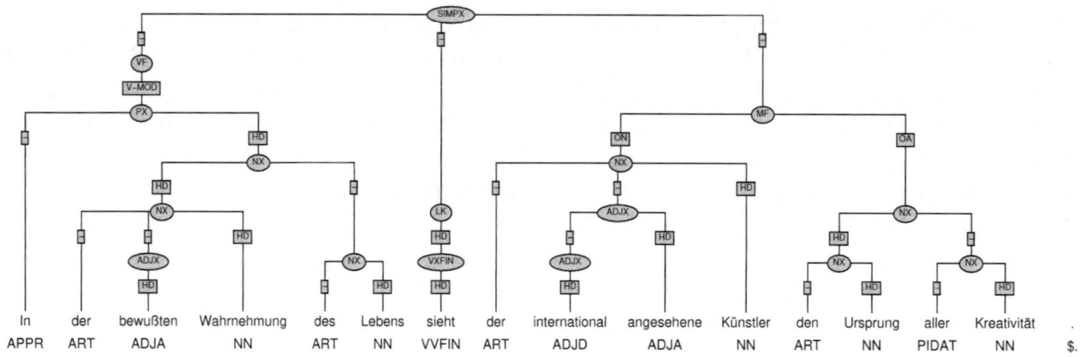


Figure 1: The TüBa-D/Z tree for sentence (1a).

```
<s broken="no">
  <cl c="V2">
    <ch fd="VF" c="PC" prep="in">
      <ch c="PC" prep="in">
        <t f="In"><P t="APPR"></P></t>
        <ch nccat="noun" hdnoun="Wahrnehmung" c="NC">
          <t f="der"><P t="ART"></P></t>
          <t f="bewußten"><P t="ADJA"></P></t>
          <t f="Wahrnehmung"><P t="NN"></P></t></ch></ch>
      <ch nccat="noun" hdnoun="Leben" c="NC">
        <t f="des"><P t="ART"></P></t>
        <t f="Lebens"><P t="NN"></P></t></ch></ch>
    <ch finit="fin" c="VCLVF" mode="akt">
      <t f="sieht"><P t="VVFIN"></P></t></ch>
    <ch nccat="noun" hdnoun="Künstler" c="NC">
      <t f="der"><P t="ART"></P></t>
      <t f="international"><P t="ADJD"></P></t>
      <t f="angesehene"><P t="ADJA"></P></t>
      <t f="Künstler"><P t="NN"></P></t></ch>
    <ch nccat="noun" hdnoun="Ur=Sprung" c="NC">
      <t f="den"><P t="ART"></P></t>
      <t f="Ursprung"><P t="NN"></P></t></ch>
    <ch nccat="noun" hdnoun="Kreativität" c="NC">
      <t f="aller"><P t="PIDAT"></P></t>
      <t f="Kreativität"><P t="NN"></P></t></ch></cl></s>
```

Figure 2: The KaRoPars analysis for sentence (1a). For better readability, the words and the chunk types are displayed in bold.

*Lebens* needs to be attached to the previous phrase. In the treebank, it is grouped into a complex noun phrase while in the KaRoPars output, this noun phrase is the sister of the prepositional chunk *In der bewußten Wahrnehmung*. Such boundary mismatches also occur on the clause level.

## 4 Chunk Sequences as Indicators for Syntax Trees

The complexity of the proposed parser depends on the proportion of chunk sequences versus syntax trees, as explained in section 2. A first indication of this proportion is given by the ratio of chunk sequence types and tree types. Out of the 22 091 sentences in the treebank, there are 20 340 different trees (types) and 14 894 different chunk sequences. This gives an average of 1.37 trees per chunk sequence. At a first glance, the result indicates that the chunk sequences are very good indicators for selecting the correct syntax tree. The negative aspect of this ratio is that many of these chunk sequences will not be part of the training data. This is corroborated by an experiment in which one tenth of the complete data set of chunk sequences (test set) was tested against the remainder of the data set (training set) to see how many of the test sequences could be found in the training data. In order to reach a slightly more accurate picture, a ten-fold setting was used, i.e. the experiment was repeated ten times, each time using a different segment as test set. The results show that on average only 43.61% of the chunk sequences could be found in the training data.

(2) Schon trifft sich die Mannschaft erst am
*Already meets REFL the team only on the*
Spieltag.
*game day.*

'So the team only meets on the day of the game.'

In a second experiment, we added more information about chunk types, namely the information from the fields *nccat* and *finit* in the XML representation to the chunk categories. Field *nccat* contains information about the head of the noun chunk, whether it is a noun, a reflexive pronoun, a relative pronoun, etc. Field *finit* contains information about the finiteness of a verb chunk. For this experiment, sentence (2) is represented by the chunk sequence "NC:noun VCL NC:refl PC NC:noun PC AVC NC:noun VCR:fin". When using such chunk sequences, the ratio of sequences found in the training set decreases to 36.59%.

In a third experiment, the chunk sequences were constructed without adverbial phrases, i.e. without the one category that functions as adjunct in a majority of the cases. Thus sentence (3) is represented by the chunk sequence "NC VCL NC NC" instead of by the complete sequence: "NC VCL NC AVC AVC AVC NC". In this case, 54.72% of the chunk sequences can be found. Reducing the information in the chunk sequence even further seems counterproductive because every type of information that is left out will make the final decision on the correct syntax tree even more difficult.

(3) Wer gibt uns denn jetzt noch einen Auftrag?
*Who gives us anyhow now still an order?*

'Who will give us an order anyhow?'

All the experiments reported above are based on data in which complete sentences were used. One possibility of gaining more generality in the chunk sequences without losing more information consists of splitting the sentences on the clause level.

(4) Ganz abgesehen davon, daß man dann schon
*Totally irrespective of it, that one then already*
mal alle die Geschlechtsgenossinnen kennt, mit
*once all the fellow females knows, with*
denen man nach der Trennung über den Kerl
*whom one after the break-up about the twerp*
ablästern kann, weil sie ja genau
*slander can, because they already exactly*
wissen, wie mies er eigentlich ist.
*know, how bad he really is.*

'Completely irrespective of the fact that one already knows all the other females with whom one can slander the twerp after the break-up because they already know what a loser he is.'

Thus, the complex sentence in (4) translates into 5 different clauses, i.e. into 5 different chunk sequences:

1. SubC NC:noun AVC AVC AVC NC:noun NC:noun VCR:fin
2. PC NC:noun PC PC VCR:fin
3. SubC NC:noun AVC AJVC VCR:fin
4. SubC AJVC NC:noun AVC VCR:fin
5. AVC VCR:fin PC

The last sequence covers the elliptical matrix clause *ganz abgesehen davon*, the first four sequences describe the subordinated clauses; i.e. the first sequence describes the subordinate clause *daß man dann schon mal alle die Geschlechtsgenossinnen kennt*, the second sequence covers the relative clause *mit denen man nach der Trennung über den Kerl ablästern kann*. The third sequence describes the subordinate clause introduced by the conjunction *weil*, and the fourth sequence covers the subordinate clause introduced by the interrogative pronoun *wie*.

On the one hand, splitting the chunk sequences into clause sequences makes the parsing task more difficult because the clause boundaries annotated during the partial parsing step do not always coincide with the clause boundaries in the syntax trees. In those cases where the clause boundaries do not coincide, a deterministic solution must be found, which allows a split that does not violate the parallelism constraints between both structures. On the other hand, the split into clauses allows a higher coverage of new sentences without extending the size of the training set. In an experiment, in which the chunk sequences were represented by the main chunk types plus subtypes (cf. experiment two) and were split into clauses, the percentage of unseen sequences in a tenfold split was reduced from 66.41% to 44.16%. If only the main chunk type is taken into account, the percentage of unseen sequences decreases from 56.39% to 36.34%.

The experiments presented in this section show that with varying degrees of information and with different ways of extracting chunk sequences, a range of levels of generality can be represented. If the maximum of information regarded here is used, only 36.59% of the sequences can be found. If, in contrast, the sentences are split into chunks and only the main chunk type is used, the ratio of found sequences reaches 63.66%. A final decision on which representation of chunks is optimal, however, is also dependent on the sets of trees that are represented by the chunk sequences and thus needs to be postponed.

## 5 Tree Sets

In the previous section, we showed that if we extract chunk sequences based on complete sentences and on main chunk types, there are on average 1.37 sentences assigned to one chunk sequences. At a first glance, this results means that for the majority of chunk sequences, there is exactly one sentence which corresponds to the sequence, which makes the final selection of the correct tree trivial. However, 1261 chunk sequences have more than one corresponding sentence, and there is one chunk sequence which has 802 sentences assigned. We will call these collections *tree sets*. In these cases, the selection of the correct tree from a tree set may be far from trivial, depending on the differences in the trees. A minimal difference constitutes a difference in the words only. If all corresponding words belong to the same POS class, there is no difference in the syntax trees. Another type of differences in the trees which does not overly harm the selection process are differences in the internal structure of phrases. In (Kübler, 2004a), we showed that the tree can be cut at the phrase level, and new phrase-internal structures can be inserted into the tree. Thus, the most difficult case occurs when the differences in the trees are located in the higher regions of the trees where attachment information between phrases and grammatical functions are encoded. If such cases are frequent, the parser needs to employ a detailed search procedure.

The question how to determine the similarity of trees in a tree set is an open research question. It is clear that the similarity measure should abstract away from unimportant differences in words and phrase-internal structure. It should rather concentrate on differences in the attachment of phrases and in grammatical functions. As a first approximation for such a similarity measure, we chose a measure based on precision and recall of these parts of the tree. In order to ignore the lower levels of the tree, the comparison is restricted to nodes in the tree which have grammatical functions.

(5) Der Autokonvoi mit den Probenbesuchern
*The car convoy with the rehearsal visitors*
fährt eine Straße entlang, die noch heute
*travels a street down, which still today*
Lagerstraße heißt.
*Lagerstraße is called.*
'The convoy of the rehearsal visitors' cars travels down a street that is still called Lagerstraße.'

For example, Figure 5 shows the tree for sentence (5). The matrix clause consists of a complex subject noun phrase (GF: ON), a finite verb phrase, which is the head of the sentence, an accusative noun phrase (GF: OA), a verb particle (GF: VPT), and an extraposed relative clause (GF: ON-MOD). Here the grammatical function indicates a long-distance relationship, the relative clause modifies the subject. The relative clause, in turn, consists of a subject (the relative pronoun), an adverbial phrase modifying the verb (GF: V-MOD), a named entity predicate (EN-ADD, GF: PRED), and the finite verb phrase. The comparison of this tree to other trees in its tree set will then be based on the following nodes: NX:ON VXFIN:HD NX:OA PTKVC:VPT R-SIMPX:ON-MOD NX:ON ADVX:V-MOD EN-ADD:PRED VXFIN:HD. Precision and recall are generally calculated based on the number of identical constituents between two trees. Two constituents are considered identical if they have the same node label and grammatical function and if they cover the same range of words (i.e. have the same yield). For our comparison, the concrete length of constituents is irrelevant, as long as the sequential order of the constituents is identical. Thus, in order to abstract from the length of constituents, their yield is normalized: All phrases are set to length 1, the yield of a clause is determined by the yields of its daughters. After this step, precision and recall are calculated on all pairs of trees in a tree set. Thus, if a set contains 3 trees, tree 1 is compared to tree 2 and 3, and tree 2 is compared to tree 3. Since all pairs of trees are compared, there is no clear separation of precision and recall, precision being the result of comparing tree A to B in the pair and recall being the result of comparing B to A. As a consequence only the $F_{\beta=1}$-measure, a combination of precision and recall, is used.

As mentioned above, the experiment is conducted with chunk sequences based on complete sentences and the main chunk types. The average F-measure for the 1261 tree sets is 46.49%, a clear indication that randomly selecting a tree from a tree set is not sufficient. Only a very small number of sets, 62, consists of completely identical trees, and most of these sets contain only two trees.

The low F-measure can in part be explained

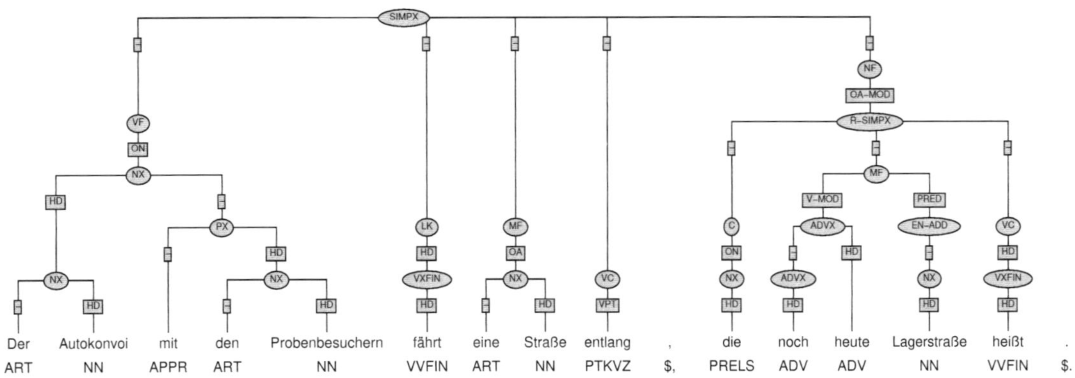


Figure 3: The TüBa-D/Z tree for sentence (5).

by the relatively free word order of German: In contrast to English, the grammatical function of a noun phrase in German cannot be determined by its position in a sentence. Thus, if the partial parser returns the chunk sequence "NC VCL NC NC", it is impossible to tell which of the noun phrases is the subject, the accusative object, or the dative object. As a consequence, all trees with these three arguments will appear in the same tree set. Since German additionally displays case syncretism between nominative and accusative, a morphological analysis can also only provide partial disambiguation. As a consequence, it is clear that the selection of the correct syntax tree for an input sentence needs to be based on a selection module that utilizes lexical information.

Another source of differences in the trees are errors in the partial analysis. In the tree set for the chunk sequence "NC VCL AVC PC PC VCR", there are sentences with rather similar structure, one of them being shown in (6). Most of them only differ in the grammatical functions assigned to the prepositional phrases, which can serve either as complements or adjuncts. However, the tree set also contains sentence (7).

(6) Die Brüder im wehrfähigen Alter
*The brothers in the fit for military service age*
seien schon vor der Polizeiaktion in die
*had already before the police operation into the*
Wälder geflohen.
*woods fled.*

'Those brothers who are considered fit for military service had already fled into the woods before the police operation.'

(7) Das gilt auch für den Umfang, in dem
*This holds also for the extent, to which*
Montenegro attakkiert wird.
*Montenegro attacked is.*

'This is also true for the extent to which Montenegro is being attacked.'

In sentence (7), the relative pronoun was erroneously POS tagged as a definite determiner, thus allowing an analysis in which the two phrases *in dem* and *Montenegro* are grouped as a prepositional chunk. As a consequence, no relative clause was found. The corresponding trees, however, are annotated correctly, and the similarity between those two sentences is consequently low.

The low F-measure should not be taken as a completely negative result. Admittedly, it necessitates a rather complex tree selection module. The positive aspect of this one-to-many relation between chunk sequences and trees is its generality. If only very similar trees shared a tree set, then we would need many chunk sequences. In this case, the problem would be moved towards the question how to extract a maximal number of different partial parses from a limited number of training sentences.

## 6 Consequences for a Case-Based Parser

The experiments in the previous two sections show that the chunk sequences extracted from a partial parse can serve as indicators for syntax trees. While the best definition of chunk sequences can only be determined empirically, the results presented in the previous section allow some conclusions on how the parser must be designed.

### 6.1 Consequences for Matching Chunk Sequences and Trees

From the experiments in section 4, it is clear that a good measure of information needs to be found for an optimal selection process. There needs to be a good equilibrium between a high coverage of different chunk sequences and a low number of trees per chunk sequence. One possibility to reach the first goal would be to ignore certain types of phrases in the extraction of chunk sequences from the partial parse. However, the experiments show that it is impossible to reduce the informativeness of the chunk sequence to a level where all possible chunk sequences are present in the training data. This means that the procedure which matches the chunk sequence of the input sentence to the chunk sequences in the training data must be more flexible than a strict left-to-right comparison. In (Kübler, 2004a; Kübler, 2004b), we allowed the deletion of chunks in either the input sentence or the training sentence. The latter operation is uncritical because it results in a deletion of some part of the syntax tree. The former operation, however, is more critical, it either leads to a partial syntactic analysis in which the deleted chunk is not attached to the tree or to the necessity of guessing the node to which the additional constituent needs to be attached and possibly guessing the grammatical function of the new constituent. Instead of this deletion, which can be applied anywhere in the sentence, we suggest the use of Levenshtein distance (Levenshtein, 1966). This distance measure is, for example, used for spelling correction: Here the most similar word in the lexicon is found which can be reached via the smallest number of deletion, substitution, and insertion operations on characters. Instead of operating on characters, we suggest to apply Levenshtein distance to chunk sequences. In this case, deletions from the input sequence could be given a much higher weight (i.e. cost) than insertions. We also suggest a modification of the distance to allow an exchange of chunks. This modification would allow a principled treatment of the relative free word order of German. However, if such an operation is not restricted to adjacent chunks, the algorithm will gain in complexity but since the resulting parser is still deterministic, it is rather unlikely that this modification will lead to complexity problems.

### 6.2 Consequences for the Tree Selection

As explained in section 5, there are chunk sequences that correspond to more than one syntax tree. Since differences in the trees also pertain to grammatical functions, the module that selects the best tree out of the tree set needs to use more information than the chunk sequences used for selecting the tree set. Since the holistic approach to parsing proposed in this paper does not lend itself easily to selecting grammatical functions separately for single constituents, we suggest to use lexical co-occurrence information instead to select the best tree out of the tree set for a given sentence. Such an approach generalizes Streiter's (2001) approach of selecting from a set of possible trees based on word similarity. However, an approach based on lexical information will suffer extremely from data sparseness. For this reason, we suggest a soft clustering approach based on a partial parse, similar to the approach by Wagner (2005) for clustering verb arguments for learning selectional preferences for verbs.

## 7 Conclusion and Future Work

In this paper, we have approached the question whether it is possible to construct a parser based on ideas from case-based reasoning. Such a parser would employ a partial analysis (chunk analysis) of the sentence to select a (nearly) complete syntax tree and then adapt this tree to the input sentence.

In the experiments reported here, we have shown that it is possible to obtain a wide range of levels of generality in the chunk sequences, depending on the types of information extracted from the partial anaylses and on the decision whether to use sentences or clauses as basic segments for the extraction of chunk sequences. Once a robust method is implemented to split trees into subtrees based on clauses, chunk sequences can be extracted on the clause level rather than from complete sentences. Consequently, the tree sets will also reach a higher cardinality. However, a tree selection method based on lexical information will be indispensable even then. For this tree selection, a method for determining the similarity of tree structures needs to be developed. The measure used in the experiments reported here, $F_1$, is only a very crude approximation, which serves well for an initial investigation, but which is not good enough for a parser depending on such a similarity measure. The optimal combination of chunk sequences and tree selection methods will have to be determined empirically.

## References

Steven Abney. 1991. Parsing by chunks. In Robert Berwick, Steven Abney, and Caroll Tenney, editors, *Principle-Based Parsing*, pages 257–278. Kluwer Academic Publishers, Dordrecht.

Rens Bod. 1998. *Beyond Grammar: An Experience-Based Theory of Language*. CSLI Publications, Stanford, CA.

Walter Daelemans, Jakub Zavrel, Peter Berck, and Steven Gillis. 1996. MBT: A memory-based part of speech tagger-generator. In Eva Ejerhed and Ido Dagan, editors, *Proceedings of the 4th Workshop on Very Large Corpora*, pages 14–27, Copenhagen, Denmark.

Walter Daelemans, Antal van den Bosch, and Jakub Zavrel. 1999. Forgetting exceptions is harmful in language learning. *Machine Learning*, 34:11–43. Special Issue on Natural Language Learning.

Claire Grover, Colin Matheson, and Andrei Mikheev. 1999. TTT: Text Tokenization Tool. Language Technology Group, University of Edinburgh.

Tilman Höhle. 1986. Der Begriff "Mittelfeld", Anmerkungen über die Theorie der topologischen Felder. In *Akten des Siebten Internationalen Germanistenkongresses 1985*, pages 329–340, Göttingen, Germany.

Sandra Kübler. 2004a. *Memory-Based Parsing*. John Benjamins, Amsterdam.

Sandra Kübler. 2004b. Parsing without grammar–using complete trees instead. In Nicolas Nicolov, Ruslan Mitkov, Galia Angelova, and Kalina Boncheva, editors, *Recent Advances in Natural Language Processing III: Selected Papers from RANLP 2003*, Current Issues in Linguistic Theory. John Benjamins, Amsterdam.

Vladimir I. Levenshtein. 1966. Binary codes capable of correcting deletions, insertions, and reversals. *Cybernetics and Control Theory*, 10(8):707–710.

Raymond J. Mooney. 1996. Comparative experiments on disambiguating word senses: An illustration of the role of bias in machine learning. In *Proceedings of the 1st Conference on Empirical Methods in Natural Language Processing EMNLP*, pages 82–91, Philadelphia, PA.

Frank Henrik Müller and Tylman Ule. 2002. Annotating topological fields and chunks–and revising POS tags at the same time. In *Proceedings of the 19th International Conference on Computational Linguistics (COLING 2002)*, pages 695–701, Taipei, Taiwan.

Frank Henrik Müller. 2005. *A Finite-State Approach to Shallow Parsing and Grammatical Functions Annotation of German*. Ph.D. thesis, Seminar für Sprachwissenschaft, Universität Tübingen. Version of 16th Nov. 2005.

Remko Scha, Rens Bod, and Khalil Sima'an. 1999. Memory-based syntactic analysis. *Journal of Experimental and Theoretical Artificial Intelligence*, 11:409–440. Special Issue on Memory-Based Language Processing.

Oliver Streiter. 2001. Recursive top-down fuzzy match, new perspectives on memory-based parsing. In *Proceedings of the 15th Pacific Asia Conference on Language, Information and Computation, PACLIC 2001*, Hong Kong.

Heike Telljohann, Erhard Hinrichs, and Sandra Kübler. 2004. The TüBa-D/Z treebank: Annotating German with a context-free backbone. In *Proceedings of the Fourth International Conference on Language Resources and Evaluation (LREC 2004)*, pages 2229–2235, Lisbon, Portugal.

Erik F. Tjong Kim Sang. 2002. Memory-based named entity recognition. In *Proceedings of CoNLL-2002*, pages 203–206. Taipei, Taiwan.

Jorn Veenstra, Antal van den Bosch, Sabine Buchholz, Walter Daelemans, and Jakub Zavrel. 2000. Memory-based word sense disambiguation. *Computers and the Humanities, Special Issue on Senseval, Word Sense Disambiguation*, 34(1/2):171–177.

Andreas Wagner. 2005. *Learning Thematic Role Relations for Lexical Semantic Nets*. Ph.D. thesis, Universität Tübingen.

# A Measure of Aggregate Syntactic Distance

**John Nerbonne and Wybo Wiersma**
Alfa-informatica, University of Groningen
P.O.Box 716, NL 9700 AS Groningen, The Netherlands
j.nerbonne@rug.nl & wybo@logilogi.org

**Abstract**

We compare vectors containing counts of trigrams of part-of-speech (POS) tags in order to obtain an aggregate measure of syntax difference. Since lexical syntactic categories reflect more abstract syntax as well, we argue that this procedure reflects more than just the basic syntactic categories. We tag the material automatically and analyze the frequency vectors for POS trigrams using a permutation test. A test analysis of a 305,000 word corpus containing the English of Finnish emigrants to Australia is promising in that the procedure proposed works well in distinguishing two different groups (adult vs. child emigrants) and also in highlighting syntactic deviations between the two groups.

## 1 Introduction

Language contact is a common phenomenon which may even be growing due to the increased mobility of recent years. It is also linguistically significant, since contact effects are prominent in linguistic structure and well-recognized confounders in the task of historical reconstruction. Nonetheless we seem to have no way of assaying the aggregate affects of contacts, as Weinreich famously noted:

> "No easy way of measuring or characterizing the total impact of one language on another in the speech of bilinguals has been, or probably can be devised. The only possible procedure is to describe the various forms of interference and to tabulate their frequency." (Weinreich, 1953, p. 63)

This paper proposes a technique for measuring the aggregate degree of syntactic difference between two varieties. We shall thus attempt to measure the "total impact" in Weinreich's sense, albeit with respect to a single linguistic level, syntax.

If such a measure could be developed, it would be important not only in the study of language contact, but also in the study of second-language acquisition. A numerical measure of syntactic difference would enable these fields to look afresh at issues such as the time course of second-language acquisition, the relative importance of factors influencing the degree of difference such as the mother tongue of the speakers, other languages they know, the length and time of their experience in the second language, the role of formal instruction, etc. It would make the data of such studies amenable to the more powerful statistical analysis reserved for numerical data.

Naturally we want more than a measure which simply assigns a numerical value to the difference between two syntactic varieties: we want to be able to examine the sources of the difference both in order to win confidence in the measure, but also to answer linguistic questions about the relative stability/volatility of syntactic structures.

### 1.1 Related Work

Thomason and Kaufmann (1988) and van Coetsem (1988) noted, nearly simultaneously, that the most radical (structural) effects in language contact situations are to be found in the language of SWITCHERS, i.e., in the language used as a second or later language. People MAINTAINING their language tend to adopt new lexical items from a contact language, but this only has structural consequences as the lexical items accumulate. Thus we hear radically different English used in immigrant



*Proceedings of the Workshop on Linguistic Distances*, pages 82–90,
Sydney, July 2006. 

communities in the English-speaking world, but the natives in contact with these groups do not tend to modify their language a great deal. This suggests that we should concentrate on those switching as we begin to develop measures of aggregate difference.

Poplack and Sankoff (1984) introduced techniques for studying lexical borrowing and its phonological effects, and and Poplack, Sankoff and Miller (1988) went on to exploit these advances in order to investigate the social conditions in which contact effects flourish best.

We follow Aarts and Granger (1998) most closely, who suggest focusing on tag sequences in learner corpora, just as we do. We shall add to their suggest a means of measuring the aggregate difference between two varieties, and show how we can test whether that difference is statistically significant.

## 2 Syntactic Footprints

In this section we justify using frequency profiles of trigrams of part-of-speech (POS) categories as indicators of syntactic differences. We shall first automatically tag second-language speakers' corpora with syntactic categories:

| | | | | | |
|---|---|---|---|---|---|
| Oh | that | 's | a | just | a |
| INT | PRON | COP | ART | EXCL | ART |
| fun | in | a | ' | Helsinki | |
| N-COM | PREP | ART | PAUSE | N-PROP | |

We then collect these into overlapping triples (trigrams). The tag-trigrams include triples such as INT-PRON-COP and PRON-COP-ART.

We consider three possible objections to proceeding this way. First, one might object that unigrams, bigrams, also should be compared. We are in fact sympathetic to the criticism that $n$-grams for $n \neq 3$ should also be compared, at least with an eye toward refining the technique, and we have performed experiments with bigrams and with combinations of $n$-grams for larger $n$, but we restrict the discussion here to trigrams in order to simplify presentation. Second, our choice of part-of-speech categories may bias the results, since other research might use other POS categories, and third, that POS trigrams do not reflect syntax completely. We first develop these last two objections further, and then explain why it is reasonable to proceed this way.

Ideally we should like to have at our disposal the syntactic equivalent of an international phonetic alphabet (IPA, 1949), i.e. an accepted means of noting (an interesting level of) syntactic structure for which there was reasonable scientific consensus. But no such system exists. Moreover, the ideal system would necessarily reflect the hierarchical structure of dependency found in all contemporary theories of syntax, whether directly based on dependencies or indirectly reflected in constituent structure. Since it is unlikely that researchers will take the time to hand-annotate large amounts of data, meaning we shall need automatically annotated data, this leads to a second problem, viz., that our parsers, the automatic data annotators capable of full annotation, are not yet robust enough for this task. (Even the best score only about 90% per constituent on edited newspaper prose.)

We have no solution to the problem of the missing consensual annotation system, but we wish to press on, since it will be sufficient if we can provide a measure which correlates strongly with syntactic differences. We note that natural language processing work on tagging has compared different tag sets, noting primarily the obvious, that larger sets result in lower accuracy (Manning and Schütze, 1999, 372ff.). Since we aim here to contribute to the study of language contact and second-language learning, we shall choose a linguistically sensitive set, that is, a large set designed by linguists. We have not experimented with different tagsets.

With regard to the second objection, the fact that syntax concerns more than POS trigrams, we wish to deny that this is a genuine problem for the development of a measure of difference. We note that our situation in measuring syntactic differences is similar to other situations in which effective measures have been established. For example, even though researchers in first language acquisition are very aware that syntactic development is reflected in the number of categories, and rules and/or constructions used, the degree to which principles of agreement and government are respected, the fidelity to adult word order patterns, etc., still they are in large agreement that the very simple MEAN LENGTH OF UTTERANCE (MLU) is an excellent measure of syntactic maturity (Ritchie and Bhatia, 1998). Similarly, life expectancy and infant mortality rates are considered reliable indications of health when large populations are compared. We therefore continue, postulating that the measure we propose will correlate with syntactic differences as a whole, even if it does not measure them directly.

In fact we can be rather optimistic about using POS trigrams given the consensus in syntactic theory that a great deal of hierarchical structure is predictable given the knowledge of lexical categories, in particular given the lexical HEAD. Sells (1982, §§ 2.2, 5.3, 4.1) demonstrates that this was common to theories in the 1980's (Government and Binding theory, Generalized Phrase Structure Grammar, and Lexical Function Grammar), and the situation has changed little in the successor theories (Minimalism and Head-Driven Phrase Structure Grammar). There is, on the other hand, consensus that the very strict lexicalism which Sells's work sketched must be relaxed in favor of "constructionalism" (Fillmore and Kay, 1999), but even in such theories syntactic heads have a privileged, albeit less dominant status.[1]

Let us further note that the focus on POS trigrams is poised to identify not only deviant syntactic uses, such as the one given as an example above, but also overuse and under-use of linguistic structure, whose importance is emphasized by researchers on second-language acquisition (Coseriu, 1970), (de Bot et al., 2005, A3,B3). According to these experts it is misleading to consider only errors, as second language learners likewise tend to overuse certain possibilities and tend to avoid (and therefore underuse) others. For example, Bot et al. (2005) suggest that non-transparent constructions are systematically avoided even by very good second-language learners).

### 2.1 Tagging

We tagged the material using Thorsten Brants's *Trigrams 'n Tags* (TnT) tagger, a hidden Markov model tagger which has performed at state-of-the-art levels in organized comparisons, achieving $96.7\%$ correct on the material of the Penn Treebank (Brants, 2000).

Since our material is spoken English (see below), we trained the tagger on the spoken part of the *International Corpus of English* (ICE) from Great Britain, which consists of 500k words. This was suboptimal, as the material we wished to analyze was the English of Finnish emigrants to Australia, but we were unable to acquire sufficient Australian material.

We used the tagset of the TOSCA-ICE consisting of 270 tags (Garside et al., 1997), of which 75 were never instantiated in our material. In a sample of $1,000$ words we found that the tagger was correct for $87\%$ of words, $74\%$ of the bigrams, and $65\%$ of the trigrams. As will be obvious in the presentation of the material (below), it is free conversation with pervasive foreign influence. We attribute the low tagging accuracy to the roughness of the material. It is clear that our procedure would improve in accuracy from a more accurate tagger, which would, in turn, allow application to smaller corpora.

We collect the material into a frequency vector containing the counts of $13,784$ different POS trigrams, one vector for each of the two sub-corpora which we describe below. We then ask whether the material in the one sub-corpus differs significantly from that in the other. We turn now to that topic.

## 3 Permutation Tests

There is no convenient test we can apply to check whether the differences between vectors containing $13,784$ elements are statistically significant, nor how significant the differences are. Fortunately, we may turn to permutation tests in this situation (Good, 1995), more specifically a permutation test using a Monte Carlo technique. Kessler (2001) contains an informal introduction for an application within linguistics.

The fundamental idea in a permutation test is very simple: we measure the difference between two sets in some convenient fashion, obtaining $\delta(A,B)$. We then extract two sets at random from $A \cup B$, calling these $A_1, B_1$, and we calculate the difference between these two in the same fashion, $\delta(A_1, B_1)$, recording the number of times $\delta(A_1, B_1) \geq \delta(A, B)$, i.e., how often two randomly selected subsets from the entire set of observations are at least as different as (usually more different than) the original sets were. If we repeat this process, say, $10,000$ times, then $n$, the number of times we obtain more extreme differences, allows us to calculate how strongly the original two sets differ from a chance division with respect to $\delta$. In that case we may conclude that if the two sets were not genuinely different, then the original division into $A$ and $B$ was likely to the degree of $p = n/10,000$. In more standard hypothesis-

[1] One referee suggested that one might test the association between POS trigram differences and head differences experimentally, and we find this suggestion sensible.

testing terms, this is the $p$-value with which we may reject (or retain) the null hypothesis that there is no relevant difference in the two sets.

We would like to guard against three dangers in our calculations. First, given the ease with which large corpora are obtained, we are uninterested in obtaining statistical significance through sheer corpus size. We aim therefore at obtaining a measure that is sensitive only to relative frequency, and not at all to absolute frequency (Agresti, 1996). Permutation tests effectively guard against this danger, if one takes care to judge samples of the same size within the permutations.

Second, we are mindful of a potential confounding factor, viz., the syntactical intra-dependence found within sentences (especially between adjoining POS trigrams). If we permuted $n$-grams, we might in part measure the internal coherence of the two initial sub-corpora, i.e., the coherence due to the fact that both sub-corpora use language conforming to the rules of English syntax. If we permuted $n$-grams, this coherence would be lost, and the measurement of difference would be affected. In the terminology of permutation statistics: the elements that are permuted must be reasonably independent. So we shall permute not $n$-grams, but rather entire sentences.

Third, the decision to permute sentences rather than $n$-grams exposes us to a confound due to systematically different sentence lengths. While the result of permuting elements in a Monte Carlo fashion always results in two sub-corpora that have the same number of elements as in the base-case, our problem is that the elements we permute are sentences, while what we measure are $n$-grams. Now if the original two sub-corpora differ substantially in average sentence length, then the result of the Monte Carlo "shuffling" will not be similar to the original split with respect to the number of $n$-grams involved. The original sub-corpus with longer sentences will therefore have many more $n$-grams in the base-case than in the random re-drawings from the combining corpora, at least on average. We address this danger systematically in the subsection below on within-permutation normalizations (§ 3.2).

We note a more subtle dependency we do not attempt to guard against. Some POS sequences (almost) only occur in relatively long sentences, e.g. the inversion that occurs in some conditionals *Were I in any doubt, I should not ....* Perhaps English subjunctives in general occur only in relatively long sentences. If this sort of structure occurs in one variety more frequently than in another, that is a genuine difference, but it might still be the reflection of the simpler difference in sentence length. One might then think that the second variety would show the same syntax if only it had longer sentences. As far as they are to be considered a problem in the first place, differences in syntax that are related to sentence length cannot be removed by (our) normalizations.

Permutation tests are a very suitable tool for finding significant syntactical differences, and for finding the POS trigrams that make a significant contribution to this difference.

### 3.1 Measuring Vector Differences

The choice of vector difference measure, e.g. cosine vs. $\chi^2$, does not affect the proposed technique greatly, and alternative measures can be used straightforwardly. Accordingly, we have worked with both cosine and two measures inspired by the RECURRENCE ($R$) metric introduced by Kessler (Kessler, 2001, 157ff). Following Kessler, we also call our measures $R$ and $Rsq$. The advantage of the $R$ and $Rsq$ metrics is that they are transparently interpretable as simple aggregates, meaning that one may easily see how much each trigram contributes to the overall corpus difference. We even used them to calculate a separate $p$-value per trigram.

Our $R$ is calculated as the sum of the differences of each cell with respect to the average for that cell. If we have collected our data into two vectors $(\mathbf{c}, \mathbf{c}')$, and if $i$ is the index of a POS trigram, $R$ for each of these two vector cells is equal, as it is defined simply as $R = \sum_i |c_i - \overline{c_i}|$, with $\overline{c_i} = (c_i + c_i')/2$. The $Rsq$ measure attributes more weight to a few large differences than to many small ones, and it is calculated: $Rsq = \sum_i (c_i - \overline{c_i})^2$, with $\overline{c_i}$ being the same as above (for $R$).

### 3.2 Within-Permutation Normalization

Each measurement of difference—whether the difference is between the original two samples or between two samples which arise through permutations—is taken over the collection of POS trigram frequencies once these have been normalized. We describe first the normalization that is required to cope with differences in sentence length which we call WITHIN-PERMUTATION NORMALIZATION, as it is applied within each permutation.

In case sub-corpora differ in sentence length, they will automatically differ in the number of $n$-grams across permutations as well. Our Monte Carlo choice of alternatives does not change the relative number of sentences across permutations, but the number of POS trigrams in the groups will vary if no normalization is applied. Longer sentences give rise to larger numbers of POS trigrams per sentence, and therefore per sub-corpora. Applying the within-permutation normalization one or more times ensures that this does not infect the measurement of difference.

Protecting the measurement from sensitivity to differing numbers of POS trigrams per sentence is for us sufficient reason to normalize, but we also normalize in order to facilitate interpretation. We return to this below, in the definition of the rescaled vectors $\mathbf{s^y}, \mathbf{s^o}$.

We thus collect from the tagger a sequence of counts $c_i$ of tag trigrams for each sample. We treat only the case of comparing two samples here, which we shall refer to as young ($y$) and old ($o$) for reasons which will become clear in the following section. We shall keep track of the sum-per-tag trigram as well, summing over the two sub-corpora.

$$\begin{array}{rcll} \mathbf{c^y} & = & < c_1^y, c_2^y, ..., c_n^y > & N^y = \sum_{i=1}^n c_i^y \\ +\mathbf{c^o} & = & < c_1^o, c_2^o, ..., c_n^o > & N^o = \sum_{i=1}^n c_i^o \\ \hline \mathbf{c} & = & < c_1, c_2, ..., c_n > & N (= N^y + N^o) \\ & & & = \sum_{i=1}^n c_i \end{array}$$

As a first step in normalization, we work with vectors holding the relative frequency fractions per group:

$$\begin{array}{rcl} \mathbf{f^y} & = & < ..., f_i^y (= c_i^y / N^y), ... > \\ \mathbf{f^o} & = & < ..., f_i^o (= c_i^o / N^o), ... > \end{array}$$

We note that $\sum_{i=1}^n f_i^y = \sum_{i=1}^n f_i^o = 1$.

We then compute the relative proportions per trigram, comparing now across the groups. This prepares for the step which redistributes the raw trigram counts to compensate for differences in sentence length.

$$\begin{array}{rcl} \mathbf{p^y} & = & < ..., p_i^y (= f_i^y / (f_i^y + f_i^o)), ... > \\ \mathbf{p^o} & = & < ..., p_i^o (= f_i^o / (f_i^y + f_i^o)), ... > \end{array}$$

We might also define a sum of $\mathbf{p^y} + \mathbf{p^o}$:

$$\mathbf{p} \quad = \quad < ..., p_i (= (p_i^o + p_i^y) = 1), ... >$$

We do not actually use $\mathbf{p}$ below, only $\mathbf{p^y}$ and $\mathbf{p^o}$, but we mention it for the sake of the check it allows that $p_i^y + p_i^o = 1, \forall i$.

We then re-introduce the raw frequencies per category to obtain the normalized, redistributed counts $\mathbf{C_n^y}, \mathbf{C_n^o}$. Note that we use the total count of the trigram in both samples to redistribute (thus redistributing these counts based on the trigram totals in both samples):

$$\begin{array}{rcl} \mathbf{C_n^y} & = & < ..., p_i^y \cdot c_i, ... > \\ \mathbf{C_n^o} & = & < ..., p_i^o \cdot c_i, ... > \end{array}$$

Up to this point the normalization has corrected for differences in sentence length, or to be more precise, for differences in the numbers of $n$-grams which may appear as a result of permuting sentences. For larger numbers of trigrams the situation will become: $N^y = \sum_{i=1}^n c_i^y \approx \sum_{i=1}^n \mathbf{C_i^y}$ so that we have effectively neutralized the increase or decrease in the number of $n$-grams which might have arisen due to sentence length. Without this normalization a skew in sentence length in the base case would cause changed, in the worst case increased, and perhaps even extreme, significance. During random permutation, where longer sentences will tend to be distributed more evenly between the sub-corpora, a disproportionately larger number of $n$-grams would be found in the sub-corpus corresponding to the base corpus with shorter sentences. We have now normalized so that that effect will no longer appear.

We illustrate the normalizations up to this point in Table 1. We see already that the overall effect is to shift mass to the smaller sample. Notice also that if we were to define $\mathbf{C} = \mathbf{C^y} + \mathbf{C^o}$, then $\mathbf{C} = \mathbf{c}$, since $\mathbf{C^y}$ and $\mathbf{C^o}$ are a redistribution of $\mathbf{c}$ using $p^y$ and $p^o$, whose sum $p$ is 1 under all circumstances, as was noted above. At the same time $\mathbf{c^y} \neq \mathbf{C^y}$ and $\mathbf{c^o} \neq \mathbf{C^o}$ (if there were differences in sentence lengths). The values obtained at this point may be measured by the vector comparison measure (cosine or $R(sq)$).

We use this redistributing normalization instead of just the relative frequency because using relative frequency would cause trigrams occurring mainly and frequently in the short-sentence group to become extremely significant. This is especially

| | Group y | | Group o | | Group y' | | Group o' | |
|---|---|---|---|---|---|---|---|---|
| | T1 | T2 | T1 | T2 | T1 | T2 | T1 | T2 |
| counts **c** | **15** | **10** | 90 | 10 | 10 | 10 | 17 | 0 |
| rel. freq. **f** | 0.6 | 0.4 | 0.9 | 0.1 | 0.5 | 0.5 | 1 | 0 |
| norm. prop. **p** | 0.4 | 0.8 | 0.6 | 0.2 | 0.33 | 1 | 0.67 | 0 |
| trigram $\mathbf{c}_i$ | 105 | 20 | 105 | 20 | 27 | 10 | 27 | 10 |
| redistrib. **C** | 42 | 16 | 63 | 4 | 9 | 10 | 18 | 0 |

Table 1: Two examples of the normalizations applied before each measurement of vector difference. On the left groups $y$ and $o$ are compared on the basis of the two trigrams $T1$ and $T2$. The counts are shown in the first row, then relative frequencies (within the group), normalized relative proportions, and finally redistributed normalized counts. The two numbers in boldface in the 'count' line are compared to calculate the underlined relative frequency (on the left) in the 'relative frequency' line (in general counts are compared within groups to obtain relative frequencies). Next, the two underlined fractions of the 'relative frequency' row are compared to obtain the corresponding fractions (immediately below) of the 'normalized proportions' row. Thus relative frequencies are compared across groups (sub-corpora) to obtain the relative proportions. The trigram count row shows the counts per trigram type, and the 'redistributed' row is simply the product of the last two. The second example (on the right) demonstrates that missing data finds no compensation in this procedure (although we might experiment with smoothing in the future).

distorting if one calculates the per trigram type $p$-value ($R$ or $Rsq$ for a single $i$).

The normalization does not eliminate all the irrelevant effects of differing sentence lengths. To obtain further precision we iterate the steps above a few times, re-applying the normalization to its own output. We are motivated to iterate the procedure for the following reason. If a trigram is relatively more frequent in the smaller sub-corpus, it must then also be relatively less frequent within the entire corpus (less frequent within the two sub-corpora together), so there is less frequency mass to re-distribute for these trigrams than for trigrams that are relatively more frequent in the larger sub-corpus (those will be more frequent within the entire corpus). A special case of this are $n$-grams that occur only in one sub-corpus. If they occur only in the larger sub-corpus then their mass will never be re-distributed in the direction of the smaller sub-corpus, since zero-frequencies within one sub-corpus will always result in zero relative weight (in the current set-up).[2] This means that after normalization the larger sub-corpus will always still be a bit larger than the smaller one. After one normalization the effect of these factors is small, but we can reduce it yet further by iterating the normalization. This is worthwhile since we wish to be certain. After five iterations the relative size-difference between our normalized sub-corpora is less than $0.1\%$ for trigrams of the full ICE-tagset (and even a thousand times smaller for the reduced tagset). We regard this as small enough to effectively eliminate corpus size differences as potential problems.

For the purposes of interpretation we also scale everything down so that the average redistributed count is 1. We do this by dividing each $C_i^y, C_i^o$ by $N/2n$, where $N$ is the total count of all trigrams and $n$ is the number of trigram categories being counted. Note that $N/2n$ is the average count of a given trigram in one of the groups.

$$\mathbf{s^y} = \mathbf{c^y} \cdot 2n/N = < ..., C_i^y \cdot 2n/N, ... >$$
$$\mathbf{s^o} = \mathbf{c^o} \cdot 2n/N = < ..., C_i^o \cdot 2n/N, ... >$$

These values might just as well be submitted to the vector comparison measure since they are just linear transformations of the redistributed **C** values. The scaling expresses the trigram count as a value with respect to the total $2n$ of counts involved in the comparison, and, since $\sum_{i=1}^n c_i^y + \sum_{i=1}^n c_i^o = N$, $\sum_{i=1}^n s_i^y + \sum_{i=1}^n s_i^o = 2n$. As there are $n$ sorts of trigrams being compared in two groups, it is clear that the average value in these last vectors will be 1.

Similarly, this normalized value will be higher than 1 for trigrams that are more frequent than average. Now if we sort the trigrams by frequency—

[2] Alternatively, we might have explored a Good-Turing estimation of unseen items (Manning and Schütze, 1999, p. 212).

or more precisely, by the weight that they have within the total $R(sq)$ value, so by their per trigram $R(sq)$ value—we get a listing of the POS trigrams that distinguish the groups most sharply. This list can be made even more telling by adding the raw frequency and a per-trigram $p$-value. It allows us to directly see significant under and overuse of POS trigrams, and thereby of syntax.

### 3.3 Between-Permutations Normalization

The purpose of this normalization is the identification of $n$-gram types which are typical in the two original sub-corpora. It is applied after comparing all the results of all the Monte Carlo re-shufflings.

The BETWEEN-PERMUTATIONS NORMALIZATION is similar to the last step of the within-permutation normalization, except that the linear transformation is applied across permutations, instead of across groups (sub-corpora): for each POS trigram type $i$ in each group (sub-corpora) $g \in \{o, y\}$, the redistributed count $\mathbf{C_i^g}$ is divided by the average redistributed count for that type in that group (across all permutations)$\overline{\mathbf{C_i^g}}$. Note that the average redistributed count is $c_i/2$ for large numbers of permutations. The values thus normalized will be 1 on average across permutations.

Trigrams with large average counts between permutations are those with high frequencies in the original sub-corpora, and these contribute most heavily toward statistical significance. The normalization under discussion strips away the role of frequency, allowing us to see which POS trigrams are most (a)typical for a group. We note additionally that this normalization is useful only together with information on frequency (or statistical significance). Infrequent trigrams are especially likely to have high values with respect to $\overline{\mathbf{C_i^g}}$. For example a trigram occurring only once, in one sub-corpus, gets the maximum value of $1/0.5 = 2$ (as it is indeed very typical for this sub-corpus), while with a count of one it clearly cannot be statistically significant (moving between equally sized sub-corpora with a chance of 50 % during permutations). So it's best to calculate this normalization together with the per trigram $p$-values.

## 4 A Test Case

We tested this procedure on data transcribed from free interviews with Finnish emigrants to Australia. The emigrants were farmers and skilled or semi-skilled working class Finns who left Finland in the 1960's at the age of 25-40 years old, some with children. Greg Watson of Joensuu University interviewed these people between 1995 and 1998, publishing about his corpus in *ICAME* 20, 1996 (Watson). He included both interviews with those who emigrated as adults (at seventeen years or older) and those who emigrated as children (before their seventeenth birthday). There are sixty conversations with adult-age emigrants and thirty with those who emigrated as children, totaling 305,000 words of relatively free conversation.

It is well established in the literature on second-language learning that the language of people who learned the second language as children is superior to that of adult learners. We will test our idea about measuring syntactic differences by applying the measure to the two samples language from adult vs. child emigrants. The issue is not remarkable, but it allows us to verify whether the measure is functioning.

### 4.1 Results

The two sub-corpora had 221,000 words for the older group and 84,000 words for the younger group, respectively. The sentences of the childhood immigrants were indeed substantially longer (27.1 tokens) than those of the older immigrants (16.3 tokens). So the within-permutation normalization was definitely needed in this case. The groups clearly differed in the distribution of POS trigrams they contain ($p < 0.001$). This means that the difference between the original two sub-corpora was in the largest $0.1\%$ of the Monte Carlo permutations.

In addition we find genuinely deviant syntax patterns if we inspect the trigrams most responsible for the difference between the two sub-corpora.

| | | | | | |
|---|---|---|---|---|---|
| it | 's | low | tax | in | here |
| PRO | COP | ADJ | N/COM | PREP | ADV |
| and | I | was | professional | fisherman | |
| CONJ | PRO | COP | ADJ | N/COM | |

Both COP-ADJ-N/COM and N/COM-PREP-ADV accounted for a substantial degree of aggregate syntactic difference. The first pattern normally corresponds to an error, as it does in the two (!) examples of it above (there is a separate tag for plural and mass nouns). These are cases where English normally requires an article.

Since Finnish has no articles, these are clear cases of transfer, i.e., the (incorrect) imposition of the first language's structure on a second language. The N/COM-PREP-ADV pattern (corresponding to the use of *in here*) is also worth noting, as it falls into the class of expressions which is not absolutely in error (*The material is in here*), but it is clearly being overused in the example above. Presumably this is a case of hypercorrection from Finnish, a language without prepositions. We conclude from this experiment that the procedure is promising.

On the other hand there were also problems, perhaps most seriously with the use of the tags denoting pauses and hesitations, where we found that the tag trigrams most responsible for the deviant measures in the corpora involved disfluencies of one sort or another. These tended to occur more frequently in the speech of the older emigrants. With the pauses removed (hesitations still in place) a list of the ten most frequent, significant trigrams for the older group is shown. Two random examples from the corpus are given for each in Table 2.

We suspect additionally that the low accuracy rate of the tagger when applied to this material also stems from the large number of disfluencies.

| | | | |
|---|---|---|---|
| 1 | roadworks | and | uh |
| | hill | and | ah |
| | N | CONJUNC | INTERJEC |
| 2 | I | reckon | it |
| | that | take | lot |
| | PRON | V | PRON |
| 3 | enjoy | to | taking |
| | my | machine | break |
| | INTERJEC | PRON | V |
| 4 | but | that | 's |
| | that | I | clean |
| | CONJUNC | PRON | V |
| 5 | I | 'm | uh |
| | it | 's | uh |
| | PRON | V | INTERJEC |
| 6 | now | what | what |
| | changing | but | some |
| | CONJUNC | INTERJEC | PRON |
| 7 | said | it | 's |
| | all | everybody | has |
| | PRON | PRON | V |
| 8 | bought | that | car |
| | lead | glass | windows |
| | V | PRON | N |
| 9 | that | was | different |
| | I | was | fit |
| | PRON | V | ADJ |
| 10 | Oh | lake | lake |
| | uh | money | production |
| | INTERJEC | N | N |

Table 2: The most significant and most frequent trigrams that were typical for the speech of the group of older Finnish emigrants to Australia compared to the speech of those who emigrated before their 17th birthday. The tag trigrams indicating pauses were removed before comparing the corpora, as these appear to dominate the differences. The examples illustrating the trigrams were chosen at random, and we note that the examples of the third sort of trigram involved tagging errors in the first and second elements of the trigram, and that other errors are noticeable at the seventh and eight positions in the list (where 'said' and 'glass' are marked as pronouns). We reserve the linguistic interpretation of the error patterns for future work, but we note that we will also want to filter interjections before drawing definite conclusions.

## 5 Conclusions and Prospects

Weinreich (1953) regretted that there was no way to "measure or characterize the total impact one language on another in the speech of bilinguals," (p. 63) and speculated that there could not be. This paper has proposed a way of going beyond counts of individual phenomena to a measure of aggregate syntactic difference. The technique may be implemented effectively, and its results are subject to statistical analysis using permutation statistics.

The technique proposed follow Aarts and Granger (1998) in using part-of-speech trigrams. We argue that such lexical categories are likely to reflect a great deal of syntactic structure given the tenets of linguistic theory according to which more abstract structure is, in general, projected from lexical categories. We go beyond Aarts and Granger in Showing how entire histograms of POS trigrams may be used to characterize aggregate syntactic distance, in particular by showing how this can be analyzed.

We fall short of Weinreich's goal of assaying "total impact" in that we focus on syntax, but we take a large step in this direction by showing how to aggregate and test for significance, using the sorts of counts he worked with.

The software implementing the permutation test, including the normalizations, is available freely at `http://en.logilogi.org/HomE/WyboWiersma/FiAuImEnRe`. It is developed to allow easy generalization to more than two sub-corpora and longer $n$-grams.

Several further steps would be useful. We should like to repeat the analysis here, eliminating the effect of hesitation tags, etc. Second, we should like to experiment systematically with the inclusion of $n$-grams for $n > 3$; to-date we have experimented with this, but not systematically enough. Third, we would like to test the analysis on other cases of putative syntactic differences, and in particular in cases where tagging accuracy might be less an issue.

## Acknowledgments

We are grateful to Lisa Lena Opas-Hänninen, Pekka Hirvonen and Timo Lauttamus of the University of Oulu, who made the data available and consulted extensively on its analysis. We also thank audiences at the 2005 *TaBu Dag*, Groningen; at the Workshop *Finno-Ugric Languages in Contact with English II* held in conjunction with *Methods in Dialectology XII* at the *Université de Moncton*, Aug. 2005; the Sonderforschungsbereich 441, "Linguistic Data Structures", Tübingen in Jan. 2006; and the Seminar on Methodology and Statistics in Linguistic Research, University of Groningen, Spring, 2006, and especially Livi Ruffle, for useful comments and discussion. Finally, two referees for the 2006 ACL/COLING workshop on "Linguistic Distances" also commented usefully.

## References

Jan Aarts and Sylviane Granger. 1998. Tag sequences in learner corpora: A key to interlanguage grammar and discourse. In Sylviane Granger, editor, *Learner English on Computer*, pages 132–141. Longman, London.

Alan Agresti. 1996. *An Introduction to Categorical Data Analysis*. Wiley, New York.

Thorsten Brants. 2000. TnT — a statistical part of speech tagger. In *6th Applied Natural Language Processing Conference*, pages 224–231, Seattle. ACL.

Eugenio Coseriu. 1970. *Probleme der kontrastiven Grammatik*. Schwann, Düsseldorf.

Kees de Bot, Wander Lowie, and Marjolijn Verspoor. 2005. *Second Language Acquisition: An Advanced Resource Book*. Routledge, London.

Charles Fillmore and Paul Kay. 1999. Grammatical constructions and linguistic generalizations: the *what's x doing y* construction. *Language*, 75(1):1–33.

Roger Garside, Geoffrey Leech, and Tony McEmery. 1997. *Corpus Annotation: Linguistic Information from Computer Text Corpora*. Longman, London/New York.

Phillip Good. 1995. *Permutation Tests*. Springer, New York. 2nd, corr. ed.

1949. *The Principles of the International Phonetic Association*. International Phonetics Association, London, 1949.

Brett Kessler. 2001. *The Significance of Word Lists*. CSLI Press, Stanford.

Chris Manning and Hinrich Schütze. 1999. *Foundations of Statistical Natural Language Processing*. MIT Press, Cambridge.

Shana Poplack and David Sankoff. 1984. Borrowing: the synchrony of integration. *Linguistics*, 22:99–135.

Shana Poplack, David Sankoff, and Christopher Miller. 1988. The social correlates and linguistic processes of lexical borrowing and assimilation. *Linguistics*, 26:47–104.

William C. Ritchie and Tej K. Bhatia, editors. 1998. *Handbook of Child Language Acquisition*. Academic, San Diego.

Peter Sells. 1982. *Lectures on Contemporary Syntactic Theories*. CSLI, Stanford.

Sarah Thomason and Terrence Kaufmann. 1988. *Language Contact, Creolization, and Genetic Linguistics*. University of California Press, Berkeley.

Frans van Coetsem. 1988. *Loan Phonology and the Two Transfer Types in Language Contact*. Publications in Language Sciences. Foris Publications, Dordrecht.

Greg Watson. 1996. The Finnish-Australian English corpus. *ICAME Journal: Computers in English Linguistics*, 20:41–70.

Uriel Weinreich. 1953. *Languages in Contact*. Mouton, The Hague. (page numbers from 2nd ed. 1968).

# A Structural Similarity Measure

**Petr Homola** and **Vladislav Kuboň**
Institute of Formal and Applied Linguistics
Malostranské náměstí 25
110 00 Praha 1, Czech republic
{homola,vk}@ufal.mff.cuni.cz

## Abstract

This paper outlines a measure of language similarity based on structural similarity of surface syntactic dependency trees. Unlike the more traditional string-based measures, this measure tries to reflect "deeper" correspondences among languages. The development of this measure has been inspired by the experience from MT of syntactically similar languages. This experience shows that the lexical similarity is less important than syntactic similarity. This claim is supported by a number of examples illustrating the problems which may arise when a measure of language similarity relies too much on a simple similarity of texts in different languages.

## 1 Introduction

Although the similarity of natural languages is in principal a very vague notion, the linguistic literature seems to be full of claims classifying two natural languages as being more or less similar. These claims are in some cases a result of a detailed comparative examination of lexical and/or syntactic properties of languages under question, in some cases they are based on a very subjective opinion of the author, in many other cases they reflect the application of some mathematical formula on textual data (a very nice example of such mathematical approach can be found at (Scannell, 2004)).

Especially in the last case the notion of language similarity is very often confused with the notion of text similarity. Even the well known paper (Lebart and Rajman, 2000) deals more with the text similarity than language similarity. This general trend is quite understandable, the mathematical methods for measuring text similarity are of a prominent importance especially for information retrieval and similar fields. On the other hand, they concentrate too much on the surface similarity of word forms and thus may not reflect the similarity of languages properly. This paper tries to advocate different approach, based on the experience gained in MT experiments with closely related (and similar) languages, where it is possible to "measure" the similarity indirectly by a complexity of modules we have to use in order to achieve a reasonable translation quality. This experience led us to formulating an evaluation measure trying to capture not only textual, but also syntactic similarities between natural languages.

## 2 Imperfections of measures based on string similarity

There are many application areas in the NLP in which it is useful to apply the measures exploiting the similarity of word forms (strings). They serve very well for example for tasks like spellchecking (where the choice of the best candidates for correction of a spelling error is typically based upon the Levenshtein metrics) or estimating the similarity of a new source sentence to those stored in the translation memory of a Machine Aided Translation system. They are a bit controversial in a "proper" machine translation, where the popular BLEU score (Papineni et al., 2002), although widely accepted as a measure of translation accuracy, seems to favor stochastic approaches based on



*Proceedings of the Workshop on Linguistic Distances*, pages 91–99,
Sydney, July 2006. 

an n-gram model over other MT methods (see the results in (Nist, 2001)).

The controversies the BLEU score seems to provoke arise due to the fact that the evaluation of MT systems can be, in general, performed from two different viewpoints. The first one is that of a developer of such a system, who needs to get a reliable feedback in the process of development and debugging of the system. The primary interest of such a person is the grammar or dictionary coverage and system performance and he needs a cheap, fast and simple evaluation method in order to allow frequent routine tests indicating the improvements of the system during the development of the system.

The second viewpoint is that of a user, who is primarily concerned with the capability of the system to provide fast and reliable translation requiring as few post-editing efforts as possible. The simplicity, speed and low costs are not of such importance here. If the evaluation is performed only once, in the moment when the system is considered to be ready, the evaluation method may even be relatively complicated, expensive and slow. A good example of such a complex measure is the FEMTI framework (Framework for the Evaluation of Machine Translation). The most complete description of the FEMTI framework can be found in (Hovy et al., 2002). Such measures are much more popular among translators than among language engineers and MT systems developers.

If we aim at measuring the similarity of languages or language distances, our point of view should be much more similar to that of a human translator than of a system developer, if we'll stick to our MT analogy. When looking for clues concerning the desirable properties of a language similarity (or distance) measure, we can first try to formulate the reasons why we consider the simple string-based (or word-form-based) measures inadequate.

If we take into account a number of languages existing in the world, the number of word forms existing in each of those languages and a simple fact that a huge percentage of those word forms is not longer than five or six characters, it is quite clear that there is a huge number of overlapping word forms which have completely different meaning in all languages containing that particular word form. Let us take for illustration some language pairs of non-related languages.

For example for Czech and English (the languages very different with regard both to the lexicon and syntax) we can find several examples of overlapping word forms. The English word *house* means a *duckling* in Czech, the English indefinite article *a* is in Czech also very frequent, because it represents a coordinating conjunction *and*, while *an* is an archaic form of a pronoun in Czech. On the other hand, if we look at the identical (or nearly identical) word forms in similar languages, we can find many examples of totally different meaning. For example, the word form *život* means *life* in Czech and *belly* in Russian; *godina* means *year* in Serbo-Croatian while *hodina* is an hour in Czech (by the way, an hour in Russian is *čas* — and the same word means *time* in Czech).

The overlapping word forms between relatively distant languages are so frequent that it is even possible to create (more or less) syntactically correct sentences in one language containing only word forms from the other language. Again, let us look at the Czech-English language pair. The English sentences *Let my pal to pile a lumpy paste on a metal pan.* or *I had to let a house to a nosy patron.* consist entirely of word forms existing also in Czech, while the Czech sentence *Adept demise metal hole pod led.* — [A resignation candidate was throwing sticks under the ice.] consists of English word forms.

Creating such a Czech sentence is more complicated — as a highly inflected language it uses a wide variety of endings, which make it more difficult to create a syntactically correct sentence from word forms of a language which has incomparably smaller repertoire of endings. This fact directly leads to another argument against the string similarity based measures — even though two languages may have very similar syntactic properties and their basic word forms may also be very similar, then if the languages are highly inflective and the only difference between those languages are different endings used for expressing identical morphosyntactic properties, the string similarity based methods will probably show a substantial difference between these languages.

This is highly probable especially for shorter words — the words with a basic form only four or five characters long may have endings longer or equal to the length of the basic form, for example: ***nov**á*/***nov**ata* "new" (Cze/Mac), ***vid**ěný*/***vid**imyj* "seen" (Cze/Rus), ***fotograf**ující*/***fotograf**uojantysis* "photographing" (Cze/Lit).

The last but not least indirect argument against the use of string-based metrics can be found in (Kuboň and Bémová, 1990). The paper describes so called transducing dictionary, a set of rules designed for a direct transcription of a certain category of source language words into a target language. The system has been tested on two language pairs (English-to-Czech and Czech-to-Russian) and although there was a natural original assumption that such a system will cover substantially more expressions when applied to a pair of related languages (which are not only related, but also quite similar), this assumption turned to be wrong. The system covered almost identical set of words for both language pairs — namely the words with Greek or Latin origin. The similarity of coverage even allowed to build an English-to-Russian transducing dictionary using Czech as a pivot language with a negligible loss of the coverage.

## 3 Experience from MT of similar languages

The Machine Translation field is a good testing ground for any theory concerning the similarity of natural languages. The systems dealing with related languages usually achieve higher translation quality than the systems aiming at the translation of more distant language pairs — the average MT quality for a given system and a given language pair might therefore also serve as some kind of a very rough metrics of similarity of languages concerned.

Let us demonstrate this idea using an example of a multilingual MT system described in several recently published papers (see e.g. (Hajič et al., 2003) or (Homola and Kuboň, 2004)). The system aims at the translation from a single source language (Czech) into multiple more or less similar target languages, namely into Slovak, Polish, Lithuanian, Lower Sorbian and Macedonian.

The system is very simple — it doesn't contain any full-fledged parser, neither rule based, nor stochastic one. It relies on the syntactic similarity of the source and target languages. It is transfer-based with the transfer being performed as soon as possible, depending on the similarity of both languages. In its simplest form (Czech to Slovak translation) the system consists of the following modules:

1. Morphological analysis of the source language (Czech)

2. Morphological disambiguation of the source language text by means of a stochastic tagger

3. Transfer exploiting the domain-related bilingual glossaries and a general (domain independent) bilingual dictionary

4. Morphological synthesis of the target language

The lower degree of similarity between Czech and the remaining target languages led to an inclusion of a shallow parsing module for Czech for some of the language pairs. This module directly follows the morphological disambiguation of Czech.

The evaluation results presented in (Homola and Kuboň, 2004) indicate that even though Czech and Lithuanian are much less similar at the lexical and morphological level (e.g. at both levels actually dealing with strings), the translation quality is very similar due to the syntactic similarity between all languages concerned.

## 4 Typology of language similarity

The experience from the field of MT of closely related languages presented in the previus sections shows that it is very useful to classify the language similarity into several categories:

- typological
- morphological
- syntactic
- lexical

Let us now look at these categories from the point of view of machine translation,

## 4.1 Typological similarity

The first type of similarity is probably the most important one. If both the target and the source language are of a different language type, it is more difficult to obtain good MT quality. The notions like word order, the existence or non-existence of articles, different temporal system and several other properties have direct consequences for the translation quality. Let us take Czech and Lithuanian as an example of the language pair, which doesn't belong to the same group of languages (Czech is a Slavic and Lithuanian Baltic language). Both languages have rich inflection and very high degree of word order freedom, thus it is not necessary to change the word order at the constituent level. On the other hand, both languages differ a lot in the lexics and morphology.

For example, both (1) and (3) mean approximately "*The father read a/the book*". What these sentences differ in is the information structure. (1) should be translated as "*The father read a book*", whereas (3) means in fact "*The book has been read by the father*".[1] The category of voice differs in both sentences because of strict word order in English, although in both Czech equivalents, active voice is used.[2] We see that in the Lithuanian translation, the word order is exactly the same.

(1) *Otec* *četl* *knihu*
father-NOM read-3SG,PAST book-ACC
"The father read a book." (Cze)

(2) *Tėvas* *skaitė* *knygą*
father-NOM read-3SG,PAST book-ACC
"The father read a book." (Lit)

(3) *Knihu* *četl* *otec*
book-ACC read-3SG,PAST father-NOM
"The father read a book." (Cze)

(4) *Knygą* *skaitė* *tėvas*
book-ACC read-3SG,PAST father-NOM
"The father read a book." (Lit)

## 4.2 Lexical similarity

The lexical similarity does not mean that the vocabulary has to have the same origin, i.e., that words have to be created from the same (proto-)stem. What is important for shallow MT (and for MT in general), is the semantic correspondence (preferably one-to-one relation).

Lexical similarity is the least important one from the point of view of MT, because the lexical differences are solved in the glossaries and general dictionaries.

## 4.3 Syntactic similarity

Syntactic similarity is also very important especially on higher levels, in particular on the verbal level. The differences in verbal valences have negative influence on the quality of translation due to the fact that the transfer thus requires a large scale valence lexicon for both languages, which is extremely difficult to build. Syntactic structure of smaller constituents, such as nominal and prepositional phrases, is not that important, because it is possible to analyze those constituents syntactically using a shallow syntactic analysis and thus it is possible to adapt locally the syntactic structure of a target sentence.

## 4.4 Morphological similarity

Morphological similarity means similar structure of morphological hierarchy and paradigms such as case system, verbal system etc. In our understanding Baltic and Slavic languages (except for Bulgarian and Macedonian) have a similar case system and their verbal system is quite similar as well. Some problems are caused by synthetic forms, which have to be expressed by analytical constructions in other languages (e.g., future tense or conjunctive in Czech and Lithuanian). The differences in morphology can be relatively easily overcomed by the exploitation of full-fledged morphology of both languages (source and target).

Similar morphological systems simplify the transfer. For example, Slavonic languages (except of Bulgarian and Macedonian) have 6-7

[1] Note that in the first sentence, an indefinite article is used, whereas in the latter one, a definite article stands in front of "book". The reason is that in the first sentence, the noun "book" is not contextually bound (it belongs to the focus), in the latter one it belongs to the topic.

[2] Passive voice (except of the reflexive one) occurs rarely in Czech (and most other Slavonic languages). It can be used if one would like to underline the direct object or if there is no subject at all (for example, *Kniha byla čtena* "The book has been read").

cases. The case system of East Baltic languages is very similar, although it has been reduced formally in Latvian (instrumental forms are equal as dative and accusative and the function of instrumentral is expressed by the preposition *ar* "with", similarly as in Upper Sorbian). (Ambrazas, 1996) gives seven cases for Lithuanian, but there are in fact at least eight cases in Lithuanian (or ten cases but only eight of them are productive[3]). Nevertheless the case systems of Slavonic and East Baltic languages are very similar which makes the languages quite similar even across the border of different language groups.

Significant differences occur only in the verbal system, East Baltic languages have a huge amount of participles and half-participles that have no direct counterpart in Czech. The Lithuanian translation of an example from (Gamut, 1991) is given in (5):

(5) *Gimė* *vaikas,*
was-born-3SG child-NOM
*valdysiantis* *pasaulį*
ruling-FUT,MASC,SG,NOM world-ACC
"A child was born which will rule the world." (Lit)

The participle *valdysiantis* is used instead of an embedded sentence, because Lithuanian has future participles. These participles have to be expresses by an embedded sentence in Slavonic languages.

## 5 An outline of a structural similarity measure

In this section, we propose a comparatively simple measure of syntactic (structural) similarity. There are generally two levels which may serve as a basis for such a structural measure, the surface or deep syntactic level. Let us first explain the reasons supporting our choice of surface syntactic level.

Compared to deep syntactic representation, the surface syntactic trees are much more closely related to the actual surface form of a sentence. It is quite common that every word form or punctuation sign is directly related to a single node of a surface syntactic tree. The deep syntactic trees, on the other hand, usually represent autosemantic words only, they may even actually contain more nodes than there are words in the input sentence (for example, when the input sentence contains ellipsis). It is also quite clear that the deep syntactic trees are much more closely related to the meaning of the sentence than its original surface form, therefore they may hide certain differences between the languages concerned, it is a generally accepted hypothesis that transfer performed on the deep syntactic level is easier than the transfer at the surface syntactic level, especially for syntactically and typologically less similar languages.

The second important decision we had to make was to select the best type of surface syntactic trees between the dependency and phrase structure trees. For practical reasons we have decided to use dependency trees. The main motivation for this decision is the enormous structural ambiguity of phrase structure trees that represent sentences with identical surface form. Let us have a look at the following Polish sentence:

(6) *Paweł* *czyta*
Paweł-NOM read-3SG
*książkę*
book-FEM,SG,ACC
"Paweł is reading a/the book."

The syntactic structure of this sentence can be expressed by two phrase structure trees representing different order of attaching nominal phrases to a verb.[4]

[3]Although some Balticists argue that illative forms are adverbs, it is a fact that this case is productive and used quite often (Erika Rimkutė, personal communication), though it has been widely replaced by prepositional phrases. Allative and adessive are used only in some Lithuanian dialects, except of a few fixed allative forms (e.g., *vakarop(i)* "in the evening", *velniop(i)* "to the hell".)

[4]The full line denotes the head of the phrase, the dotted line a dependent.

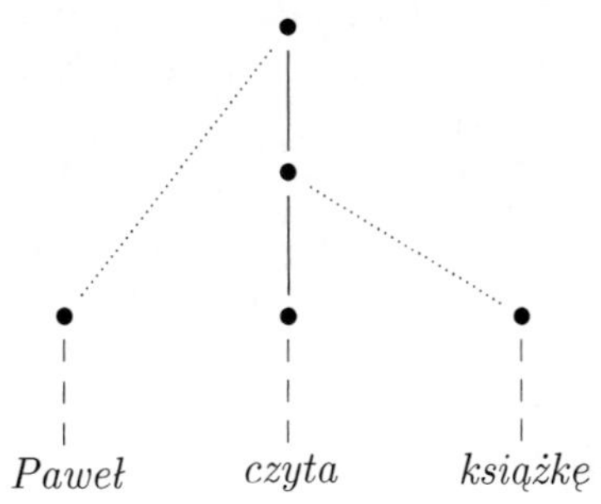


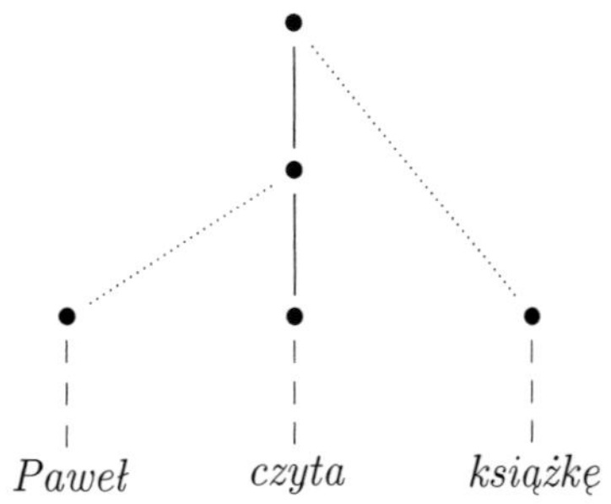


There is no linguistically relevant difference between these two trees. Although generally useful, the information hidden in both trees is purely superfluous for our goal of designing a simple structural metrics. The dependency tree obtained from the phrase structure ones by contraction of all head edges seem to be much more appropriate for our purpose. In our example, we therefore get the following form of the dependency tree:

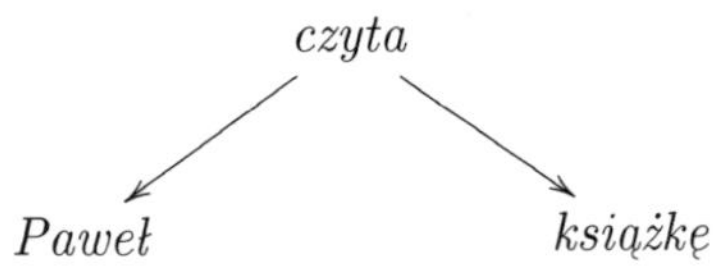


The nodes of the dependency trees representing surface syntactic level directly correspond to word forms present in the sentence. For the sake of simplicity, the punctuation marks are not represented in our trees. They would probably cause a lot of technical problems and might distort the whole similarity measure. The node of a tree are ordered and reflect the surface word-order of the sentence. Different labels of nodes in both languages (see the example below) don't influence the value of the measure, however they are important for the identification of corresponding nodes (a bilingual dictionary is used here).

The structural measure we are suggesting is based on the analogy to the Levenshtein measure. It is therefore pretty simple — the distance of two trees is the minimal amount of elementary operations that transform one tree to the other. We consider the following elementary operations:

1. adding a node,
2. removing a node,
3. changing the order of a node,
4. changing the father of a node.

The similarity of languages can be obtained as an average distance of individual sentences in a parallel corpus.

The following examples show the use of the measure on individual trees. The correspondence between individual nodes of both trees can be handled by exploiting the bilingual dictionary wherever necessary:

(7) *Vesna* *je*
Vesna-NOM is-3SG
*prišla*
come-RESPART,FEM,SG
"Vesna has come." (Slo)

(8) *Vesna* *przyszła*
Vesna-NOM come-RESPART,FEM,SG
"Vesna has come." (Pol)

The distance between (7) and (8) is equal 1, since one node has been removed (the dotted line gives the removed node).

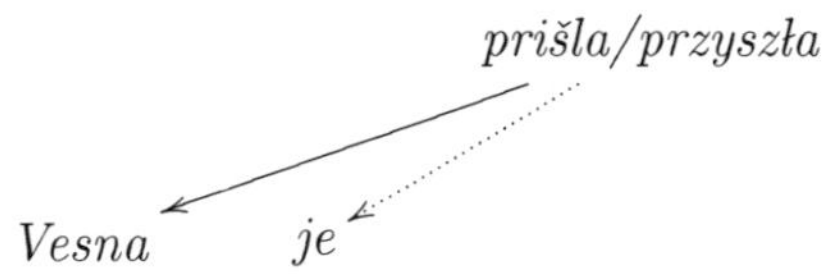


(9) *Grem* *z* *avtom*
go-1SG with car-MASC,SG,INS
"I am going by car." (Slo)

(10) *Jadę* *samochodem*
go-1SG car-MASC,SG,INS
"I am going by car." (Pol)

The distance between (9) and (10) is equal 1, since one node has been removed (the dotted line gives the removed node).

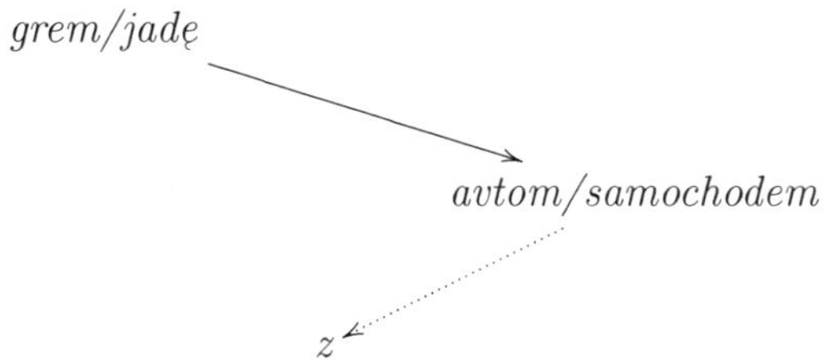


### 5.1 Formalization

(11) *On* *rád* *plave*
he-NOM with-pleasure swims-3SG
"He likes swimming." (Cze)

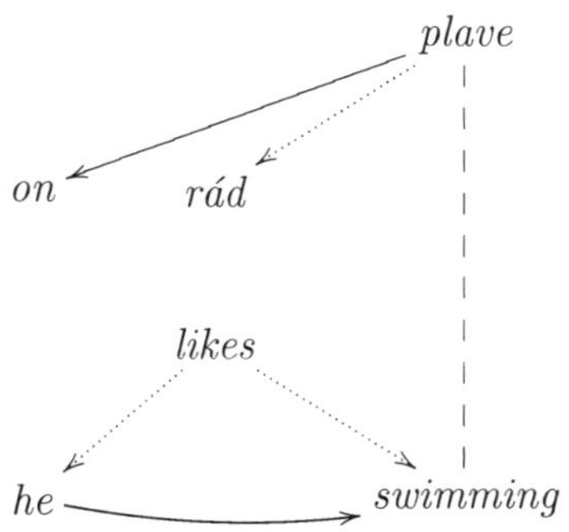


The Czech-English example (11) shows two sentences which have a mutual distance equal to 3 — if we start changing the Czech tree into an English one, then the first elementary operation is the deletion of the node *rád*, the second operation adds the new node corresponding to the English word *likes* and the third and last operation is the change of the father of the node corresponding to the personal pronoun *on* [he] from *swimming* to *likes*. As mentioned above, the node labels are not taken into account, the fact that the Czech finite verbal form *plave* changes into an English gerund has no effect on the distance.

A similar case are sentences with a dative agent, for example:

(12) *Je* *mi* *zima*
is me-DAT cold-F,SG,NOM
"I am cold" (Cze)

In this sentence, the Czech *mi* does not match to *I* since it is no subject. Similarly, the substantive *zima* does not match to *cold*, since it is a different part of speech. Hence two nodes are removed and two new nodes are added, which gives us a distance of 4. This example demonstrates that the measure tends to behave naturally - even short sentences containing syntactically different constructions get a relatively high score.

To formalize the process described above, let us introduce a notion of lexical and analytical equality of nodes in analytical trees:

- Two nodes equal lexically if and only if they share the same meaning in the given context. Nevertheless to simplify automatic processing, we treat two nodes as lexically equal if they share a particular meaning (defined e.g. as a non-empty intersection of Wordnet classes).

- Two nodes equal analytically if and only if they have the same analytical label (e.g. subject, spacial adverbial etc.).

As for the measure, two nodes match to each other if they 1) occur at the same position in the subtree of their parent and 2) equal lexically and analytically.

If a subtree (greater than 1) is added or removed, the operation contributes to the measure with the size of the subtree (the amount of its nodes), for example in the following idiomatic phrase:

(13) *puścić* *z* *dymem*
leave-INF with smoke-MASC,SG,INS
"burn down" (Pol)

(14) *zapálit*
burn-down-INF
"burn down" (Cze)

In the above example, the distance is equal 2.

The automatic procedure can be described as follows (given two trees):

1. Align all sons of the root node.

2. Count discrepancies.

3. For all matched nodes, go to step 1 to process subtrees and sum up distances.

### 5.2 Discussion

It is obvious that our measure expresses the typological similarity of languages. We get comparatively high values even for genetically related languages if their typology is different. Let us demonstrate this fact on Czech and Macedonian examples.

(15) *Ivan* *dal*
Ivan-NOM gave-RESPART,MASC,SG
*knihu* *Stojanovi*
book-FEM.SG,ACC Stojan-DAT
"Ivan gave the book to Stojan." (Cze)

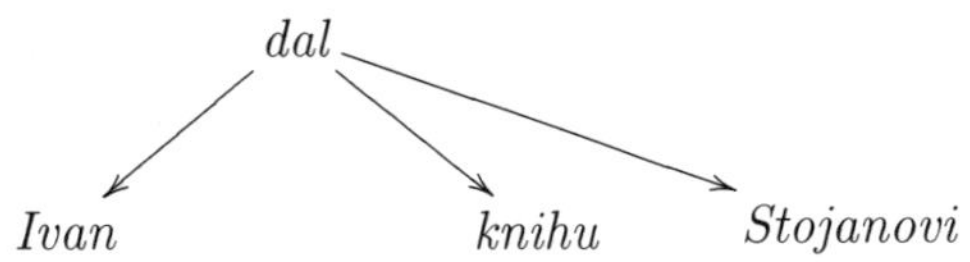


(16) *Ivan* *mu* *ja*
Ivan-NOM him her-FEM,SG,ACC
*ima* *dadeno*
has-3SG given-PPART,NEUT,SG
*knigata* *na* *Stojan*
book-FEM.SG,DEF on Stojan
"Ivan gave the book to Stojan." (Mac)

The distance equals 5. The score is relatively high, taken into account that both languages are related. It indicates again that for a given purpose the measure seems to provide consistent results.

The proposed measure takes into account only the structure of the trees, completely ignoring node and edge labels. Let us analyze the following example:

(17) *Ta* *książka*
this-FEM,SG,NOM book-FEM.SG,NOM
*się* *często* *czyta*
REFL well read-3SG
"This book is read often."

(18) *Tę* *książkę*
this-FEM,SG,ACC book-FEM.SG,ACC
*się* *często* *czyta*
REFL well read-3SG
"This book is read often."

The syntactic trees of both sentences have the same structure, but (17) is passive and (18) active (with a general subject). This is of course a significant difference and as such it should be captured in the measure, nevertheless our simple measure doesn't reflect it. There are several reasons why a current version of the measure doesn't include morphological and morphosyntactic labels. One of the reasons is a different nature of the problem — to design a reliable measure combining structural information with the information contained in node labels is very difficult. From the technical point of view, a great obstacle is also the variety of systems of tags used for this purpose for individual languages, which may not be compatible. For example, Macedonian has almost no cases at nouns, therefore it would make no sense to use cases in the noun annotation, while for other Slavic languages (and not only for Slavic ones) is this information very important. To find a good integration of morphosyntactic features into the structural measure is definitely a very interesting topic for future research.

## 6 Conclusions

This paper contains an outline of a simple language similarity measure based upon the surface syntactic dependency trees. According to our opinion, such a measure expresses more adequately the similarity of languages than simple string-based measures used for the text similarity. The measure is defined on pairs of trees from a parallel corpus. In its current form it doesn't account for differences in morphosyntactic labels of corresponding nodes or edges, although it is an important parameter of language similarity. The proper combination of our basic structural similarity measure with some measure reflecting the differences of labels opens a wide range of options for a future research. Equally important seems to be a task of gathering properly syntactically annotated parallel corpora of a reasonable size. The only corpus of such kind which we have at our disposal, the Prague Czech-English Dependency Treebank (Cuřín et al., 2004) relies on imperfect automatic annotation which might distort the results. The human annotation of the PCEDT is just starting, so there's a

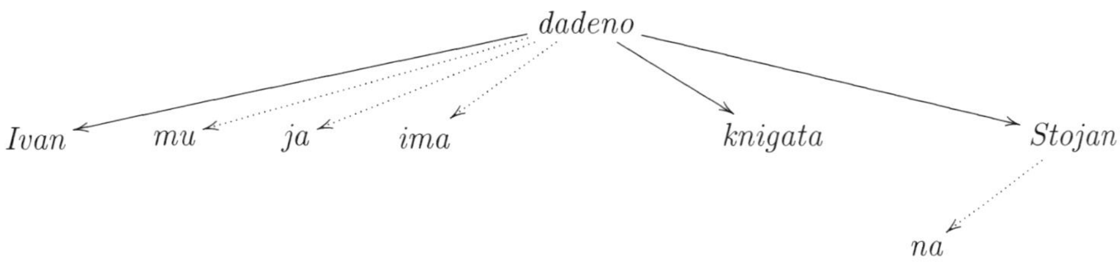


Figure 1: The dependency tree of (16)

good chance that the measure will bring some reliable results at least for those two lenguages soon.

## 7 Acknowledgements

This research was supported by the Ministry of Education of the Czech Republic, project MSM0021620838, by the grant No. GAUK 351/2005 and by the grant No. 1ET100300517. We would like to thank the anonymous reviewers for their valuable comments and recommendations.

## References

Vytautas Ambrazas. 1996. *Dabartinės lietuvių kalbos gramatika.* Mokslo ir enciklopedijų leidykla, Vilnius.

Jan Cuřín, Martin Čmejrek, Jiří Havelka, Jan Hajič, Vladislav Kuboň, and Zdeněk Žabokrtský. 2004. Prague Czech-English Dependency Treebank Version 1.0. Linguistic Data Consortium.

LTF Gamut. 1991. *Login, loanguage and meaning 2: Intensional logic and logical grammar.* University of Chicago Press, Chicago.

Jan Hajič, Petr Homola, and Vladislav Kuboň. 2003. A simple multilinguale machine translation system. In *Proceedings of the MT Summit IX*, New Orleans.

Petr Homola and Vladislav Kuboň. 2004. A translation model for languages of accessing countries. In *Proceedings of the 9th EAMT Workshop*, La Valetta, Malta.

Eduard Hovy, Margaret King, and Andrei Popescu-Beli. 2002. Principles of Context-Based Machine Translation Evaluation. *Machine Translation*, 1(17).

Vladislav Kuboň and Alevtina Bémová. 1990. Czech-to-Russian Transducing Dictionary. In *Proceedings of the XIIIth conference COLING '90*, volume 3.

Ludovic Lebart and Martin Rajman, 2000. *Handbook of Natural Language Processing*, chapter Computing similarity. Dekker, New York.

Nist. 2001. Automatic evaluation of machine translation quality using n-gram co-occurrence statistics. Technical report, NIST.

Kishore Papineni, Salim Roukos, Todd Ward, and Wei-Jing Zhu. 2002. BLEU: a Method for Automatic Evaluation of Machine Translation. In *Proceedings of the 40th Annual Meeting of the Association for Computational Linguistics*, Philadelphia.

Kevin P. Scannell. 2004. Corpus building for minority languages. http://borel.slu.edu/crubadan/index.html.

# Variants of tree similarity in a Question Answering task

**Martin Emms**
Dept of Computer Science
Trinity College
Ireland

## Abstract

The results of experiments on the application of a variety of distance measures to a question-answering task are reported. Variants of tree-distance are considered, including whole-vs-sub tree, node weighting, wild cards and lexical emphasis. We derive string-distance as a special case of tree-distance and show that a particular parameterisation of tree-distance outperforms the string-distance measure.

## 1 Introduction

This paper studies the deployment in a question answering task of methods which assess the similarity of question and answer representations. Given questions such as

Q1 *what does malloc return ?*
Q2 *What year did poet Emily Dickinson die?*

and a collection of sentences (eg. a computer manual, a corpus of newspaper articles), the task is to retrieve the sentences that answer the question, eg.

A1 *the malloc function returns a null pointer*
A2 *In 1886 , poet Emily Dickinson died in Amherst , Mass*

One philosophy for finding answers to questions would be to convert questions and candidate answers into logical forms and to compute answerhood by apply theorem-proving methods. Another philosophy is to assume that the answers are *similar* to the questions, where similarity might be defined in many different ways. While not all answers to all questions will be similar, there's an intuition that most questions can be answered in a way which shares quite a bit with the question, and that accordingly with a large enough corpus, a similarity-based approach could be fruitful.

## 2 Distance Measures

In pursuing such a similarity-based approach to question-answering, the key decisions to be made are the representations of the questions and answers, and relatedly, distance measures between them.

We will primarily be concerned with measures which refer to a linguistic structure assigned to a word sequence – variants of *tree-distance*, but we will also consider *string-distance*.

### 2.1 Tree Measures

Following (Zhang and Shasha, 1989), one can arrive at *tree-distance* in the following way. Given source and target ordered, labelled trees, $S$ and $T$, consider the set $\mathcal{H}(S,T)$ of all 1-to-1 *partial* maps, $\sigma$, from $S$ into $T$, which are *homomorphisms* preserving left-to-right order and ancestry[1]. Let the *alignment*, $\sigma'$, be the enlargment of the map $\sigma$ with pairs $(S_i, \lambda)$ for nodes $S_i \notin dom(\sigma)$ and $(\lambda, T_j)$ for nodes $T_j \notin ran(\sigma)$. Let $\mathcal{D}$ define *deletion* costs for the $(S_i, \lambda)$, $\mathcal{I}$ *insertion* costs for the $(\lambda, T_j)$, and $\mathcal{R}$ *replacement* costs for the $(S_i, T_j)$ which represent nodes with non-identical labels. Then a total cost for the alignment, $\mathcal{C}(\sigma')$ can be defined as the sum of these components costs, and the **tree distance** can then be defined as the cost of the least-cost map:

$$\Delta(S,T) = min(\{\mathcal{C}(\sigma') \mid \sigma \in \mathcal{H}(S,T)\})$$

For any 3 trees, $T^1, T^2, T^3$, the triangle inequality holds $\Delta(T^1,T^3) \leq \Delta(T^1,T^2) + \Delta(T^2,T^3)$.

[1]If $T_{j_1} = \sigma(S_{i_1})$ and $T_{j_2} = \sigma(S_{i_2})$ then (i) $S_{i_1}$ is to the left of $S_{i_2}$ iff $T_{j_1}$ is to the left of $T_{j_2}$ and (ii) $S_{i_1}$ is a descendant of $S_{i_2}$ iff $T_{j_1}$ is a descendant of $T_{j_2}$, with descendency understood as the transitive closure of the daugher-mother relation.



*Proceedings of the Workshop on Linguistic Distances*, pages 100–108,

Briefly the argument is as follows. Given mappings $\sigma \in \mathcal{H}(T^1, T^2)$, and $\tau \in \mathcal{H}(T^2, T^3)$, $\sigma \circ \tau \in \mathcal{H}(T^1, T^3)$[2], so $(\sigma \circ \tau)'$ is an alignment between $T^1$ and $T^3$, and $\Delta(T^1, T^3) \leq \mathcal{C}((\sigma \circ \tau)')$. The cost of the composition is less than the sum of the costs of the composed maps: $\sigma$'s insertions and replacements contribute only if they fall in $dom(\tau)$, $\tau$'s deletions and replacements contribute only if they act on $ran(\sigma)$.

From this basic definition, one can depart in a number of directions. First of all, there is a **part-vs-whole** dimension of variation. Where $\Delta(S, T)$ gives the cost of aligning the *whole* source tree $S$ with the target $T$, one can consider variants where one minimises over a set of *sub-parts* of $S$. This is equivalent to letting all but the nodes belonging to the chosen sub-part to delete at zero cost[3]. Let $\delta(S, T)$ be the **sub-tree** distance. Let $\vec{\delta}(S, T)$, be the **sub-traversal** distance, in which sub-traversals of the left-to-right, post-order traversal of $S$ are considered. As for $\Delta$, the triangle inequality holds for $\delta$ and $\vec{\delta}$ – one needs to extend the notion of alignment with a set of free deletions. Unlike $\Delta$, $\delta$ and $\vec{\delta}$ are not symmetric.

All of $\Delta$, $\delta$ and $\vec{\delta}$ are implicitly parametrised by the cost functions, $\mathcal{D}$, $\mathcal{I}$ and $\mathcal{R}$. In the work below 4 other parameters are explored

**Node weighting** $\mathcal{W}$: this is a function which assigns a real-number weight to each each node. The cost function then refers to the weights. In experiments reported below, $\mathcal{D}_w((S_i, w), \lambda) = w$, $\mathcal{I}_w(\lambda, (T_j, w)) = w$, $\mathcal{R}_w((S_i, w_s), (T_j, w_t)) = max(w_s, w_t)$, if $S_i$ and $T_j$ have unequal labels. The experiments reported below use 2 weighting function $\mathcal{STR}$, and $\mathcal{LEX}$. $\mathcal{STR}$ assign weights according to the syntactic structure, via a classification of nodes as heads vs. complements vs. adjuncts vs. the rest, with essentially adjuncts given 1/5th the weights of heads and complements, and other daughters 1/2, via essentially the following top-down algorithm:

$Str(node, rank)$ :
*assign weight* $1/rank$ *to node*
*for each daughter* $d$
*if (d is head or complement)* {
*assign weight* = $1/rank$,
$Str(rank, d)$ }
*else if (d is adjunct)* {
*assign weight* = $1/(5 \times rank)$,
$Str(5 * rank, d)$ }
*else* {
*assign weight* = $1/(2 \times rank)$
$Str(2 * rank, d)$ }

$\mathcal{LEX}$ is a function which can be composed with $\mathcal{STR}$, and scales up the weights of leaf nodes by a factor of 3.

**Target wild cards** $T(*)$: this is a function which classifies certain target sub-trees as *wild-card*. If source $S_i$ is mapped to target $T_j$, and $T_j$ is the root of a wild-card tree, all nodes within the $S_i$ sub-tree can be deleted for 0 cost, and all those within the $T_j$ sub-tree can be inserted for 0 cost. A wild card $np$ tree might can be put in the position of the gap in wh-questions, allowing for example *what is memory allocation*, to closely match any sentences with *memory allocation* as their object, no matter what their subject – see Figure 3.

**Source self-effacers** $S/\lambda$: this is a function which classifies source sub-trees as *self-effacers*. Such trees can be deleted in their entirety for zero cost. If $S/\lambda$ classifies *all* source sub-trees as self-effacing, then $\Delta(S/\lambda)$ will coincide with notion of 'tree-distance with Cut' given in (Zhang and Shasha, 1989).

**Target self-inserters** $\lambda/T$: this is a function which classifies certain target sub-trees as self-inserters. Such trees can be inserted in their entirety for zero cost. A candidate might be optional adjuncts.[4]

## 2.2 Sequence Measures

The tree-distance measures work with an elaboration of the original questions and answers. (Levenshtein, 1966) defined the 1 dimensional precursor of tree distance, which works directly on the 2 word sequences for the answer and question. For two sequences, $s$, $t$, and vertical (or horizontal) tree encodings $l\_tree(s)$ and $l\_tree(t)$, if

[2] $\forall x \in T_1 \forall z \in T_3((x, z) \in \sigma \circ \tau$ iff $\exists y \in T_2((x, y) \in \sigma, (y, z) \in \tau)$

[3] Note that if one minimises also over sub-parts of the target, you do not get an interesting notion, as the minimum will inevitably involve at most one node of source and target.

[4] Thus a target wild-card is somewhat like a target self-effacer, but one which also licenses the classification of a matched source sub-tree as a being self-effacer.

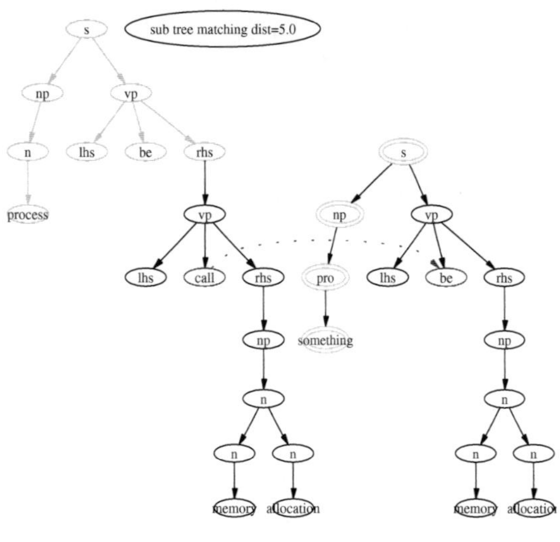


Figure 1: Sub tree example

we define $\Pi(s,t)$, as $\Delta(l\_tree(s), l\_tree(t))$, and $\pi(s,t)$, as $\vec{\delta}(l\_tree(s), l\_tree(t))$, then $\Pi$ and $\pi$ coincide with the standard **sequence edit distance** and **sub-sequence edit distance**. As special cases of $\Delta$ and $\delta$, $\Pi$ and $\pi$ inherit the triangle inequality property.

To illustrate some of the tree-distance definitions, in the following example, a $\Delta$ distance of 3 between 2 trees is obtained, assuming unit costs for deletions (shown in red and double outline), insertions (shown in green and double outline), and substitutions (shown in blue and linked with an arrow):

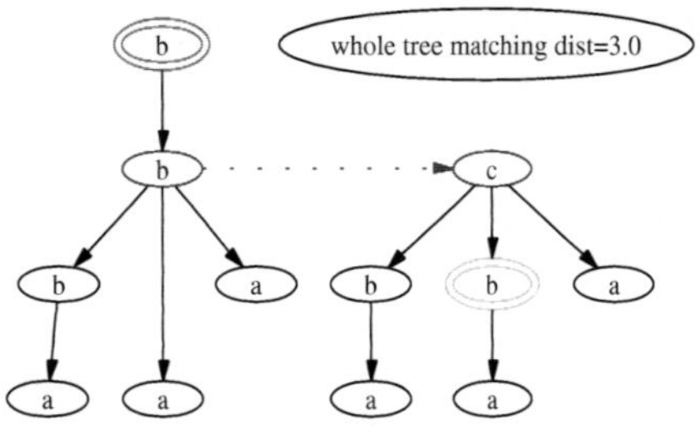


Note also in this picture that nodes that are mapped without a relabelling are shown at the same horizontal level, with no linking arrow.

Figure 1 shows a sub-tree example – $\delta$. The source tree nodes which do not belong to the chosen sub-tree are shown in grey. The lowest vp subtree in the source is selected, and mapped to the vp in the target. The remaining target nodes must be inserted, but this costs less than a match which starts higher and necessitates some deletions and substitutions.

Figure 2 shows a sub-tree example where the structural weighting $\mathcal{STR}$ has been used: size of a node reflects the weight. 4 of the nodes in the source represent the use of an auxiliary verb, and receive low weight, changing the optimum match to one covering the whole source tree. There is some price paid in matching the dissimilar subject nps.

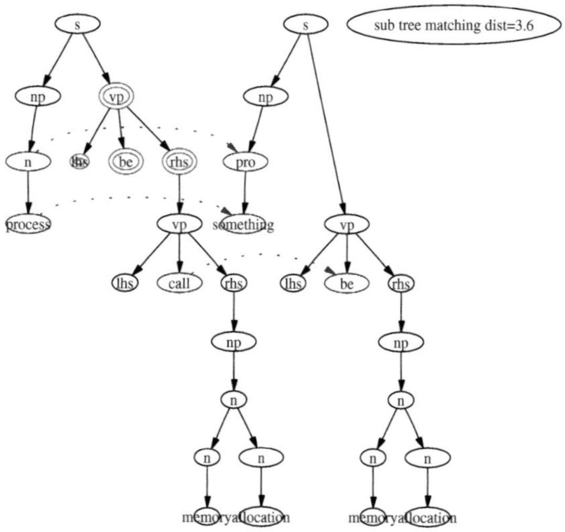


Figure 2: Structurally weighted example

Figure 3 continues the example, but this time in the subject position there is a sub-tree which is classified as a wild-card $np$ tree, and it matches at 0 cost with the subject np in the source tree.

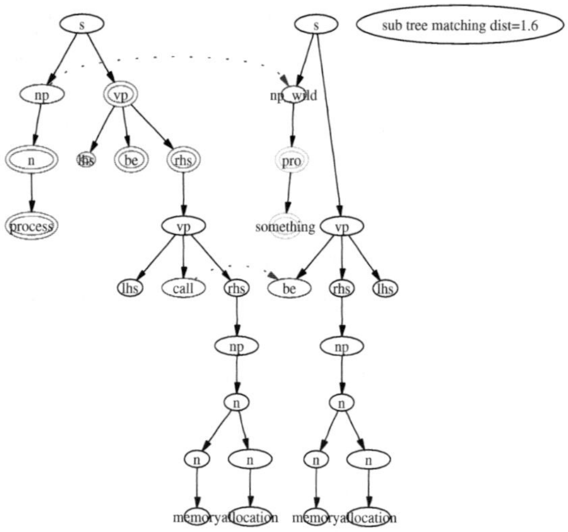


Figure 3: Wild-card example

The basis of the algorithm used to calculate $\Delta$ is the *ZhangShasha algorithm* (Zhang and Shasha, 1989): the Appendix summarises it. The implementation is based on code implementing $\Delta$ (Fontana et al., 2004), adapting it to allowing for the $\delta$ and $\vec{\delta}$ variants and $T(*)$, $S/\lambda$, and $\lambda/T$ parameters, and to generate the human-readable displays of the alignments (such as seen in figures 1,2 and 3).

### 2.3 Order invariant measures

Assessing answer/question similarity by variants of tree distance or sequence edit-distance, means that distance will not be word-order invariant. There are also measures which are word-order invariant, sometimes called *token-based* measures. These measures are usually couched in a *vector* representation of questions and answers, where vector dimensions are words from (some chosen enumeration) of words (see (Salton and Lesk, 1968)). In the simplest case the values on each dimensions are in $\{0, 1\}$, denoting presence or absence of a word. If $\bullet$ is vector product and $a^w$ is the set of words in a sequence $a$, then $\vec{a} \bullet \vec{b} = |a^w \cap b^w|$, for the binary vectors representing $a^w$, $b^w$. Three well known measures based on this are given below, both in terms vectors, and for binary vectors, the equivalent formulation with sets:

| | |
|---|---|
| Dice | $2(\vec{a} \bullet \vec{b})/(\vec{a} \bullet \vec{a}) + (\vec{b} \bullet \vec{b}))$ |
| | $= 2(\|a^w \cap b^w\|)/(\|a^w\| + \|b^w\|)$ |
| Jaccard | $(\vec{a} \bullet \vec{b})/(\vec{a} \bullet \vec{a}) + \vec{b} \bullet \vec{b} - \vec{a} \bullet \vec{b})$ |
| | $= (\|a^w \cap b^w\|)/(\|a^w \cup b^w)$ |
| Cosine | $(\vec{a} \bullet \vec{b})/(\vec{a} \bullet \vec{a})^{.5}(\vec{b} \bullet \vec{b})^{.5}$ |
| | $= (\|a^w \cap b^w\|)/((\|a^w\|)^{0.5}(\|b^w\|)^{0.5})$ |

These measure *similarity*, not difference, ranging for 1 for identical $a^w$,$b^w$, to 0 for disjoint. In the binary case, Dice/Jaccard similarity can be related to the alignment-based, difference counting perspective of the edit-distances. If we define $\Pi^w(a, b)$ as $|a^w \cup b^w| - |a^w \cap b^w|$ – the size of the *symmetric difference* between $a^w$ and $b^w$ – this can be seen as a set-based version of edit distance[5], which (i) considers mappings on the sets of words, $a^w$, $b^w$, not the sequences $a$, $b$, and (ii) sets replacement cost to infinity. A difference measure (ranging from 0 for identical $a^w$,$b^w$ to 1 for disjoint) results if $\Pi^w(a, b)$ is divided by $|a^w| + |b^w|$ (resp. $|a^w \cup b^w|$) and this difference measures will give the reverse of a ranking by Dice (resp. Jaccard) similarity.

The Cosine is a measure of the *angle* between the vectors $\vec{a}, \vec{b}$, and is not relatable in the binary-case to the alignment-based, difference-counting perspective of the edit-distances: dividing $\Pi^w(a, b)$, the symmetric difference, by $|a^w|^{.5}|b^w|^{.5}$ does not give a measure with maximum value 1 for the disjoint case, and does not give the reverse of a ranking by Cosine similarity.[6]

Below we shall use $\theta$ to denote the Cosine distance.

## 3 The Question Answering Tasks

For a given representation $r$ (parse trees, word sequences etc.), and distance measure $d$, we shall generically take a Question Answering by Distance (QAD) task to be given by a set of queries, $\mathcal{Q}$, and for each query $q$, a corpus of potential answer sentences, $\mathcal{COR}_q$. For each $a \in \mathcal{COR}_q$, the system determines $d(r(a), r(q))$, the distance between the representations of $a$ and $q$, then uses this to sort $\mathcal{COR}_q$ into $\mathcal{A}_q$. This sorting is then evaluated in the following way. If $a_c \in \mathcal{A}_q$ is the *correct* answer, then the *correct-answer-rank* is the rank of $a_c$ in $\mathcal{A}_q$:

$$| \{a \in \mathcal{A}_q : d(r(a), r(q)) \leq d(r(a_c), r(q))\} |$$

whilst the *correct-answer-cutoff* is the proportion of $\mathcal{A}_q$ cut off by the correct answer $a_c$:

$$| \{a \in \mathcal{A}_q : d(r(a), r(q)) \leq d(r(a_c), r(q))\} | \ / \ | \mathcal{A}_q |$$

*Lower* values for this connote better performance. Another figure of merit is the *reciprocal correct-answer-rank*. *Higher* values of this connote better performance.

Note the notion of answerhood is not one requiring answers to be the sub-sentential phrases associated with wh-phrases in the question. Also not all the questions are wh-questions.

Note also that the set of candidate answers $\mathcal{COR}_q$ is sorted by the answer-to-query distance, $d(r(a), r(q))$, not the query-to-answer distance, $d(r(q), r(a))$. The intuition is that the queries are short and the answers longer, with sub-part that really contains the answer.

The performance of some of the above mentioned distance measures on 2 examples of QAD tasks has been measured:

> **GNU Library Manual QAD Task**: in this case $\mathcal{Q}$ is a set of 88 hand-created

[5] $\Pi^w(a, b)$ could be equivalently defined as $|(\vec{a} - \vec{b})|^2$

[6] if the vectors are normalised by their length, then you can show $|(\vec{a}/|\vec{a}| - \vec{b}/|\vec{b}|)|^2$ reverses the Cosine ranking

queries, and $\mathcal{COR}_q$, shared by all the queries, is the sentences of the manual of the GNU C Library[7] ($| \mathcal{COR}_q | \approx 31,000$).

**The TREC 11 QAD task**: In this case $\mathcal{Q}$ was the 500 questions of the TREC11 QA track (Voorhees and Buckland, 2002), whose answers are drawn from a large corpus of newspaper articles. $\mathcal{COR}_q$ was taken to be the sentences of the top 50 from the top-1000 ranking of articles provided by TREC11 for each question ($| \mathcal{COR}_q | \approx 1000$). Answer correctness was determined using the TREC11 answer regular expressions.

For the tree-distance measures, 2 parsing systems have been used. For convenience of reference, we will call the first parser, the *trinity* parser. This is a home-grown parser combining a disambiguating part-of-speech tagger with a bottom-up chartparser, refering to CFG-like syntax rules and a subcategorisation system somewhat in a categorial grammar style. Right-branching analyses are prefered and a final selection of edges from all available is made using a leftmost/longest selection strategy – there is always an output regardless of whether there is a single input-encompassing edge. Preterminal node labels are a combination of a main functor with other feature terms, but the replacement cost function $\mathcal{R}$ is set to ignore the feature terms. Terminal node labels are base forms of words, not inflected forms. For the structural weighting algorithm, $\mathcal{STR}$, the necessary node distinctions are furnished directly by the parser for vp, and by a small set of structure matching rules for other structures (nps, pps etc). The structures output for wh-questions are essentially deep structures, re-ordering an auxiliary inversion, and placing a tree in the position of a gap.

The Collins parser (Collins, 1999) (*Model 3* variant) is a probabilistic parser, using a model of trees as built top-down with a repertoire of moves, learnt from the Penn Treebank. The preterminal node labels are a combination of a Penn Treebank label with other information pertaining to the head/complement/adjunct distinction, but the replacement cost function $\mathcal{R}$ is set to ignore all but the Penn Treebank part of the label. The terminal node labels are inflected forms of words, not base forms. For the structural weighting algorithm, $\mathcal{STR}$, the necessary node distinctions are furnished directly by the parser. For the question parses, a set of transformations is applied to the parses directly given by the parser, which comparable to the *trinity* parser, re-order auxiliary inversion, and place a tree in the position of a gap.

[7] `http://www.gnu.org`

## 4 Relating Parse Quality to Retrieval Performance

As a kind of sanity-check on the idea of the using syntactic structures in retrieving answers, we performed some experiments in which we varied the sophistication of the parse trees that the parsers could produce, the expectation being that the less sophisticated the parse, the less successful would be question-answering performance. The left-hand data in Table 1 refers to various reductions of the linguistic knowledge bases of the *trinity* parser(*thin50* = random removal of 50% subset, *manual* = manual removal of a subset, *flat* = entirely flat parses, *gold* = hand-correction of query parses and their correct answers). The right-hand data in Table 1 refers to experiments in which the repertoire of moves available to the Collins parser, as defined by its grammar file, was reduced to different sized random subsets of itself.

Figure 4 shows the empirical cumulative density function (ecdf) of the *correct-answer-cutoff* obtained with the weighted sub-tree with wild cards measure. For each possible value $c$ of *correct-answer-cutoff*, it plots the percentage of queries with a *correct-answer-cutoff* $\leq c$.

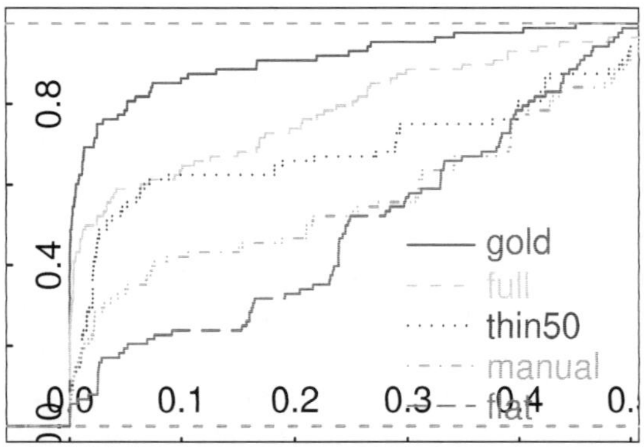


Figure 4: *Success vs Cut-off for different parse settings: $x$ = correct-answer-cutoff, $y$ = proportion of queries whose correct-answer-cutoff $\leq$ $x$ (ranking by weighted sub-tree with wild cards) (Library task)*

What these experiments show is that the ques-

Table 1: *Distribution of* Correct Cutoff *across query set* $\mathcal{Q}$ *in different parse settings. Left-hand data = GNU task, trinity parser, right-hand data = TREC11 task, Collins parser*

| Parsing | 1st Qu. | Median | Mean | 3rd Qu. |
|---|---|---|---|---|
| flat | 0.1559 | 0.2459 | 0.2612 | 0.3920 |
| manual | 0.0215 | 0.2103 | 0.2203 | 0.3926 |
| thin50 | 0.01418 | 0.02627 | 0.157 | 0.2930 |
| full | 0.00389 | 0.04216 | 0.1308 | 0.2198 |
| gold | 0.00067 | 0.0278 | 0.1087 | 0.1669 |

| Parsing | 1st Qu. | Median | Mean | 3rd Qu. |
|---|---|---|---|---|
| 55 | 0.3157 | 0.6123 | 0.5345 | 0.766400 |
| 75 | 0.02946 | 0.1634 | 0.2701 | 0.4495 |
| 85 | 0.0266 | 0.1227 | 0.2501 | 0.4380 |
| 100 | 0.01256 | 0.08306 | 0.2097 | 0.2901 |

tion answering performance is a function of the sophistication of the parses that the parsers are able to produce.

## 5 Comparing Distance Measures

Table 2 gives results on the Library task, using the trinity parser, for some variations of the distance measure.

Considering the results in 2, the best performing measure ($mrr = 0.27$) was the sub-traversal distance, $\vec{\delta}$, assigning weights structurally using $\mathcal{STR}$, with lexical emphasis $\mathcal{LEX}$, and treating a gap position as an $np$ wild card. This slightly out performs the sub-tree measure, $\delta$ ($mrr = 0.25$). An alternative approach to discounting parts of the answer tree, allowing any sub-tree of the answer the option to delete for free ($\Delta(\mathcal{W} = Str \circ Lex, T(*) = np\_gap, S/\lambda = \forall)$) performs considerably worse ($mrr = 0.16$). Presumably this is because it is too enthusiastic to assemble the query tree from disparate parts of the answer tree. By comparison, $\vec{\delta}$ and $\delta$ can only assembly the query tree from parts of the answer tree that are more closely connected.

The tree-distance measures ($\vec{\delta}$, $\delta$) using structural weights, lexical emphasis and wild cards ($mrr = 0.27$) out-perform the sub-sequence measure, $\pi$ ($mrr = 0.197$). It also out-performs the cosine measure, $\theta$ ($mrr = 0.190$). But $\pi$ and $\theta$ either out-perform or perform at about the same level as the tree-distance measure if the lexical emphasis is removed (see $\delta(\mathcal{W} = Str, T(*) = np\_gap)$, $mrr = 0.160$).

The tree-distance measure $\delta$ works better if structural weighting is used ($mrr = 0.09$) than if it is not ($mrr = 0.04$).

The tree-distance measure $\delta$ works better with wild-cards (see $\delta(\mathcal{W} = Str, T(*) = np\_gap)$, $mrr = 0.160$, than without (see $\delta(\mathcal{W} = Str)$, $mrr = 0.090$).

Table 3 gives some results on the TREC11 task, using the Collins parser. Fewer comparisons have been made here.

The sub-traversal measure, using structural weighting, lexical emphasis, and wild-cards performs better ($mrr = 0.150$) than the sub-sequence measure ($mrr = 0.09$), which in turn performs better than the basic sub-traversal measure, withouth structural weighting, lexical emphasis or wild-cards ($mrr = 0.076$). The cosine distance, $\theta$, performed best.

## 6 Discussion

For the parsers used, you could easily have 2 sentences with completely different words, and very different meanings, but which would have the same pre-terminal syntactic structure: the preterminal syntactic structure is not a function of the meaning. Given this, it is perhaps not surprising that there will be cases that the sequence distance easily spots as dissimilar, but which the tree distance measure, without any lexical emphasis, will regard as quite similar, and this perhaps explains why, without any lexical emphasis, the tree-distance measure performs at similar level to, or worse than, the sub-sequence distance measure.

With some kind of lexical emphasis in place, the tree-distance measures out-perform the subsequence measures. We can speculate as to the reason for this. There are two kinds of case where the tree-distance measures could be expected to spot a similarity which the sequence-distance measures will fail to spot. One is when the question and answer are more or less similar on their head words, but differ in determiners, auxiliaries and adjuncts. The sequence distance measure will pay more of a price for these differences than the structurally weighted tree-distance. Another kind of case is when the answer supplies words which match a wild-card in the middle of the query tree, as might happen for example in:

> Q: what do child processes inherit from their parent processes
> A: a child process inherits the owner and permissions from the ancestor process

Table 2: *For different distance measures (Library task, trinity parser), distrution of correct-answer-cutoff, mean reciprocal rank $mrr$*

| distance type | cutoff 1st Qu. | Median | Mean | mrr |
|---|---|---|---|---|
| $\vec{\delta}(\mathcal{W} = Str \circ Lex, T(*) = np\_gap)$ | 8.630-05 | 8.944-04 | 2.460-02 | 0.270 |
| $\delta(\mathcal{W} = Str \circ Lex, T(*) = np\_gap)$ | 9.414e-05 | 1.428e-03 | 7.133e-02 | 0.255 |
| $\pi$ bases | 1.569e-04 | 2.087e-03 | 5.181e-02 | 0.197 |
| $\theta$ bases | 1.569e-04 | 8.630e-04 | 1.123e-02 | 0.190 |
| $\Delta(\mathcal{W} = Str \circ Lex, T(*) = np\_gap, S/\lambda = \forall)$ | 4.080e-04 | 9.352-03 | 5.853-02 | 0.160 |
| $\delta(\mathcal{W} = Str, T(*) = np\_gap)$ | 3.923e-04 | 1.964e-02 | 1.162e-01 | 0.160 |
| $\delta(\mathcal{W} = Str)$ | 5.060e-03 | 3.865e-02 | 1.303e-01 | 0.090 |
| $\delta$ | 1.324e-03 | 1.046e-01 | 1.852e-01 | 0.040 |
| $\Delta$ | 8.398e-02 | 2.633e-01 | 3.531e-01 | 0.003 |

Table 3: *For different distance measures (TREC task, collins parser) the distribution of correct-answer-cutoff and mean reciprocal rank ($mrr$)*

| distance type | cutoff 1st Qu. | Median | Mean | mrr |
|---|---|---|---|---|
| $\theta$ forms | 7.847e-03 | 2.631e-02 | 1.068e-01 | 0.167 |
| $\vec{\delta}(\mathcal{W} = Str \circ Lex, T(*) = np\_gap)$ | 8.452e-03 | 4.898e-02 | 1.558e-01 | 0.150 |
| $\pi$ forms | 2.113e-02 | 7.309-02 | 2.051e-01 | 0.092 |
| $\vec{\delta}$ | 1.815e-02 | 1.030e-01 | 3.269e-01 | 0.076 |

The tree-distance measures will see these as similar, but the sub-sequence measure will pay a large price for words in the answer that match the gap position in the query. Thus one can argue that the use of structural weighting, and wild-card trees in the query analysis will tend to equate things which the sequence distance sees as dissimilar.

Another possible reason that the tree-distance measure out-performs the sub-sequence measure is that it may be able to distinguish things which the sequence distance will tend to treat as equivalent. A question might make the thematic role of some entity very clear, but use very few significant words as in:

*what does malloc do ?*

Using tree distance will favour answer sentences with *malloc* as the subject, such as *malloc returns a null pointer*. The basic problem for the sequence distance here is that it does not have much to work with and will only be able to partition the answer set into a small set of equivalence classes.

These are speculations as to why tree-distance would out-perform sequence distance. Whether these equating and discriminating advantages which theoretically should accrue to $\delta$, $\vec{\delta}$ actually will do so, will depend on the accuracy of the parsing: if there is too much bad parsing, then we will be equating that which we should keep apart, and discriminating that which we should equate.

In the two tasks, the relationship between the tree-distance measures and the order-invariant cosine measure worked out differently. The reasons for this are not clear at the moment. One possibility is that our use of the Collins parser has not yet resulted in good enough parses, especially question parses – recall that the indication from 4 was that improved parse quality will give better retrieval performance. Also it is possible that relative to the queries in the Library task, the amount of word-order permutation between question and answer is greater in the TREC task. This is also indicated by the fact that on the TREC task, the sub-sequence measure, $\pi$, falls considerably behind the cosine measure, $\theta$, whereas for the Library task they perform at similar levels.

Some other researchers have also looked at the use of tree-distance measures in semantically-oriented tasks. Punyakonok(2004) report work using tree-distance to do question-answering on the TREC11 data. Their work differs from that presented here in several ways. They take the parse trees which are output by Collins parser and convert them into dependency trees between the leaves. They compute the distance from query to the answer, rather than from answer to query, using essentially the variant of tree-distance that allows arbitrary sub-trees of the target to insert for zero-cost. Presumably this directionality difference is not a significant one, and with distances calculated from answers to queries, this would correspond to the variant that allows arbitrary source sub-trees to delete with zero cost. The cost functions are parameterised to refer in the case of wild-card replacements to (i) information derived from Named Entity recognisers so different kinds of wh wild-cards can be given low-cost replacment with vocabulary categorised as belong to the right kind by NE recognition and (ii) base-form information.

There is no way to make a numerical comparison because they took a different answer corpus $\mathcal{COR}_q$ – the articles containing the answers suggested by TREC11 participants – and a different criterion of correctness – an answer was correct if it belonged to an article which the TREC11 adjudicators judges to contain a correct answer.

Their adaptation of cost functions to refer to essentially semantic annotations of tree nodes is an avenue we intend to explore in future work. What this paper has sought to do is to investigate intrinsic syntactic parameters that might influence performance. The hope is that these parameters still play a role in an enriched system.

## 7 Conclusion and Future Work

For two different parsers, and two different question-answering tasks, we have shown that improved parse quality leads to better performance, and that a tree-distance measure out-performs a sequence distance measure. We have focussed on intrinsic, syntactic properties of parse-trees. It is not realistic to expect that exclusively using tree-distance measures in this rather pure way will give state-of-the-art question-answering performance, but the contribution of this paper is the (start of an) exporation of the syntactic parameters which effect the use of tree-distance in question answering. More work needs to be done in systematically varying the parsers, question-answering tasks, and parametrisations of tree-distance over all the possibilities.

There are many possibilities to be explored involving adapting cost functions to enriched node descriptions. Already mentioned above, is the possibility to involve semantic information in the cost functions. Another avenue is introducing weightings based on corpus-derived statistics, essentially making the distance comparision refer to extrinsic factors. One open question is whether analogously to $idf$, cost functions for (non-lexical) nodes should depend on tree-bank frequencies.

Another question needing further exploration is the dependency-vs-constituency contrast. Interestingly Punyakonok(2004) themselves speculate:

> *each node in a tree represents only a word in the sentence; we believe that appropriately combining nodes into meaningful phrases may allow our approach to perform better.*

We found working with constituency trees that it was the sub-traversal distance measure that performed best, and it needs to be seen whether this holds also for dependency trees. Also to be explored is the role of structural weighting in a system using dependency trees.

A final speculation that it would be interesting to explore is whether one can use feed-back from performance on a QATD task as a driver in the machine-learning of probabilities for a parser, in an approach analogous to the use of the language-model in parser training.

## References

Michael Collins. 1999. *Head-driven statistical models for natural language parsing*. Ph.D. thesis, University of Pennsylvania.

Walter Fontana, Ivo L. Hofacker, and Peter F. Stadler. 2004. Vienna rna package. www.tbi.univie.ac.at/~ivo/RNA.

V. I. Levenshtein. 1966. Binary codes capable of correcting insertions and reversals. *Sov. Phys. Dokl*, 10:707–710.

Vasin Punyakanok, Dan Roth, and Wen tau Yih. 2004. Natural language inference via dependency tree mapping: An application to question answering. *Computational Linguistics*.

G. Salton and M. E. Lesk. 1968. Computer evalation of indexing and text processing. *Journal of the ACM*, 15:8–36, January.

Ellen Voorhees and Lori Buckland, editors. 2002. *The Eleventh Text REtrieval Conference (TREC 2002)*. Department of Commerce, National Institute of Standards and Technology.

K. Zhang and D. Shasha. 1989. Simple fast algorithms for the editing distance between trees and related problems. *SIAM Journal of Computing*, 18:1245–1262.

## Appendix

This appendix briefly summarises the algorithm to compute the tree-distance, based on (Zhang and Shasha, 1989) (see Section 2.1 for definition of tree-distance). The algorithm operates on the left-to-right post-order traversals of trees. Given source and target trees $S$ and $T$, the output is a table $\mathcal{T}$, indexed vertically by the traversal of $S$ and horizontally by the traversal of $T$, and position $\mathcal{T}[i][j]$ is the tree-distance from the $S$ subtree rooted at $i$, to the $T$ subtree rooted at $j$. Thus the bottom righthand corner of the table represents the tree distance between $S$ and $T$.

If $k$ is the index of a node of the tree, the *left-most leaf*, $l(k)$, is the index of the leaf reached by following the left-branch down. For a given leaf there is a highest node of which it is the left-most leaf. Let such a node be called a *key-root*. Let $KR(T)$ be the sequence of *key-roots* in $T$. The algorithm is a doubly nested loop ascending throught the key-roots of $S$ and $T$, in which for each pair of key-roots $(i, j)$, a routine $tree\_dist(i, j)$ updates the $\mathcal{T}$ table.

Suppose $i$ is any node of $S$. Then for any $i_s$ with $l(i) \leq i_s \leq i$, the subsequence of $S$ from $l(i)$ to $i_s$ can be seen as a *forest* of subtrees of $S$, denoted $F(l(i), i_s)$. $tree\_dist(i, j)$ creates a table $\mathcal{F}$, indexed vertically from $l(i)$ to $i$ and horizontally from $l(j)$ to $j$, such that $\mathcal{F}[i_s][j_t]$ represents the distance between the forests $F(l(i), i_s)$ and $F(l(j), j_t)$. Also the $F$ table should be seen as having an extra left-most column, representing for each $i_s$, $l(i) \leq i_s \leq i$, the $F(l(i), i_s)$ to $\emptyset$ mapping (pure deletion), and an extra uppermost row representing for each for each $j_t$, $l(j) \leq j_t \leq j$, the $\emptyset$ to $F(l(j), j_t)$ mapping (pure insertion).

$tree\_dist(i, j)\{$

*initialize*:

$\mathcal{F}[l(i)][\emptyset], \ldots, \mathcal{F}[i][\emptyset] = 1, \ldots, i - l(i) + 1$

$\mathcal{F}[\emptyset][l(j)], \ldots, \mathcal{F}[\emptyset][j] = 1, \ldots, j - l(j) + 1$

*loop*: $\forall i_s, l(i) \leq i_s \leq i, \forall j_t, l(j) \leq j_t \leq j$

**case 1**: $l(i_s) = l(i)$ and $l(j_t) = l(j)$

$\mathcal{T}[i_s][j_t] = \mathcal{F}[i_s][j_t]$ = min of $swap$, $delete$, $insert$, where

$swap = \mathcal{F}[i_s - 1][j_t - 1] + swap(i_s, j_t)$

$delete = \mathcal{F}[i_s - 1][j_t] + delete(i_s)$

$insert = \mathcal{F}[i_s][j_t - 1] + insert(j_t)$

**case 2**: either $l(i_s) \neq l(i)$ or $l(j_t) \neq l(j)$

$\mathcal{F}[i_s][j_t]$ = min of $delete$, $insert$, $for + tree$, where

$swap$, $delete$, $insert$ as before and

$for + tree = \mathcal{F}[l(i_s) - 1][l(j_t) - 1] + \mathcal{T}[i_s][j_t]$

}

}

In case 1, the 'forests' $F(l(i), i_s)$ and $F(l(j), j_t)$ are both single trees and the computed forest distance is transferred to the tree-distance table $\mathcal{T}$. In case 2, at least one of $F(l(i), i_s)$ or $F(l(j), j_t)$ represents a forest of more than one tree. This means there is the possibility that the final trees in the two forests are mapped to each other. This quantity is found from the $\mathcal{T}$ table.

This formulation gives the *whole-tree* distance between $S$ and $T$. For the *sub-tree* distance, you take the minimum of the final column of $\mathcal{T}$. For the *sub-traversal* case, you do the same but on the final iteration, you set the pure deletion column of $\mathcal{F}$ to all 0s, and take the minimum of the final column of $\mathcal{F}$.

To accommodate wild-card target trees, **case 1** in the above is extended to allow $\mathcal{T}[i_s][j_t] = \mathcal{F}[i_s][j_t] = 0$ in case $j_t$ is the root of a wild-card tree. To accommodate self-effacing source trees, **case 2** in the above is extended to also consider $for + tree\_del = \mathcal{F}[l(i_s) - 1, j_t]$.

# Total rank distance and scaled total rank distance: two alternative metrics in computational linguistics

**Anca Dinu**
University of Bucharest,
Faculty of Foreign Languages/
Edgar Quinet 17,
Bucharest, Romania
anca_d_dinu@yahoo.com

**Liviu P. Dinu**
University of Bucharest, Faculty of
Mathematics and Computer Science/
Academiei 14, 010014,
Bucharest, Romania
ldinu@funinf.cs.unibuc.ro

## Abstract

In this paper we propose two metrics to be used in various fields of computational linguistics area. Our construction is based on the supposition that in most of the natural languages the most important information is carried by the first part of the unit. We introduce total rank distance and scaled total rank distance, we prove that they are metrics and investigate their max and expected values. Finally, a short application is presented: we investigate the similarity of Romance languages by computing the scaled total rank distance between the digram rankings of each language.

## 1 Introduction

Decision taking processes are common and frequent tasks for most of us in our daily life. The ideal case would be that when the decisions can be taken deterministically, based on some clear, quantifiable and unambiguous parameters and classifiers. However, there are many cases when we decide based on subjective or sensorial criteria (e.g. perceptions), but which prove to function well. The domains in which decisions are taken based on perceptions vary a lot: the qualitative evaluation of services, management, financial predictions, sociology, information/intelligent systems, etc (Zadeh and Kacprzyk, 1999).

When people are asked to approximate the height of some individual, they prefer to use terms like: very tall, rather tall, tall enough, short, etc. We can expect the same linguistic variable to have a different metrical correspondence according to the community to which the individual belongs (i.e. an individual of 170 cm can be considered short by the Australian soldiers and tall by the Eskimos). Similar situations also arise when people are asked to hierarchically order a list of objects.

For example, we find it easy to make the top of the best five novels that we read, since number one is the novel that we like best and so on, rather than to say that we liked in the proportion of 40% the novel on the first position, 20 % the novel on the second place and so on. The same thing is happening when we try to talk about the style of a certain author: it is easier to say that the author $x$ is closer to $y$ than $z$, then to quantify the distance between their styles. In both cases we operate with a "hidden variable" and a "hidden metric".

Especially when working with perceptions, but not only, we face the situation to operate with strings of objects where the essential information is not given by the numerical value of some parameter of each object, but by the position the object occupies in the strings (according to a natural hierarchical order, in which on the first place we find the most important element, on the second place the next one and on the last position the least important element).

As in the case of perceptions calculus, in most of the natural languages, the most important information is also carried by the first part of the unit (Marcus, 1974). Cf. M. Dinu (1997), it is advisable that the essential elements of a message to be situated in the first part of the utterance, thus having the best chances to be memorized[1] (see Table 1).

Based on the remark that in most of the natural

[1]On the contrary, M. Dinu notices that at the other end, we find the wooden language from the communist period, text that was not meant to inform, but to confuse the receiver with an incantation empty of content, and that used the reversed process: to place the important information at the end of very long phrases that started with irrelevant information



*Proceedings of the Workshop on Linguistic Distances*, pages 109–116,
Sydney, July 2006. 

| The length of the phrase | Memorized words (%) | | |
|---|---|---|---|
| | all | first half | second half |
| 12 | 100 % | 100 % | 100 % |
| 13 | 90 % | 95 % | 85 % |
| 17 | 70 % | 90% | 50% |
| 24 | 50 % | 70 % | 30 % |
| 40 | 30 % | 50 % | 10 % |

Table 1: The percentage of memorized words from phrases

languages the most important information is carried out by the first part of the unit, in this paper we introduce two metrics: total rank distance and scaled total rank distance.

Some preliminary and motivations are given in Section 2. In Section 3 we introduce total rank distance; we prove that it is a metric (Section 3.1), we investigate its max and expected values (Section 3.2) and its behavior regarding the median ranking problem (Section 3.3). An extension for strings is proposed in Section 4. Scaled total rank distance is introduced in Section 4, where we prove that it is a metric and we investigate its max and expected values. In Section 6 a short application is presented: we investigate the similarity of Romance languages by computing the scaled total rank distance between the digram rankings of each language. Section 7 is reserved to conclusions, while in Section 8 we give a mathematically addendum where we present the proofs of the statements.

## 2 Rank distance

By analogy to computing with words, natural language and genomics, we can say that if the differences between two strings are at the top (i.e., in essential points), the distance has to have a bigger value then when the differences are at the bottom of the strings.

On the other hand, many of the similarity measures used today (edit distance, Hamming distance etc.) do not take into account the natural tendency of the objects to place the most important information in the first part of the message.

This was the motivation we had in mind when we proposed Rank distance (Dinu, 2003) as an alternative similarity measure in computational linguistics. This distance had already been successfully used in computational linguistics, in such problems as the similarity of Romance languages (Dinu and Dinu, 2005), or in bioinformatics (in DNA sequence comparision problem, Dinu and Sgarro).

### 2.1 Preliminaries and definitions

To measure the distance between two strings, we use the following strategy: we scan (from left to right) both strings and for each letter from the first string we count the number of elements between its position in first string and the position of its first occurrence in the second string. We sum these scores for all elements and obtain the rank distance. Clearly, the rank distance gives a score zero only to letters which are in the same position in both strings, as Hamming distance does (we recall that Hamming distance is the number of positions where two strings of the same length differ).

On the other hand, the reduced sensitivity of the rank distance w.r.t. deletions and insertions is of paramount importance, since it allows us to make use of *ad hoc extensions to arbitrary strings*, such as its low computational complexity is not affected. This is not the case for the extensions of the Hamming distance, mathematically optimal but computationally heavy, which lead to the *edit-distance*, or *Levenshtein distance*, and which are at the base of the standard alignment principle. So, rank distance sides with Hamming distance rather than Levenshtein distance as far as computational complexity is concerned: the fact that in the Hamming and in the rank case the median string problem is tractable (Dinu and Manea), while in the edit case it is is NP-hard (Higuera and Casacuberta, 2000), is a very significant indicator.

The rank distance is an *ordinal* distance tightly related to the so-called *Spearman's footrule* (Diaconis and Graham, 1977) [2], which has long been used in non-parametric statistics. Unlike other ordinal distances, the Spearman's footrule is linear in $n$, and so very easy to compute. Its average value is at two-thirds of the way to the maximum value (both are quadratics in $n$); this is because, in a way, the Spearman footrule becomes rather "undiscriminating" for highly different orderings. Rank distance has the same drawbacks and the same advantages of Spearman's foootrule. As for "classical" ordinal distances for integers, with averages values, maximal values, etc., the reader is

[2]Both Spearman's footrules and binary Hamming distances are a special case of a well-known metric distance called sometimes taxi distance, which is known to be equivalent to the usual Euclidian distance. Computationally, taxi distance is obviously linear.

referred to the basic work (Diaconis and Graham, 1977).

Let us go back to strings. Let us choose a finite alphabet, say $\{N, V, A, O\}$ (Noun, Verb, Adjective, Object) and two strings on that alphabet, which for the moment will be constrained to be a permutation of each other. E.g. take two strings of length 6: $NNVAOO$ and $VOANON$; put indexes for the occurrences of repeated letters in increasing order to obtain $N_1N_2V_1A_1O_1O_2$ and $V_1O_1A_1N_1O_2N_2$. Now, proceed as follows: in the first sequence $N_1$ is in position 1, while it is in position 4 in the second sequence, and so the difference is 3; compute the difference in positions for all letters and sum them. In this case the differences are 3, 4, 2, 1, 3, 1 and so the distance is 14. Even if the computation of the rank distance as based directly on its definition may appear to be quadratic, in (Dinu and Sgarro) two algorithms which take it back to linear complexity are exhibit.

In computational linguistics the rank distance for strings *without repetitions* had been enough. In a way, *indexing* converts a sequence *with repetitions* into a sequence without repetitions, in which the $k$ occurrence of a letter $a$ are replaced by single occurrences of the $k$ indexed letters $a_1, a_2, \ldots, a_k$. Let $u = x_1x_2 \ldots x_n$ and $v = y_1y_2 \ldots y_m$ be two strings of lengths $n$ and $m$, respectively. For an element $x_i \in u$ we define its *order* or *rank* by $ord(x_i|u) = n+1-i$: we stress that the rank of $x_i$ is its position in the string, counted from the **right** to the **left**, *after* indexing, so that for example the second $O$ in the string $VOANON$ has rank 2.

Note that some (indexed) occurrences appear in both strings, while some other are *unmatched*, i.e. they appear only in one of the two strings. In definition (1) the last two summations refer to these unmatched occurrences. More precisely, the first summation on $x \in u \cap v$ refers to occurrences $x$ which are common to both strings $u$ and $v$, the second summation on $x \in u \setminus v$ refers to occurrences $x$ which appear in $u$ but not in $v$, while the third summation on $x \in v \setminus u$ refers to occurrences $x$ which appear in $v$ but not in $u$.

**Definition 1** *The rank distance between two strings without repetitions $u$ and $v$ is given by:*

$$\Delta(u, v) = \sum_{x \in u \cap v} |ord(x|u) - ord(x|v)| + + \sum_{x \in u \setminus v} ord(x|u) + \sum_{x \in v \setminus u} ord(x|v) \quad (1)$$

**Example 1** *1. Let $u = abcde$ and $v = beaf$ be two strings without repetitions. $\Delta(u, v) = |ord(a|u) - ord(a|v)| + |ord(b|u) - ord(b|v)| + |ord(e|u) - ord(e|v)| + ord(c|u) + ord(d|u) + ord(f|v) = 3 + 0 + 2 + 3 + 2 + 1 = 11$.*

*2. Let $w_1 = abbab$ and $w_2 = abbbac$ be two strings with repetitions. Their corresponding indexed strings will be: $\overline{w_1} = a_1b_1b_2a_2b_3$ and $\overline{w_2} = a_1b_1b_2b_3a_2c_1$, respectively. So, $\Delta(w_1, w_2) = \Delta(\overline{w_1}, \overline{w_2}) = 8$.*

**Remark 1** *The ad hoc nature of the rank distance resides in the last two summations in* **(1)**, *where one compensates for unmatched letters, i.e. indexed letters which appear only in one of the two strings.*

Deletions and insertions are less worrying in the rank case rather than in the Hamming case: if one incorrectly moves a symbol by, say, one position, the Hamming distance loses any track of it, but rank distance does not, and the mistake is quite light. So, generalizations in the spirit of the edit distance are unavoidable in the Hamming case, even if they are computationally very demanding, while in the rank case we may think of *ad hoc* ways-out, which are computationally convenient.

## 3 Total Rank Distance

We remind that one of the goals of introducing rank distance was to obtain a tool for measuring the distance between two strings which is more sensitive to the differences encountered in the beginning of the strings than in the ending.

Rank distance satisfies in a good measure the upper requirement (for example it penalizes more heavily unmatched letters in the initial part of strings), but some black points are yet remaining. One of them is that rank distance is invariant to the transpositions on a given length.

The following example is eloquent:

**Example 2** *1. Let $a = (1, 2, 3, 4, 5)$, $b = (2, 1, 3, 4, 5)$, $c = (1, 2, 4, 3, 5)$ and $d = (1, 2, 3, 5, 4)$ be four permutations. Rank distance between $a$ and each of $b$, $c$ or $d$ is the same,* 2.

*2. The same is happening with $a = (1, 2, 3, 4, 5, 6, 7, 8)$ and $b = (3, 2, 1, 4, 5, 6, 7, 8)$, $c = (1, 4, 3, 2, 5, 6, 7, 8)$, or $d = (1, 2, 3, 4, 5, 8, 7, 6)$ (here rank distance is equal to* 4*).*

In the following we will repair this inconvenient, by introducing the *Total Rank Distance*, a measure which gives us a more comprehensive information (compared to rank distance) about the two strings which we compare.

Since in many situations occurred in computational linguistics, the similarity for strings *without repetitions* had been enough, in the following we introduce first a metric between rankings[3] and then we generalize it to strings.

### 3.1 Total rank distance on permutations

Let $A$ and $B$ be two rankings over the same universe $U$, having the same length, $n$. Without loss of generality, we suppose that $U = \{1, 2, \ldots, m\}$.

For each $1 \le i \le n$ we define the function $\delta$ by:

$$\delta(i) \stackrel{\text{def}}{=} \Delta(A_i, B_i). \tag{2}$$

where $A_i$ and $B_i$ are the partial rankings of length $i$ obtained from the initial rankings by deleting the elements below position $i$ (i.e. the top $i$ rankings).

**Definition 2** *Let $A$ and $B$ be two rankings with the same length over the same universe, $U$. The Total Rank Distance between A and B is given by:*

$$D(A, B) = \sum_{i=1}^{n} \delta(i) = \sum_{i=1}^{n} \Delta(A_i, B_i).$$

**Example 3** 1. *Let $a$, $b$, $c$ and $d$ be the four permutations from Example 2, item 1. The total rank distance between $a$ and each of $b$, $c$, $d$ is: $D(a, b) = 10$, $D(a, c) = 6$, $D(a, d) = 4$.*

2. *The visible differences are also in the item 2 of the upper example if we apply total rank distance: $D(a, b) = 30$, $D(a, c) = 28$, $D(a, d) = 10$.*

The following theorem states that our terminology *total rank distance* is an adequate one:

**Theorem 1** *Total rank distance is a metric.*

**Proof:**

It is easy to see that $D(A, B) = D(B, A)$.

We prove that $D(A, B) = 0$ iff $A = B$. If $D(A, B) = 0$, then $\Delta(A_i, B_i) = 0$ for each $1 \le i \le n$ (since $\Delta$ is a metric, so a nonnegative number), so $\Delta(A_n, B_n) = \Delta(A, B) = 0$, so $A = B$.

For the triangle inequality we have: $D(A, B) + D(B, C) = \sum_{i=1}^{n} \Delta(A_i, B_i) + \sum_{i=1}^{n} \Delta(B_i, C_i)$
$= \sum_{i=1}^{n} (\Delta(A_i, B_i) + \Delta(B_i, C_i))$
$\ge \sum_{i=1}^{n} \Delta(A_i, C_i) = D(A, C)$. □

### 3.2 Expected and max values of the total rank distance

Let $S_n$ be the group of all permutations of length $n$ and let $A$, $B$ be two permutations from $S_n$. We investigate the max total rank distance between $A$ and $B$ and the average total rank distance between $A$ and $B$.

**Proposition 1** *Under the upper hypothesis, the expected value of the total rank distance between $A$ and $B$ is:*

$$E(D) = \frac{(n^2 - 1)(n + 2)}{6}.$$

**Proposition 2** *Under the same hypothesis as in the previous proposition, the max total rank distance between two permutations from $S_n$ is:*

$$\max_{A, B \in S_n} D(A, B) = \frac{n^2(n + 2)}{4}$$

*and it is achieved when a permutation is the reverse of the other one.*

### 3.3 On the aggregation problem via total rank distance

Rank aggregation is the problem of combining several ranked lists of objects in a robust way to produce a single ranking of objects.

One of the most natural way to solve the aggregation problem is to determine the median (sometimes called *geometric median*) of ranked lists via a particular measure.

Given a multiset $T$ of ranked lists, a median of $T$ is a list $L$ such that

[3] A ranking is an ordered list of objects. Every ranking can be considered as being produced by applying an ordering criterion to a given set of objects. More formally, let $U$ be a finite set of objects, called the universe of objects. We assume, without loss of generality, that $U = \{1, 2, \ldots, |U|\}$ (where by $|U|$ we denote the cardinality of $U$). A ranking over $U$ is an ordered list: $\tau = (x_1 > x_2 > \ldots > x_d)$, where $\{x_1, \ldots, x_d\} \subseteq U$, and $>$ is a strict ordering relation on $\{x_1, \ldots, x_d\}$, (*an ordering criterion*. It is important to point the fact that $x_i \ne x_j$ if $i \ne j$. For a given object $i \in U$ present in $\tau$, $\tau(i)$ represents the position (or rank) of $i$ in $\tau$. If the ranking $\tau$ contains all the elements of $U$, than it is called a *full ranking*. It is obvious that all full rankings represent all total orderings of U (the same as the permutations of $U$). However, there are situations when some objects cannot be ranked by a given criterion: the ranking $\tau$ contains only a subset of elements from the unverse $U$. Then, $\tau$ is called *partial ranking*. We denote the set of elements in the list $\tau$ with the same symbol as the list.

$$d(L,T) = \min_X d(X,T),$$

where $d$ is a metric and $X$ is a ranked list over the universe of $T$.

Depending on the choice of measure $d$, the upper problem may contain many unpleasant surprises. One of them is that computing the median set is NP-complete for some usual measure (including edit-distance or Kendal distance) even for binary universe.

We will show in the following that the median aggregation problem via Total rank distance can be computed in polynomial time.

**Theorem 2** *Given a multiset T of full ranked lists over the same universe, the median of T via total rank distance can be computed in polynomial time, namely proportional to the time to find a minimum cost perfect matching in a bipartite graph.*

**Proof:** Without loss of generality, we suppose that the universe of lists is $U = \{1, 2, \ldots, n\}$. We define a weighted complete bipartite graph $G = (N, P, W)$ as follows. The first set of nodes $N = \{1, 2, \ldots, n\}$ denotes the set of elements to be ranked in a full list. The second set of nodes $P = \{1, 2, \ldots, n\}$ denotes the $n$ available positions. The weight $W(i, j)$ is the contribution, via total rank distance, of node $i$ to be ranked on place $j$ in a certain ranking.

We can give a close formula for computing the weights $W(i, j)$ and this ends the proof, because we reduced the problem to the solving of the minimum cost maximum matching problem on the upper bipartite graph ((Fukuda and Matsui, 1994), (Fukuda and Matsui, 1992), (Dinu and Manea)). □

## 4 An extension to strings of total rank distance

We can extend total rank distance to strings.

Similar to the extensions of rank distance to strings, we index each letter in a word with the number of its previous occurrences.

First, we extent the total rank distance to rankings with unequal lengths as it follows:

**Definition 3** *Let $u$ and $v$ be two rankings of length $|u|$ and $|v|$, respectively. We can assume that $|u| < |v|$. The total rank distance between $u$ and $v$ is defined by:*

$$D(u,v) = \sum_{i=1}^{|u|} \Delta(v_i, u_i) + \sum_{i=|u|+1}^{|v|} \Delta(v_i, u).$$

**Theorem 3** *The total rank distance between two rankings with unequal lengths is a metric.*

To extent the total rank distance to strings, firstly we index both strings and than we apply the upper definition to the newly obtained strings (which are now rankings).

**Example 4** *Let $u = aabca$, $v = aab$ and $w = bca$ be three strings. We obtained the following results:*

1. *Rank distance:* $\Delta(u,v) = \Delta(a_1a_2b_1c_1a_3, a_1a_2b_1) = 9$ *and* $\Delta(u,w) = \Delta(a_1a_2b_1c_1a_3, b_1c_2a_1) = 9$;
2. *Total rank distance:* $D(u,v) = D(a_1a_2b_1c_1a_3, a_1a_2b_1) = 13$ *and* $D(u,w) = D(a_1a_2b_1c_1a_3, b_1c_2a_1) = 33$.

What happens in item 1 is a consequence of a general property of rank distance which states that $\Delta(uv, u) = \Delta(uv, v)$, for any nonempty strings $u$ and $v$.

Total rank distance repairs this fact, as we can see from item 2; we observe that the total rank distance is more sensitive than rank distance to the differences from the first part of strings.

## 5 Scaled Total Rank Distance

We use the same ideas from Total rank distance, but we normalize each partial distance. To do this, we divide each rank distance between two partial rankings of length $i$ by $i(i+1)$, which is the maximal distance between two rankings of length $i$ (it corresponds to the case when the two rankings have no common elements).

**Definition 4** *The Scaled Total Rank distance between two rankings $A$ and $B$ of length $n$ is:*

$$S(A,B) = \sum_{i=1}^{n} \frac{\Delta(A_i, B_i)}{i(i+1)}.$$

**Theorem 4** *Scaled total rank distance is a metric.*

**Proof:** The proof is similar to the one from the total rank distance. □

**Remark 2** *It is easy to see that $S(A,B) \leq H(A,B)$, where $H(A,B)$ is the Hamming distance.*

**Example 5** *Let* $A = (a, b, c, d, e)$, $B = (b, a, c, d, e)$ *and* $C = (a, b, d, e, c)$ *be three permutations. We have the following values for* $\Delta$, *D and S, respectively:*

1. *Rank distance:* $\Delta(A, B) = 2$, $\Delta(A, C) = 4$, *so* $\Delta(A, B) < \Delta(A, C)$.
2. *Total Rank Distance:* $D(A, B) = 2 + 2 + 2 + 2 + 2 = 10$, $D(A, C) = 0 + 0 + 2 + 4 + 4 = 10$, *so* $D(A, B) = D(A, C)$.
3. *Scaled Total Rank Distance:* $S(A, B) = \frac{2}{2} + \frac{2}{6} + \frac{2}{12} + \frac{2}{20} + \frac{2}{30} = \frac{5}{3}$, $S(A, C) = \frac{0}{2} + \frac{0}{6} + \frac{2}{12} + \frac{4}{20} + \frac{4}{30} = \frac{1}{2}$, *so* $S(A, B) > S(A, C)$.

It is not hard to see that $S(A, B) \leq n$, so we can normalize scaled total rank distance by dividing it to $n$.

We obtained the following two values for max and average values of scaled total rank distance:

**Proposition 3**

1. *If* $n \to \infty$, *then* $\max\limits_{A,B \in S_n} \frac{1}{n} S(A, B) = \frac{7}{2} - 4 \ln 2$.
2. *The average value of scaled total rank distance is:* $E(S) = \frac{2(n-1)}{3}$. *When* $n \to \infty$, $\frac{E(S)}{n} \to \frac{2}{3}$.

**Remark 3** *It is a nice exercise to show that* $\frac{7}{2} - 4 \ln 2 \leq 1$.

**Proof:** $\frac{7}{2} - 4 \ln 2 \leq 1$ *iff* $1 \leq 4(\ln 4 - 1)$. *But* $4(\ln 4 - 1) > 4(\ln 4 - \ln 3)$. *From Lagrange Theorem, there is* $3 < \xi < 4$ *such that* $\ln 4 - \ln 3 = \frac{1}{\xi}$, *so* $4(\ln 4 - \ln 3) = \frac{4}{\xi} > 1$, *so* $4(\ln 4 - 1) > 4(\ln 4 - \ln 3) > 1$. □

## 6 Application

We present here a short experiment regarding the similarity of Romance languages. The work corpus is formed by the representative vocabularies of the following six Romance languages: Romanian, Italian, Spanish, Catalan, French and Portuguese languages (Sala, 1988). We extracted the digrams from each vocabularies and then we constructed a ranking of digrams for each language: on the first position we put the most frequent digram of the vocabulary, on the second position the next frequent digram, and so on.

We apply the scaled total rank distance between all pairs of such classifications and we obtain a series of results which are presented in Table 2.

Table 2: Scaled total rank distances in Romance languages

| | Ro | It | Sp | Ca | Po | Fr |
|---|---|---|---|---|---|---|
| Ro | 0 | 0.36 | 0.37 | 0.39 | 0.41 | 0.36 |
| It | 0.36 | 0 | 0.21 | 0.24 | 0.26 | 0.30 |
| Sp | 0.37 | 0.21 | 0 | 0.20 | 0.18 | 0.27 |
| Ca | 0.39 | 0.24 | 0.20 | 0 | 0.20 | 0.28 |
| Po | 0.41 | 0.26 | 0.18 | 0.20 | 0 | 0.30 |
| Fr | 0.36 | 0.30 | 0.27 | 0.28 | 0.30 | 0 |

Some remarks are immediate:

- If we analyze the Table 2, we observe that every time Romanian finds itself at the biggest distance from the other languages. This fact proves that the evolution of Romanian in a distanced space from the Latin nucleus has lead to bigger differences between Romanian and the rest of the Romance languages, then the differences between any other two Romance languages.
- The closest two languages are Portuguese and Spanish.
- It is also remarkable that Catalan is equally distanced from Portuguese and Spanish.

The upper remarks are in concordance with the conclusions of (Dinu and Dinu, 2005) obtained from the analise of the syllabic similarity of the Romance languages, where the rank distance was used to compare the rankings of syllables, based on the frequency of syllables for each language.

During the time, different comparing methods for natural languages were proposed. We mention here the work of Hoppenbrouwers and Hoppenbrouwers (2001). Their approach was the following: using the letter frequency method for each language variety the unigram frequencies of letters are found on the basis of a corpus. The distance between two languages is equal to the sum of the differences between the corresponding letter frequencies. They verify that this approach correctly shows that the distance between Afrikaans and Dutch is smaller than the distance between Afrikaans and the Samoan language.

## 7 Conclusions

In this paper we provided some low-complexity metrics to be used in various subfields of computational linguistics: total rank distance and scaled total rank distance. These metrics are inspired from the natural tendency of objects to put the main information in the first part of the units. Our analyze was especially concentrated on the mathematical and computational properties of these metrics: we showed that total rank distance and scaled total rank distance are metrics, computed their expected and max values on the permutations group and showed that total rank distance can be used in classification problem via a polynomial algorithm.

## 8 Mathematical addendum

This addendum may be skipped by readers who are not interested in mathematical technicalities; below some statements are sketched and other are unproved, but then the proofs are quite straightforward.

**Proposition 1**:

**Proof:** It is not hard to see that $D(A, S_n) = D(B, S_n)$ for any two permutation $A, B \in S_n$. So, the expected value can be computed by computing first $D(A, S_n)$ for a convenable permutation and then by dividing the upper sum to $n!$. If we choose $A = e_n$ (i.e. the identical permutation of the group $S_n$), then the expected value is:

$$E(D) \quad = \quad \frac{1}{n!} \sum_{\sigma \in S_n} D(e_n, \sigma).$$

The upper sum can be easily computed if we take into account the fact that each number $1, 2, \ldots, n$ appears the same number of times (i.e. (n-1)!) on the ranks $1, 2, \ldots n$. So, we obtain that the expected value is equal to:

$$E(D) = \frac{(n^2-1)(n+2)}{6}.$$

□

**Proposition 2**:

**Proof:** W.l.g. we can suppose that first permutation is the identical one, i.e. $e_n$ (otherwise we will relabelled it). To compute the max value, the following preliminary results must be proven (we skipped the proofs).

We say that an integer from $\sigma$ is *low* if its position is $\leq \frac{n}{2}$ and it is *high* if its position is $> \frac{n}{2}$.

Let $\sigma \in \mathcal{S}_n$ be a permutation. We construct the set $\Theta_\sigma$ as following:

$$\Theta_\sigma = \{\tau \in \mathcal{S}_n \mid \forall x \in \{1 \ldots n\},\ x \text{ is low in } \tau \text{ iff } x \text{ is high in } \sigma \text{ and viceversa}\}$$

**Result 1** *For each $\sigma \in \mathcal{S}_n$ and every two permutation $\tau$, $\pi$ in $\Theta_\sigma$ we have: $D(\sigma, \tau) = D(\sigma, \pi)$.*

**Result 2** *For each $\sigma \in \mathcal{S}_n$ and every two permutation $\tau, \pi$ such that $\pi \in \Theta_\sigma$ and $\tau \notin \Theta_\sigma$, we have: $D(\sigma, \tau) < D(\sigma, \pi)$.*

To prove Result 2 we use the following Lemma:

**Lemma 1 (Dinu, 2003)** *If $a > b$, then the function $f(x) = |x - b| - |x - a|$ is an increasing one.*

**Result 3** *Let $\sigma \in \mathcal{S}_n$ be a permutation. The maximum total rank distance is reached by the permutation $\tau$ where $ord(x|\tau) = n + 1 - ord(x|\sigma)$, $\forall x \in V(\mathcal{P}_n)$. Under this conditions the maximum total rank distance is:*

$$\max_{A,B \in S_n} D(A, B) = \frac{n^2(n+2)}{4} \tag{3}$$

In other words, we obtained a more general result:

**Theorem 5** *For a given permutation $\sigma$, the maximum rank distance is achieved by all permutations from $\Theta_\sigma$ and it is equal to (3).*

□

**Proposition 3**:

**Proof:**

1. Similar to Proposition 2, given a permutation $\sigma \in S_n$, the max value is reached by its invert. So, to give a close formula for the max value it is enough to compute $S(e_n, e_n^{-1})$. To make easier our life, we can suppose that $n = 2k$.

   $S(e_n, e_n^{-1}) = k + \sum_{i=1}^{k} \frac{2i^2+(k-i)(k-i+1)}{(k+i)(k+i+1)} = \ldots = 4k - \frac{2k^2}{2k+1} - 2(4k+1)(\sum_{i=1}^{k} \frac{1}{k+i} - \frac{k}{2k+1});$

   When $k \to \infty$, $\sum_{i=1}^{k} \frac{1}{k+i} \to \ln 2$, so $\frac{S(e_n, e_n^{-1})}{n} = \frac{7}{2} - 4 \ln 2$ □

2. To compute the expected value we use the same motivation as in expected total rank distance. The rest is obvious.

**Acknowledgements 1** *We want to thank to reviewers for their comments and suggestions. Research supported by CNR-NATO and MEdC-ANCS.*

## References

P. Diaconis, R.L. Graham, 1977. *Spearman footrule as a Measure of Disarray*, Journal of Royal Statistical Society. Series B (Methodological), Vol. 39, No. 2, 262-268.

L. P. Dinu, 2003. *On the classification and aggregation of hierarchies with different constitutive elements*, Fundamenta Informaticae, 55(1), 39-50.

A. Dinu, L.P. Dinu, 2005. *On the Syllabic Similarities of Romance Languages*. In Proc. CICLing 2005, Lecture Notes in Computer Science, Volume 3406, pp. 785-789.

L.P. Dinu, F. Manea. *An efficient approach for the rank aggregation problem.* Theoretical Computer Science (to appear).

L.P. Dinu, A. Sgarro. *A low-complexity distance for DNA strings*, Fundamenta Informaticae (to appear).

M. Dinu, 1997. *Comunicarea* (in Romanian). Ed. Ştiinţifică, Bucureşti.

K. Fukuda, T. Matsui, 1992. *Finding all minimum cost perfect matchings in bipartite graphs*, Networks, 22, 461-468.

K. Fukuda, T. Matsui, 1994. *Finding all the perfect matchings in bipartite graphs*, Appl. Math. Lett., 7(1), 15-18.

C. de la Higuera, F. Casacuberta, 2000. *Topology of strings: Median string is NP- complete,* Theoretical Computer Science, 230:39-48.

C. Hoppenbrouwers, G. Hoppenbrouwers, 2001. *De indeling van de Nederlandse streektalen. Dialecten van 156 steden en dorpen geklasseerdvolgens de FFM*. Koninklijke Van Gorcum, Assen.

S. Marcus, 1974. Linguistic structures and generative devices in molecular genetics. Cahiers Ling. Theor. Appl., 11, 77-104.

M. Sala, (coord.) 1982. Vocabularul reprezentativ al limbilor romanice, Bucureşti.

L.A. Zadeh, J. Kacprzyk, 1999. *Computing with words in information/intelligent systems 1: Foundations, 2: Application*. Physica-Verlag, Heidelberg and New York.

# Author Index

**Association for Computational Linguistics**
209 N. Eighth Street
Stroudsburg, Pennsylvania 18360

# 26th Conference on Computational Linguistics and Speech Processing

# (ROCLING 2014)

**Zhongli, Taiwan**
**25 – 26 September 2014**

ISBN: 978-1-63439-624-0